ARRAZAT'S
AUBERGINES

ARRAZAT'S AUBERGINES

Inside a Languedoc Kitchen

Patrick Moon

PROFILE BOOKS

First published in Great Britain in 2005 by
Profile Books Ltd
58A Hatton Garden
London EC1N 8LX
www.profilebooks.co.uk

1 3 5 7 9 10 8 6 4 2

Typeset in Palatino by MacGuru Ltd
info@macguru.org.uk

Printed and bound in Great Britain by
Clays, Bungay, Suffolk

The moral right of the author has been asserted.

A CIP catalogue record for this book is available from the British Library.

ISBN 1 86197 706 9

For Michelle
and in memory of Paul

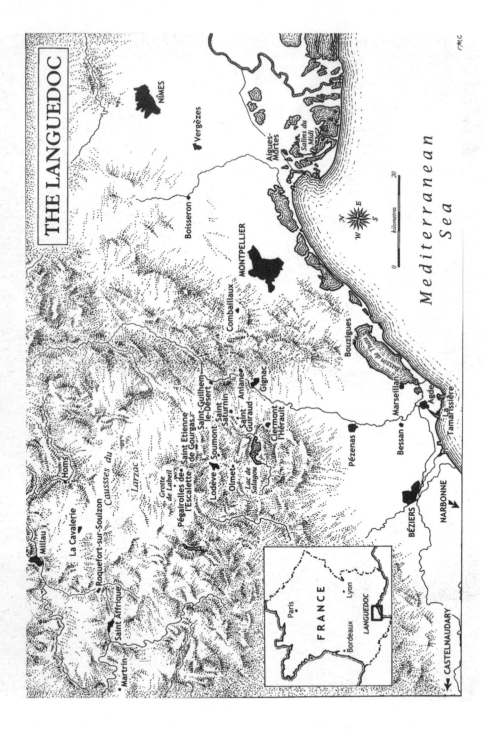

THE LANGUEDOC

NÎMES

Vergèzes

Aigues-Mortes

Salins du Midi

Boisseron

MONTPELLIER

Combaillaux

Mediterranean Sea

N
E
W
S

0   kilometres   20

Bouzigues

Bassin de Thau

Marseillan

Agde

La Tamarissière

Gignac

Saint-Guilhem le-Désert

Saint Antane

Saint Saturnin

Saint Étienne de Gourgas

Saint Guiraud

Clermont l'Hérault

Pézenas

Bessan

Caussses au Larzac

Hons

Grotte de Labeil

Pégairolles de l'Escalette

Soumont

Lodève

Olmet

Lac de Salagou

NARBONNE

BÉZIERS

Roquefort-sur-Soulzon

La Cavalerie

Millau

Saint Affrique

Martrin

FRANCE

Paris

Lyon

Bordeaux

LANGUEDOC

CASTELNAUDARY

Spring

'Do you feel as bad as you look?' asked Manu, pausing briefly at the top of my drive to let his heart slow down after the sprint across the bridge from his neighbouring cottage.

'It's the birds,' I explained, as a couple of litres of homemade *rouge* emerged ominously from a pair of faded blue dungarees. It was useless to point to my half-finished breakfast. If Emmanuel Gros was determined to celebrate my return to the Languedoc, then celebrate we both would.

'It seemed I'd only just gone to bed,' I continued, as he brushed aside the dining-room cobwebs that separated him from my wineglasses and started pouring. 'I'd hardly turned out my light but there I was – woken by the dawn chorus. I struggled up, thinking I must already be late for the market, but when I opened the shutters, I discovered it was still pitch dark. The birds were singing at the tops of their voices but it was only two o'clock in the morning.'

'Nightingales,' said Manu authoritatively, having evicted an item of unopened luggage from his favourite armchair to settle in comfortably. 'The first ones of spring. They arrived a couple of days ago. I'm surprised you don't remember from your what-sisname . . .'

'My sabbatical?'

'*Voilà!* From two years ago . . . But, *oh mon dieu*, you do look bad,' he laughed, as he replenished his already empty glass.

'Of course I look bad,' I grumbled, looking wistfully at my fast-cooling mug of coffee. 'So would you, if you'd driven all the way from England and had barely two hours' sleep.'

'Have you had a chance to look round?' he asked, with the

air of someone bracing himself to receive praise. 'I think you'll find we made a pretty good job of things, me and the wife, looking after the place while you were away. Bit of mowing, bit of strimming. Even your precious vines,' he added, with a new note of bitterness. 'Miraculously, even those survived without the interference of the great Monsieur Joly. You'd never think I'd had vines of my own for decades. Coming up here, trying to poke his nose in . . .'

Virgile Joly was the talented young winemaker from Saint Saturnin whose work I had been lucky enough to shadow in my first year here. When I decided to plant some vines, he tried to encourage me to plant wine-producing varieties but, more timidly, I'd opted for table grapes. I wasn't sure how long it would be before I could be here all the time to look after them and, anyway, perhaps the most important thing that I learned about winemaking during my year at his side was how difficult it was. Even so, I was relieved when Virgile offered to look after them in my absence. Far better his pursuit of quality than Manu's dogged adherence to quantity. But now it appears that Virgile's perfectionism has been shown the gate, leaving everything at the mercy of Manu's *laissez-faire*.

'The only thing is, we did have a few problems with the strimmer. Well, the lawnmower too, really,' confesses Manu, reverting to his normal jovial manner. 'Nothing that the garage won't be able to fix, I'm sure. In fact, I meant to get them mended by the time you arrived. But what with all the fruit to pick and so on . . .'

I resisted enquiring what unseasonal harvesting could have monopolized his recent months. It was about to be Easter and nothing could have needed picking since the autumn olive crop.

I could see from the kitchen window that I had missed the fruit blossoms by several weeks. Even the late-flowering cherries had started setting their fruits, and the bright yellow mimosa on the tree that I'd planted eighteen months ago had already turned a dusty brown.

Beyond this, I had scarcely begun to explore, but what little I had seen suggested that Monsieur and Madame Gros had confined their horticultural efforts to the preservation of access routes to everything remotely edible. It had been the same on the handful of holiday visits that I'd managed in my fifteen months away: weeds and brambles gradually reasserting themselves in every corner of the ancient stone-built terraces – except where there were things to be eaten.

Somehow, my short periods of occupancy had never quite coincided with the harvests. Either the fruits were frustratingly under-ripe ('a crime to pick them yet,' was the oft-repeated verdict from the other side of the stream) or a well-developed sense of neighbourly duty had required a total stripping of the trees in the preceding days ('another day and they'd have rotted,' the alternative judgement).

'Such a pity about your freezer breaking down,' said Manu, cheerfully draining the first bottle. 'Otherwise, we'd have filled it for you. But then I was always telling your Uncle Milo it was on its last legs. Outlived him, though, poor fellow,' he added, with a respectful raising of his glass to the memory of the generous, childless relative who had made me the heir to this house.

'Surprised were they?' asks Manu, in more expansive, enquiring mode, now that the second bottle has been broached. 'When you told you them you were leaving the office for good?'

'I'm sure they could see I was tempted,' I tell him. 'From the moment I got back from that first year. But they didn't think I'd actually be daft enough to do it. Too late to worry now though . . .'

'That's what the wife was asking the other night,' says Manu with an embarrassed cough. 'I mean, it *would* be too late to change your mind, would it? If you decided you couldn't afford to keep this place going without a regular income? I know poor Milo found it a bit of a struggle, even before his illness . . . Ah, there you are, *ma chère!*'

A tall female figure in a tightly buttoned nylon housecoat has appeared at the doorway, casting a long, dark shadow across the room, as she favours me with the briefest of nods.

'Have you asked him?' she demands of her husband.

'I . . . I was just working round to it,' he stammers, looking quickly over his shoulder, as if for a means of escape. His questioner tuts an 'as usual I have to do everything myself' kind of tut; then two surprising things happen.

The first is Mme Gros's smile. This is an eerily unaccustomed phenomenon under any circumstances but even more exceptional on this occasion in being targeted unmistakably, almost beamingly, on me. I have no idea what I can be about to do to deserve it.

The second is a lacerating reprimand to Manu. 'Your neighbour's glass is empty!' she snaps, as he leaps to his feet to remedy the omission. This is even more astonishing. Historically, Mme Gros was always relentlessly unforgiving of the fact that my proximity afforded potentially round-the-clock pretexts for her husband's deeply disapproved-of liquid hospitality. Yet amazingly, this morning she is abetting the crime.

'Such a view,' she sighs, striding purposefully past me to the panoramic window at the end of the barrel-vaulted dining-room. 'But such a waste.' She encapsulates several overgrown and under-exploited terraces in a single decisive gesture. 'I mean, look at that silly little vegetable garden of your uncle's. I know he was unwell but, if you really intend to make a go of this place . . .' She squares her sizeable shoulders in the way that she always does when coming to the point. 'We wondered whether you might consider a bigger potager. You could fill the whole of that bottom terrace with vegetables. Maybe the one above it as well, now that your income's not what it was.' She adjusts the earlier smile to something more sympathetic and solicitous. 'Some more fruit trees perhaps? Extend the greenhouse even?'

'All the things we wish we could do,' chips in Manu supportively.

'If it weren't for the vines,' his wife adds acerbically. The sacrifice of most of their own half hectare to wine production has long been a source of bitter recrimination between them.

'Manu will help all he can,' Mme Gros volunteers. 'Though of course, he's not as young as he was.'

*

'I know you're tired but it has to be tonight,' said Virgile, when he telephoned at lunchtime. 'They're fully booked for the whole of the weekend. It's Easter, remember.'

'But I thought it was a new restaurant . . .'

'New to you. And to me, if it comes to that. Although I do know the chef. He's bought my wine. But he opened before you left. I can't think how you missed it, being so near.'

'It's on the campsite, you say?'

'It's next to the campsite. It used to be the campsite café. But trust me,' he laughed, 'it's changed.'

So I agreed to meet him at Le Temps de Vivre at eight.

'We did it all ourselves,' says a welcoming figure in immaculate chef's whites. He leads me into a large and airy white room, full of well-spaced tables dressed with stiff white cloths. The high-backed chairs, upholstered alternately in terracotta pink and ochre yellow, provide a restrained note of colour. 'Just my wife and I,' he elaborates. 'Day and sometimes night, for a month. It was in a terrible state after being empty for two and a half years.' He shakes his head in disbelief at his own recollection, as he shows me to a circular table in a long, glazed veranda overlooking the valley. 'We opened just thirty-two days after I left Le Jardin des Sens.'

Now even I have heard of Montpellier's 'Jardin'. It's a byword locally for unaffordably outstanding cooking. When the postman's wife won the lottery a couple of years ago, there was no other possible place for them to celebrate.

'Working there was a revelation,' the chef continues. 'I did my early training at La Tamarissière, down on the coast near Agde.' He pauses shyly, as if banter with his guests is not the part of the job that he finds easiest. 'He's a very good cook, Nicolas Albano. But not like the Pourcel twins at the Jardin. They completely changed my view of what cooking and eating could be.'

'But what brought you here?' I ask, looking out at the under-populated river valley, winding up from Lodève towards the dramatic white cliffs in the distance and the desolate Larzac plateau beyond them.

'I was born in Lodève,' he answers, offering a menu devoted exclusively to aperitifs. 'I spent most of my childhood in Pégairolles, the next village along this little road, where my grandparents lived. Fishing trout in the village stream, with my bare hands and the villagers complaining that I was fishing *their* trout. I mean, how could they be *their* trout, in a stream?'

Laughter briefly penetrates the air of formality as he leaves me to contemplate the view in the fading light. It is every bit as impressive as Uncle Milo's, except that from here you can just see the dual carriageway cutting up through the heart of the valley towards Millau. It formed the last lap of yesterday's drive and, to judge by the preparatory roadworks near the village, the long-dreaded upgrade to full-blown motorway must be coming sooner than I'd thought.

A tall young man in a double-breasted suit that emphasizes his slimness comes to take my aperitif order and, turning my attention back to the table to wonder whether I should wait for Virgile, I notice that it is laid for three.

'Monsieur Joly rang to say they'd be a little late,' says the man whom I assume to be the head waiter. So I order a glass of Muscat and he leaves me to speculate about this unexpected third person.

Someone who doesn't share his preference for punctuality, I have concluded, when a familiar-looking, dark-haired girl arrives a quarter of an hour later.

'Sorry, I always make him late,' she says in slightly breath-less, intriguingly accented English, and I try to remember where I've seen this warm, generous smile before. 'I try to be a good influence in other ways ... *Mais Virgile arrive. Il stationne la voiture,*' she adds in French, as I find myself exchanging the triple kiss of greeting that is de rigueur in the Languedoc. 'You see how much better my French is now?' she resumes in English. 'I'm doing a course in Montpellier.'

And then I recognize her.

'Magda!' I exclaim in surprise. We worked together on Virgile's *vendange* two years ago. She had come with a girlfriend from Poland, for the second year in succession. Her English was then much better than her French, forcing Virgile to venture hesitantly into my own language. But she looks so different tonight without the grape stains.

'Didn't he tell you?' she laughs, as she sits beside me. 'I came again last year, for a third harvest . . .'

'But this time she stayed,' says Virgile, blushing slightly as he appears at our table to make it complete. 'It's a shame,' he adds, at the sight of my Muscat. 'We should have ordered champagne.'

'To celebrate your return,' endorses Magda warmly.

The man who, I have decided, must be not so much the head as the one and only waiter has materialized optimistically at the mention of champagne but Virgile and Magda order some thirst-quenching beers instead. They have both been working hard at Virgile's *ébourgeonnage* – the stripping off of surplus shoots from his vines to help achieve the low yields that he insists are so important for the quality of his wine.

'This year's going to be different,' he tells me, when we have made our selection from the humblest of the three set menus. 'Last winter was by far the wettest since I've worked in the Languedoc. In fact, the only significantly wet one. The vines will have a much easier time producing grapes, unless Magda and I work even harder to make it difficult. Good news for your springs, though,' he adds.

As the owner of a house with no mains water and entirely dependent for my survival on three natural *sources* that give the property its name, I am delighted to receive this intelligence of replenished water-tables. Manu assures me that my springs have never stopped but, when I was here last August, the flow of drinking, washing and swimming water was unmistakably slower.

My water worries are interrupted by the arrival of the waiter, reinvented as sommelier. He sets down our bottle of wine – a red made by one of Virgile's fellow rising stars – along with a decanter and a wineglass of his own. He pours a little wine into the decanter, swills it round and empties it into the glass. He sniffs it, concludes that the contents are sound and decants the remainder. Then he exits with the glass to the kitchen.

The kitchen doors have hardly swung closed before he re-emerges, now reverse-incarnated as a waiter, and sets before each of us a tiny dish of something looking not at all like the *roulés* of trout that I remember us ordering.

To 'put us in appetite' he is presenting a small but ambitiously elaborate *amuse-bouche* involving *foie gras*, miniature vegetables and something new to me, pig's cheek – all served in a chilled, Muscat-flavoured jelly. It takes only a spoonful to persuade me that cheek of pork is a widely under-esteemed commodity.

'How are your own vines?' asks Virgile, as soon as the *amuse-bouche* has ceased to demand our full attention.

'A bit of a disaster,' I admit. 'Did I explain? I planted five different sorts – all table varieties, as I warned you. Cinsault, Chasselas, the two different Muscats, green and black, and that late-ripening grape that you had.'

'Servent?'

'Exactly. Eight of each, all in nice neat rows on a perfect south-facing, well-drained slope behind the house, with a label tied at the end of each row, so I'd know which was which. You'd have been proud. But long before I could come back to check on them, the rain washed the writing off the labels, so I no longer had a clue which was which. Not that it mattered much, because the wild boar had been in before me to dig about a quarter of them up. Then those that they'd left alone, the rabbits came and stripped off half their leaves . . .'

'Are you sure there's no sign of life?' asks Virgile, distracted somewhat by the waiter's return, in sommelier mode again, to offer us our own opportunity to taste the wine. 'Vines are pretty resilient things,' he adds, with a nod of approval for a general pouring.

'Oh they're alive,' I assure him. 'The leaves are starting to sprout. It's just that I seem to be right back where I was a year ago – with an extra year to wait before there's any fruit.'

'I did try to keep an eye on them but your neighbour, Monsieur Gros . . .'

'I know, he told me. He can be strangely proprietorial about other people's plants.'

'*Et voici, messieurs-dame*' – the waiter begins a word-perfect recitation of the menu's various pledges in respect of our first course – '*les roulés de truites de Labeil à la tapenade, roquette en vinaigrette basilic, tuile de parmesan.*' And happily all of them seem to be honoured: our fillets of trout (we must take the 'Labeil' provenance on trust) have been coated with dark olive *tapenade* paste, then rolled like swiss rolls and served with a basil-vinaigretted rocket-leaf salad and wafer-thin parmesan biscuit.

'How about the oaks?' whispers Virgile.

Just before I left, he gave me three tiny saplings, only about thirty centimetres tall but allegedly impregnated with the precious spores that might – on a chance of one in three and conceivably within my life expectancy – produce truffles.

'They've grown about a centimetre,' I tell him. 'You said I'd have to be patient. But the important thing is . . .' – I find myself whispering too – 'I don't think Manu's guessed.'

'I wouldn't count on it,' laughs Virgile. 'But listen, have I told you about Puech?'

Virgile hasn't but I remember that Puech was his *négociant*, the middleman who acquired a hundred per cent of his early production. He was even partially financing the vintages before they were made but, at the same time, pushing prices up to levels that many considered unrealistic. Virgile's wobbly gesture suggests that the business must now be either failing or failed.

'I'll be doing a lot of marketing myself this year,' is all that he actually says before the waiter returns with our main courses.

11

'*Messieurs-dame, je vous propose . . .*' (fortunately for all of us, the proposals irreproachably match our orders) '*pour Madame, la daurade royale, fine ratatouille à l'oeuf et beurre d'olive. Et pour messieurs . . .*' (Virgile and I have made the chef work a little harder, with a different selection for this course) '*la tarte friande d'agneau aux aubergines et son jus au thym. Bon appétit, messieurs-dame.*'

'I think we've won,' says Virgile, cutting into his savoury lamb tart.

Magda's fillet of sea bream and accompanying ratatouille look delicious but our own dish is perhaps more impressive, certainly more original. The waiter said that the tart was one of the chef's most popular dishes: there were howls of protest when he tried to take it off the menu. However, it is not really a tart, rather a circular disc of puff pastry on which sits a circular disc of lamb, topped by a circular mound of intensely flavoured aubergine purée and an upper layer (circular, naturally) of roasted tomato slivers.

So, yes, I think we've won.

'I don't know how you do it,' I marvel, when the chef appears in person. Only two other covers have been served tonight so he is less than fully stretched (although the waiter said that the rest of the Easter weekend will be manic – almost over-booked, with two services a day, for three days).

'I don't mean the dish,' I hasten to explain. 'Or at least, I *would* like to know how you make it. But what amazes me is, how you manage to produce so many different things, all at the right moment, even with . . . You do have some assistants, I assume?'

'Just the one at the moment,' he says regretfully. (He presumably needs to fill the other tables before he can afford another.) 'But would you really like to find out?'

'Oh, no . . . I mean, it was just a figure of speech,' I falter.

'He means "yes",' says Virgile who, it seems, has already told the chef about the year I shared with him. 'And like I told you, he's quite well-behaved. Occasionally even useful. Just not very good at getting up in the mornings.'

'That was different,' I prevaricate. It was one thing to play at winemaking when I was only here for a year but, now that I'm back for good, the idea of such frivolous extra-curricular activity fills me with puritan guilt.

But Virgile is adamant. 'You can't spend all your time in your vegetable patch,' he insists, and I hear myself agreeing to meet the chef at dawn on the Wednesday after Easter, because that is when he goes shopping in Montpellier's Métro market. I then spend most of the cheese, dessert and coffee courses wondering what I have let myself in for.

'So we'll be seeing you next week,' says the waiter, when he brings us our coats. His tone leaves me not quite sure that he approves, as does the valedictory warning: 'If you thought the winemaker's life was strenuous, wait till you've spent a day in a restaurant!'

With that, he summons the chef from behind the swing doors to bid us goodnight.

'I'm sorry, but I don't even know your name,' I confess, as we shake hands on the doorstep.

'Laurent Arrazat,' he answers and points with a smile to the name embroidered on his still immaculately white jacket. '*À mercredi, donc.*'

*

'Have you met your new neighbour?'

Manu shivered slightly as he wrapped the sheet of plastic tarpaulin more snugly round his shoulders and continued watching my pickaxe rise and fall in the rain. Extending my insignificant potager to fill the bottom terrace was proving more of a challenge than I had expected, especially in a downpour. But the seedlings I'd purchased in Lodève's Saturday morning market had to be planted, whatever the weather.

I paused to get my breath back and to look at Manu blankly. I didn't think I was capable of having a new neighbour because his house and mine stand all alone, at the end of a long and bumpy lane leading out from the village.

'Old Rouffia's place,' said Manu, reminding me of the tiny abandoned shepherd's *maset* a little way beyond our properties, where the lane peters out into vineyards. Everyone had said it was never likely to be sold. There were too many heirs apparently, all entitled under the Code Napoléon to absurd little fractions of Rouffia's insignificant fortune, and the *notaires* had spent decades failing to find them all. 'A cousin turned up in Béziers,' explained Manu, against the sound of rainwater bouncing off his tarpaulin. 'The lawyers were too busy looking in Canada to see the ends of their noses. So it's been sold at last.'

'To a poet,' added Mme Gros, in tones that others might reserve for 'child-molester'. Despite the climatic conditions, she was detouring briefly from her walk to the village Easter Mass to judge when the first of my harvests could be budgeted for.

'Poetess,' corrected Manu, as if that made the calling many times more acceptable. 'Garance Something-or-other,' he added for my benefit.

'Garance?' I queried. 'I thought that was the name of this weed.' I held up a clump of one of the potager's most persistent menaces, which then clung to my hand as I tried to shake it off.

Manu simply laughed and pulled his 'need I say more?' face, but Mme Gros snorted sharply from beneath her severe black umbrella. 'She's worse than your uncle. Thinks it's all very romantic, living up there without electricity, until she's got some little job that needs a power drill. Then suddenly she's round at our place, wanting Manu to rig up an extension lead from the back bedroom.'

The intervention of the church bell reminded her that further character assassination would have to wait. Determined, whatever the weather, to mortify the flesh with a walk to her Sunday devotions, she splashed her way down through the rivulets of water descending the drive. Those forty-odd customers at Le Temps de Vivre had the right idea, I reflected, as I resumed my efforts with the pickaxe. This was definitely a day to spend having lunch.

'What you want is a motor cultivator,' said Manu, which I

quickly translated to mean, 'Manu wants a motor cultivator for some yet-to-be-disclosed activity of his own.' Or, more immediately, 'Manu wants to get out of the rain.' Or, most pressingly of all, 'Manu wants a drink and his keeper's Easter observances have now made this possible.' But I was sufficiently wet to need little encouragement to take a break, even if it did entail a substantial glass of his illicitly home-distilled brandy.

'Took the precaution of bringing a bottle,' says Manu, with a rummage deep inside his habitual blue dungarees. 'But wait till you hear her on the subject of the motorway,' he continues, wringing the water from his faded red baseball cap, as we shelter beneath the deep arcades of the courtyard at the front of the house. 'Says we should all be made to ride pushbikes.'

I look blankly again, never having pictured Mme Gros as a cyclist. Then I realize he means Garance.

'Does she have water up there?' I ask, wondering whether she will soon be asking for a hosepipe out of my own back bedroom.

'A well, apparently,' says Manu, already savouring a second pouring of the infamous firewater. 'Don't ask what she does about the other. I don't want to think about it. She'd have to sell a lot of poems to buy a septic tank. But talking of water . . .'

He glances across to the fountain at the side of the terrace. It is fed by the most important of my three springs. The water runs constantly from a decorative spout on the wall. It runs equally constantly from the basin at the bottom, down an underground pipe to the natural, blessedly chlorine-free swimming pool a couple of terraces below, and thence eventually to the river. The perpetual flow, from the *source* to the fountain, helps ensure that the water for the house, arriving by the same route, is always fresh.

'Is the fountain normally as slow as that?' asks Manu casually.

'I'm sure it's all right,' I answer. Surely, with this much rain, it has to be.

Manu changes the subject to the discount that a cousin of his might allow on the motor cultivator; then again to the notion that our visit to the cousin might be advantageously combined with 'one of our little outings'. A substantial part of my first twelve months was spent exploring the Languedoc wine region in Manu's little red van, a series of wine-tasting excursions which Mme Gros would never have allowed him on his own but which she reluctantly countenanced in my company.

'I need to finish this potager,' I excuse myself, worrying all the time that he does have a point. The fountain is definitely slower than usual.

'Can you hear your water pump?' he asks, as casually as before. 'You haven't used any water in the house for an hour but the pump's still running.'

He's right. I hadn't really noticed above the rattle of the rain in the terracotta drainpipes, but the pump is straining, as if there is no longer any water in the house for it to circulate. When something similar happened in my early days, Manu introduced me to a little reserve tank beside the garage, where an all-important ballcock had stuck. Today it takes me several soaking minutes to remove the pile of stones on top of the tank but, when I do, I find the ballcock fully functioning.

'*Formidable*,' says Manu, relaxing serenely behind another refill.

'*Pas formidable*,' I correct him. 'The reserve tank's empty.'

'It can't be,' he protests. 'The *source* can't be drying up, not after the wettest winter for three or four years and all this rain today.'

'We'll have to go and see.'

'We'll be soaked,' he whines. 'And the wife won't be back for at least an hour.'

'It's an emergency,' I insist, setting off through the deluge, as Manu trails behind me, still obstinately clutching the tarpaulin draped round his shoulders in a vain attempt to keep dry.

The principal *source* that supplies the house is situated several hundred metres away, on the other side of the stream, where the wildest part of my land loops round the back of Manu's vines.

The spring rises somewhere inside a wall – the retaining wall of the topmost terrace, in fact. Behind the bottom row of stones is a hollow collecting chamber, where Uncle Milo adapted some plastic guttering to channel the precious commodity into pipes. These travel at first discreetly underground, resurfacing more obtrusively several metres later, to run all the way back across the stream and down through the orchard as far as the house. But standing right here beside it, the only clue to the *source*'s location is the gushing sound inside the wall.

Except, for gushing sound, read trickling sound this morning.

'Give me a hand,' I ask Manu, as I wrestle with the heaviest of the boulders masking whatever dwindling quantity of water remains.

It takes longer than it should to unveil the cavity, partly because a year's neglect has allowed so much vegetation to sprout and partly because neither the brandy nor the plastic sheeting round his shoulders is doing anything for Manu's dexterity. Eventually, however, we can see inside. Or we could, if the rainclouds hadn't made the day so dark.

'We should have brought a torch,' I offer uselessly, but Manu is already fumbling for a cigarette lighter somewhere deep inside his overalls.

'Here's the culprit,' he announces, as he gropes inside the chamber by the light of the flickering flame. 'You've got a tree root nearly blocking the collecting pipe. There's plenty of water. It just can't get down the hole. That's why it's all so overgrown. Half the water's escaping underground.'

'It must be that oak,' I deduce, pointing over our heads. 'Should we cut it down? . . . I mean, not this morning, but sometime when the rain's stopped?'

'It's a tricky one.' He screws his dripping features into an expression of suitable sagacity. 'It might be the tree that's drawing the water up from the water-table. If you cut it down, the *source* might go somewhere else. It's better not to meddle more than you have to.'

'But we'll have to cut out the root.'

'Better when the rain's stopped,' advises Manu, his sights now set on a last consoling brandy before his wife's return from church.

'It might be completely blocked by tomorrow,' I persist. 'It won't take a minute to get a saw.'

But it does take more than a minute because a visitor is waiting for me at the house.

'I'm Garance, your neighbour,' says a tense-looking, rain-bedraggled young female on my doorstep. 'I'm sorry not to have called before,' she continues in a high-pitched, highly strung tone that I could quickly grow tired of.

'Quite all right,' I would have liked to assure her. 'Can't really stop. Just dashing back for a saw,' would have explained my position admirably. But Garance doesn't stop talking for long enough for me to say any of this. Instead, she catalogues the domestic disasters and personal afflictions that have come between her and her social duty.

As the monologue drifts past me, I realize that she is not as young as I'd first thought. It must be the rain that made her look so waif-like – that and the ethnic cape, smock and sandals that she's wearing.

'. . . so that's why I had to come this morning,' I half hear her say, as an unaccustomed silence pulls me back to consciousness.

'Sorry, I was miles away,' I confess.

'My roof,' she explains. 'The hole in it. The leak . . .'

'Are you coming or aren't you?' says Manu, returning grumpily to the courtyard, still swaddled in the plastic tarpaulin.

'Perfect!' cries Garance at the sight of his rainwear. 'Exactly what I need for the roof.'

Manu starts to explain about the *source* but Garance launches into a second unabridged account of her recent vicissitudes and he realizes there is no other route to a quiet life than to follow her back to her little *maset* and there surrender the tarpaulin. He mimes an apology to me and I set off alone with my saw.

The tree root is awkwardly inaccessible but I manage to hack it out with only minimal damage to the pipe. Then, flushed with this accomplishment, I give the collecting chamber a bare-handed dredging to remove as much as possible of the mud silted up at the bottom. I even succeed in juggling most of the stones back into place unaided, so I am feeling unusually proud of myself when I return to the courtyard.

I can hear how vigorous the fountain has become before I even turn the corner but, when I do so, it is Mme Gros who dominates the view. She is pacing up and down the arcade, wondering why the pickaxe operations have been suspended. But when I tell her of my triumphs at the *source*, she laughs contemptuously and points to the deep muddy brown of the water pouring from the spout.

'Better to have disconnected the supply,' she observes with ill-disguised satisfaction. 'Better still to have waited till the rain stopped. When your uncle made the same mistake, it took most of the day to wash the system clear. Not counting the mud that you'll have in the pool.'

*

It is not yet light when my Wednesday morning alarm goes off. It is not even light when I leave the house, and I can barely see to lock the door.

The sky is just beginning to lighten as I reach the Le Temps de Vivre car park but there are no signs of life. Two vehicles – a small white van and a blue Subaru with flashy, gold-painted hubcaps – are parked by the basement door, beneath the restaurant, implying that Laurent must live somewhere on the premises, though I have no idea where. Apart from the entrance to the dining-room at the top of a steep ramp, there are two glazed doors into the kitchen on the same level and another giving access to what appears to be a small office in the basement. However, everything seems to be locked and deserted.

'I hope you've got an alarm-clock,' laughed Virgile, when he heard how early we were meeting. Well, I have but it seems that Laurent hasn't.

I return to my car, wondering how long I should wait and whether the basement space on either side of the office can really be big enough for anyone to live in. Then, unexpectedly, there is a jangle of keys from the dining-room entrance.

'*Un café?*' asks a bleary-eyed Laurent, almost unrecognizable this morning in multi-coloured pullover and shapeless leather jacket.

Muttering grumpily that you'd have to be *malade* to want to run a restaurant, he leads me through the familiar swing doors separating the dining-room from everything behind the scenes. I am surprised at how domestic the first of the backstage rooms seems to be. The kitchen proper can be glimpsed through an open doorway on the opposite side; but here the line of anti-quated, louvre-fronted wall cupboards and the large central table, covered with a well-worn plastic cloth, look more like some down-at-heel farmhouse – until I notice the espresso machine of almost industrial proportions and the left-hand wall of shelving crammed with glassware and white crockery, some of it discreetly decorated with the handwritten words: 'Le Temps de Vivre'.

'How did you decide on the restaurant's name?' I ask him, as he fumbles with the coffee-making apparatus, looking as if he has had only an hour's sleep, instead of a whole day off, since the great Easter marathon.

'I wanted a place where people would come and breathe . . . take time to enjoy life,' he begins with a yawn. But soon the draught of caffeine has galvanized him and he is energetically loading the van with polystyrene boxes to accommodate the more perishable purchases.

'I leave even earlier in summer,' he tells me, as we set off, 'avoiding the Métro crowds, as well as the traffic. But imagine the chaos here this summer,' he sighs, as we negotiate the road-builders' latest reconfiguration of the route from the restaurant down to Lodève and on towards Montpellier. 'I mean, I ask you, how can all this *not* discourage customers?'

I know just what he means. Already, in the short time since I arrived, the chicanery through the bollards has been radically altered on at least three occasions in as many working days. Familiar little landmarks, the only surviving clues to our where-abouts, are fast being flattened. And with Easter over, the blasting of a new tunnel through the hills above Lodève has required the closure of the old one beside it. The resulting tailbacks via the town are the talk of the *département* and would certainly make me think twice about driving up from the coast for a meal.

'Have you always wanted to be a chef?' I ask when the worst of the frustrations are behind us.

'I was never much of a student,' he confesses. 'It was always clear that I'd have to do something with my hands. I left school at fifteen and went to work for the local radio station in Lodève. That led to me organizing discos for restaurants, including one where they let me help with the barbecues.'

'And the rest is history?'

'Not quite,' he laughs. 'I had to spend four years at catering college. My parents sent me to a place run by monks in the Lozère. Stricter than the army, it was; but my family reckoned it was only the twenty-four-hour discipline that would stop me fooling around.'

'You must learn an awful lot of recipes in four years.'

'Would you believe it, there was only one cooking lesson a week? The rest was management and accountancy.'

'After which you trained at La Tamarissière?'

'Yes. Then in '92 I gave it all up for a year . . .'

'A sabbatical?' I ask with a sense of fellow-feeling.

'I spent a year on a ranch. I love that contact with horses,' he says with more passion than I have so far heard him expend on food. 'Such strong, intelligent animals . . . But then I went back to cooking, at Le Jardin des Sens.'

'The turning-point.'

'Exactly.' We have reached the Métro car park. 'Look, there's Bridget's car from Le Mimosa. And Eric Cellier from Montpel-lier. I told you, everyone comes here.' He loads his polystyrene boxes on to the biggest supermarket trolley that I have ever seen – the platform only a few centimetres off the ground and the surface area more like a trailer that might be pulled behind the van. 'They have every sort of thing a chef or hotelier could need.'

I soon see what he means. It is not just the fruit, vegetables, fish, meat and every other kind of food; not even just the plates and glasses. They sell tables and chairs and beds here. They sell light bulbs and potted plants, even reception counters and computers, stacked on shelves that must be nearly five metres high. But we start with the fruit and vegetables.

Whole boxes of peppers, courgettes and rocket are ruthlessly examined for deficiencies before being accorded a place on the trolley. No less than four boxes of glossy black aubergines are added to the heap, then two of big beef tomatoes – barely ripe enough, Laurent says, but he selects the best he can find. Various sacks of onions are poked and prodded. He wants to experiment with a new first course on his least expensive menu, involving something stuffed inside an onion, and the onions must not be too dry.

'I'll have to sort them.' He compromises, having failed to find total satisfaction in any one bag, and we wheel the trolley into a separate room that feels like January. This is where they keep the cheeses cool, and Laurent chooses some parmesan for his trout-accompanying *tuiles*. Then he steers the shopping into a room that feels like January in the north of Scotland: the home of the fish, where the fishmongers are very sensibly wearing three pullovers each. For those of us wearing only a shirt, Laurent's critical selection of his *daurades royales* feels painfully protracted (the skin must be glistening, he explains, the eyes still bright).

'Normally, I'd buy more,' he says, taking only eight, 'but we're not expecting crowds. We were turning people away at Easter, but now it's dead.'

In the marginally more temperate climes of the meat room, Laurent tells me how the boned legs of lamb for his *tarte friande* are normally supplied directly, every Thursday, from a farm on the Larzac plateau. The *tarte*, however, proved far and away his most popular Easter dish and he needs an emergency leg to tide him over the next twenty-four hours.

Turning away from the food, he loads a giant bottle of bleach, checking first that the lid is tightly closed (he once lost a van-load of food by not checking), and a special kind of ungluable glue, enabling him to substitute pages in his wine list, as availability alters. Then we pay and set off back to Lodève before the traffic builds up.

'You don't do this to make money,' says Laurent. 'Run my kind of restaurant, I mean. Take the staff costs. I'm working with the absolute minimum. One *sous-chef*, one washer-up and one waiter, with my wife helping out in the dining-room, if we're busy. Just the social security bill – never mind the wages – comes to 7,000 Euros, four times a year.'

Two hundred and fifty times the price of his most popular menu, my mental arithmetic tells me, as we grind our way back through the roadworks. Without counting the wages. Or the rent. Or the food. Or the need to make some sort of profit.

Laurent brakes heavily behind a slow-moving machine of house-like proportions, which is arriving to mince the boulders from the new tunnel into hardcore for the road.

'You'd have to be *malade* to want to live in this country,' he growls, banging the steering-wheel.

'The famous thirty-five-hour week can't help,' I suggest sympathetically.

Laurent gives me a sideways look, which says that I must be *malade* as well. The *sous-chef*'s typical morning shift, he explains, lasts from 8.30 to maybe 3.30 in the afternoon. That's already seven hours. Then a couple of hours off and its 5.30 till who knows when? Often 12.30. Another seven. And this is five days a week. Even six in summer.

'The legislation was supposed to create more jobs,' he says. 'But how can a business like mine afford twice as many staff without putting the prices up to something customers can't afford?'

'What are most people doing then?'

'Opening fewer days a week, having longer winter closures, taking last orders earlier, serving less elaborate food . . . And, of course, increasing prices where they can.'

'So, just when everyone's got all this free time for eating out, the places they want to go to are either closed or offering worse value for money.'

'Try telling that to the government,' laughs Laurent, as we finally turn down the slope to the restaurant car park. 'As it is, my wife and I do everything possible ourselves. She does all the napkins and tablecloths, for instance. The washing-machine never stops.' And sure enough, in the middle room behind the swing doors, Mme Arrazat is resignedly folding what looks like a whole week's napkin supply into Laurent's favoured pleats.

Laurent introduces her as 'Laurence'. The potential for confusion must be endless, I think to myself, as she shakes my hand with a napkin-weary smile. 'Jean-Pierre, the maître d'hôtel, you've met already.' Like Laurent, the waiter is almost unrecognizable today in a white T-shirt, white cardigan, white track-suit bottoms and white clogs. He is polishing cutlery alongside Laurence and welcomes me with a cutlery-weary half-smile: I am still not sure that he approves of my being here. 'And this is Georges,' says Laurent, leading me through to the kitchen itself.

I can see that the *sous-chef* is Georges because his white chef's jacket is, like Laurent's, embroidered with his name: Georges Lemarié. However, even without the distinctive jacket, I think I would know him as a chef. His ample girth and plump, well-fed features look much more the part than Laurent's wiry figure and angular, altogether craggier mien.

The kitchen is smaller than I'd expected, even for just two cooks. A well-worn wooden work table dominates the centre of the room. An ankle-level shelf beneath it is close to collapse under the weight of saucepans, sieves and platters crammed into too little space. The back wall is lined with ovens, gas rings and hotplates, except where a sink sits inaccessibly in the right-hand corner, next to a further narrow work surface, running along the side wall to the point where a staircase leads steeply down to the basement. Behind me, filling the wall that divides the kitchen from the middle room, are a head-high, double-doored refrigerator and a brightly coloured, sliding-topped ice-cream fridge that would be more at home in a village sweet shop. The final left-hand wall offers no scope for anything but one of the two glazed doors that I already know from the outside. The gap between it and the central table is barely wide enough for the well-padded *sous-chef* to squeeze past.

Georges is busy cutting a pile of small birds into smaller pieces. 'Pigeons,' he tells me, extending a forearm instead of a bloody hand for shaking. It's what every dirty-handed Frenchman does but, even with a year of practice behind me, my arm-shaking skills remain awkwardly under-developed. Georges, in harmony with the prevailing mood, is too pigeon-weary to notice. The single day off since the Easter multitudes has been insufficient for everyone.

'*Bonjour Monsieur! Bonjour Madame!*' pipes the only discordantly cheerful member of the team, as he bounces in through the second glazed door to what appears to be a washing-up station, tucked away behind the crockery shelves, on one side of the middle room. '*Bonjour Georges! Bonjour Jean-Pierre!*' he continues, impervious to their 'how can he be so spirited?' grimaces. '*Bonjour tout le monde!*' he adds to include me, as he skips, bizarrely light-hearted, into the main kitchen, in search of something to purify.

'*Bonjour Eric,*' they chorus, barely civilly.

The *plongeur*'s buoyancy seems calculated to make everyone else's Wednesday 'Monday morning feeling' many times worse. He has hardly rolled up his sleeves before Laurent summons him menacingly to compare their respective notions of saucepan cleanliness. Even the placid-looking Georges vents unexpected aggression on a box of aubergines. I rapidly conclude that there will be better occasions to linger and, with a diffident '*Au revoir tout le monde,*' I start to slink quietly away.

'Tired already?' quips Jean-Pierre, without looking up from the cutlery. 'Wait till you've worked a service.'

'Take no notice,' laughs Laurent. Then, as impeccably polite as when I came here as a customer, he accompanies me down to my car, where I remember an unasked question.

'I was thinking about what you said about money,' I begin hesitantly. 'You never told me what it is that does motivate you.'

'*Oh, ça, c'est simple,*' he answers without a moment's pause. 'It's the pleasure of giving pleasure. *A très bientôt!*'

*

The weather can't decide whether this is summer or winter. Two days ago, at Jean-Marc's wine bar in Montpeyroux, I not only sat outside for lunch, I had to drag my table round the square in search of shade. Then yesterday, I needed every last log in the wood store for a fire.

It is only when shopping that you can really tell that it is spring. Most obviously, the markets have entire stalls selling nothing but local asparagus – just as in later seasons they will sell nothing but peaches or melons or mushrooms – and I am eating it once or twice a day without tiring.

More subtly, the supermarkets can be relied upon to remind you whether it is seedling-planting or bulb-planting time; the moment for filling your garden with plastic furniture or your satchel with stationery for the return to school. In the same way, huge expanses of shelf space are cleared to accommodate whatever arsenal of products is about to be needed to combat the next wave of wildlife invading your home. In my first year, it was enormously consoling to find row upon row of beetle killer just when a particularly outsized variety had taken over my kitchen. Likewise, the mice in my food cupboard could hardly have singled me out, if Super U had chosen that particular week to display such a comprehensive range of traps and poisons.

Today it is ants that appear to be the pest of the moment.

Manu says he dealt with a major infestation while I was away, distributing special arsenic drops that ants find irresistible. Apparently, they gobble up as much of it as they can, then totter back contentedly to base, gasping 'have a taste of this', thereby poisoning the whole of the nest, before they expire. Well, Manu the pest-controller certainly seems to have succeeded because there is no sign of any repeat incursion this year. Unfortunately, however, none of the local traders has thought to stock a goat repellent.

It was a week ago that the incumbents of the new *bergerie* started making a nuisance of themselves. I still think of the goat shed as 'new' because it sprang up halfway through my first year. In a single day the once empty hillside, less than half a kilometre from my bedroom, gained a brash modern barn. For the remainder of that year, however, the goatherd's daily perambulations never really bothered me. Indeed, I grew to enjoy the distant tinkling of bells. Then last Friday I was woken by a tinkling that seemed far from distant. The entire herd was trotting down the path running just inside the eastern boundary of my land.

I donned an absurd combination of boots and dressing-gown and strode across the field behind the house to remonstrate. It was *propriété privée*, I explained. The right of way was farther over. Yes, I knew it was overgrown but that wasn't my fault. I'd turned a blind eye to ramblers but a herd of goats . . .

The herder listened, smirking quietly behind his moustache. I tried to make the dressing-gown look more dignified but that seemed only to increase his amusement. When I finally ran out of steam, he told me the path belonged to the commune. I demurred but he was unpersuadable. 'I've lived in the village all my life,' he said, as if that settled the matter. '*C'est communal.*'

'No idea,' said Manu, when I asked him what he knew about its ownership. 'I've never needed to go that way. Maybe the roadworks are making him find new routes. But I warned you, he's a rogue. You could do with some wire netting.'

'To close off the lane?'

'No, to put a fence down the vineyard side of it. You'll never keep him off the lane but you might be able to keep the goats off your vines.'

This morning in the Clermont l'Hérault market, I was too distracted by the spring produce to remember the wire-netting requirement and, returning with another week's supply of asparagus, I find a goat peering nosily round the back of the house. From farther away, near the vines, I can hear an assortment of what I take to be goat-rallying expletives and, climbing up the slope to investigate, I see the goatherd chasing the last of the stragglers back to the lane.

'You could do with some wire netting,' he tells me with his apparently customary smirk. Then he leaves me to assess the damage.

I try to think positively. Perhaps the goats have simply achieved by mouth the kind of 'thinning' that Virgile might have instigated by hand. But I know in my heart that the rules are different for table vines, especially ones which are less than two years old and have been all but eaten alive in their first year. The supermarkets need to get their priorities right: a bit more emphasis on fence-erection and less on fringe pursuits such as ant-killing.

But I soon have cause to reconsider.

On the rug outside my bedroom is a conical heap of dead ants, seven or eight centimetres high. Inside the room are two slightly larger piles, the first in one of my slippers, the other half-floating in my bedside water-glass; and they were not there this morning.

Manu omitted to mention that the ants' nests that he poisoned were located in the narrow space between the wooden ceiling boards and the terracotta roof tiles above; but a very desirable location it must be, if the new generation's herculean spring-cleaning efforts are anything to go by. A small but determined battalion is doggedly dragging thousands of fallen ancestors out through the joins in the wood, then dumping them with precision on to one of the unappetizing accumulations below.

There is nothing for it but to return to the supermarket, in the hope that surging seasonal demand will have left me a phial of the lethal potion.

*

I hadn't seen Garance since the tarpaulin morning. I had tried calling round to be neighbourly but a quavery voice from behind her small, low door said she was lying in the dark with a migraine. I popped a note under the door inviting her round for a glass of wine when she was better. She replied with a lengthy epistle, delivered to my letter box at the bottom of the drive, explaining how much she loved wine but how bad it was for her heart; how tea and coffee also made it beat too fast. Even the mint infusions, which she found so good for creative concentration, could be dangerously over-stimulating unless they were tempered with just the right amount of calming lemon balm. But subject to these provisos, yes, she'd love to come over for a drink.

'Not now,' I pleaded silently, as I saw her walking up the drive this morning. I was busy putting a circle of fine-meshed rabbit wire round the base of each vine. I knew it wouldn't save the topmost leaves from further goat incursions; but it would at least protect the tender young shoots at the bottom from shorter-legged predators.

I blurted out a lame excuse about having to go shopping. 'Completely out of goat's cheese,' I threw in idiotically for verisimilitude.

'You're off to see Rens?'

My expression told her I had never heard of Rens.

'The *bergerie* in Pégairolles.'

'I didn't know there was one.'

'I must take you there,' she insisted. 'After our infusion.'

I pretended to be worried about the time, foolishly adding that I was devoted to a particular *chèvre* seller in the weekend market. Then it occurred to me that this hardly squared with the midweek shopping alibi, so I told her I was certain he supplied the supermarket.

'How can you?' she shuddered. '*His* goats never go out. It's a factory. And the cheese isn't even Pélardon.'

'What's Pélardon?' I queried.

'That settles it. You have to meet Rens,' she answered unequivocally.

So I went to meet Rens; but not before Garance had told me a great deal about Pélardon.

As with many of the good things in the Languedoc, it was the Romans who first introduced cheese-making. They more or less had to because cheese, like wine, formed part of the legionnaire's rations. Then, when the Empire collapsed and the barbarians invaded, the monasteries preserved the skill, much as they did with winemaking.

I managed to interrupt, asking how it was that she knew these things. For a moment she looked deeply ashamed, then she confessed that she was editing a book – selling her artistic soul to pay for a roof repair. 'It's a children's book,' she stressed, as if that made the dishonour less complete. But the children, it seemed, were to be favoured with a level of detail usually reserved exclusively for Garance's personal misfortunes.

It was an eighteenth-century abbot who first defined Pélardon as a small, flat, round goat's cheese. Or rather, that was how he defined 'Peraldou', which was exactly the same. But the monasteries didn't have a monopoly: the know-how survived in mountain villages where the cheese was made mainly for family consumption . . . Did I know why chèvre never succeeded commercially?

I didn't but Garance soon remedied that. First, cow's cheeses kept and travelled better; second, goats were seen as the poor man's cow and their products despised by the better-off; third, the unfortunate animal was believed to be a reincarnation of the devil.

'I'll take the risk,' I told her, impatient now to leave.

Garance couldn't after all face the dust of the roadworks. The coughing did something else to her heart. So she gave me both directions and her personal cheese order and, calling ahead to check that Rens was open, I set off alone, up the road past Laurent's restaurant, to the place where he spent his childhood.

Pégairolles is the last village in the valley, the final gasp of vines and herby *garrigue* before the sheer white cliffs divide it from the bleakness of the Causses du Larzac above. The village's proper name is Pégairolles de l'Escalette. According to Monsieur and Madame Vargas, almost the oldest inhabitants of our own village, this is a reference to the *escalade* of giant ladders, used by travellers and traders alike to scale these cliffs, before the road builders drove a tunnel through. Zigzag donkey tracks offered less vertical alternatives but many chose the punishing direct-ness of the Escalette. The Vargases even found a grainy, turn-of-the-nineteenth-century photograph to prove it.

The village, sunk deep in the sharp end of the valley, must have fewer sunlit hours than its neighbours only a little farther south, which is probably why my cheese-maker is sitting waiting for me on the sunny side of the main square. A short, plump, jolly-looking woman of about thirty, she has been basking content-edly on a wall in the company of a cigarette, but she quickly jumps up to join me in the Renault.

'Rens van Doorne,' she confirms with a big, bespectacled smile, explaining that her husband has the van today; and anyway, she doesn't drive. 'We can't drive all the way though. Not in your nice car,' she adds, which is quite the kindest thing that anyone has ever said about my ancient little Renault. I like her immedi-ately. 'Best to stop here,' she advises, when a narrow lane leading north from the village comes to an end in a leafy glade, and we continue, in single file, down a well-worn footpath.

'Smell the air up here,' she enthuses over her shoulder, as she lights a second cigarette. 'Good for us as well as the goats. They spend virtually every daylight hour outside. It's one of the stip-ulations for Pélardon. Natural foods – in this case, grasses, oak leaves, broom and thyme. *Ça va pour vous?*' Somewhat short of breath herself, she turns to check on my progress. 'I normally do this on my scooter. But listen. So quiet! You'd never think there was a motorway at the top there. *Mais qu'est-ce qu'il y a?'* She notices my sharp intake of breath.

'You mentioned the "M" word.'

'We're lucky,' she laughs sympathetically. 'Our bit was finished five or six years ago, before we came. That's where the goats must be now, right up by the hard shoulder, or you'd see them. They'll come back down in the afternoon for some shade by the stream.'

'Is this all your land?' I pause to enjoy the sun-dappled water beside us, thinking there must be worse lives to live than that of a goat.

'Goodness, no,' she laughs. 'Just a couple of hectares round the *bergerie* and those are used for hay. It's communal land that the goats graze, about 125 hectares. We've had a lot of support from the mayor. And from neighbours, who are delighted that the goats keep the undergrowth down. Better than strimmers!'

Perhaps I should have a word with my own local goatherd, I think to myself; but then I remember the damage to my vines.

'Have you been here long?' I ask, as a crudely constructed, wooden, barn-like structure comes into view.

'Since 6 January last year. We'd been looking for a property for a year, when at last we found this, through a chance contact. If you'd seen it then! Totally abandoned for two years. It was invisible, completely covered with brambles. But we got it tidied up, extended and ready to receive the goats by 22 February – a date I'll never forget. We had to. We needed to get some money in.'

'Where were the goats in the meantime?'

'We didn't have any. We were starting from scratch. We'd never done this. My father bred goats in the Cantal and Bernard's father bred cattle so we knew a bit about that side. But cheese production, no. I was studying accountancy before. I needed a cheese-making diploma to qualify for the young farmers' grants, so I registered for a correspondence course. Thirty kilos of books they sent me! Sorry, what was it you were asking?'

'The goats?'

'Oh yes, that was chance too. Someone down at Aigues Mortes was giving up. He sold us forty goats and eight kids. We're milking forty-four now, plus there are two billy goats and these.'

In a wooden pen inside the barn, about sixteen young kids rush excitedly to lick her hand, clambering on to each other's backs to check for anything of gastronomic interest. I put out a hand as well but they have no such illusions in my case.

'They all have names,' she explains. 'There's a national convention of using a different letter of the alphabet for each year. All very well last year with T, but this year with U ... Utha ... Uppsala ...' She points to different animals. 'It's a struggle.' All girls, of course. The idea is to renew a fifth of the herd each year, on a rotating basis. An expert comes to say which will produce the most milk. And the best quality. Then we select the top ten.'

'And the others?'

She mimes an apologetic throat-slitting gesture.

'You've no plans to expand then?'

'Our herd's a pretty typical size. The right amount of milk for the number of hours in the day.' She leads me round to the other end of the building, to show me the milking and *chèvre*-making areas. 'You must come back when Bernard's milking,' she decides on the threshold of the milking parlour, then she opens a door beside it. 'The *salle de fabrication*,' she announces, but all I see inside is another door (doubtless gratifying some bureaucratic directive on separating the *chèvres* from the goats). I am about to open the second door when she restrains me.

'No one's allowed in there except me,' she says. 'Not even Bernard. It upsets the cheeses. When I let the man from the Pélardon authority in, it ruined several days' production. The trouble is, cheeses are like children. The more you protect them, the more protection they need.'

'I was hoping to see how it's done.'

'Then come back to the house. I'll see what I can find to show you.'

'I've never seen you in the market,' I call from behind her on the footpath. 'Do you mainly sell from the *bergerie*?'

'I'll be doing the Marché du Terroir – the Tuesday afternoon affair that starts in June in Lodève. An Avignon cheese merchant takes twenty per cent of our production and the Pégairolles wine co-operative's selling them. But otherwise, yes, we sell a lot directly – as many as a hundred cheeses a day in summer.'

'No wonder this path's so well-trodden! How many do you make?'

'Two hundred and forty a day. You need just over half a litre of milk per cheese and each of the goats gives roughly three litres, split between morning and evening milkings. Except for eight weeks between December and February, when they're otherwise engaged producing kids, which means a couple of months without income. It's not a lavish life,' she adds, settling comfortably back into the Renault. 'A family of four can manage and we came here more for the quality of life than money but, all the same, I'd like to be putting something aside, to breathe a bit more easily.'

'When could I come to see the milking?' I ask, turning back into the village square.

'What are you like at six in the morning?' she laughs. 'I get up even earlier than Bernard myself. I cycle down to the *bergerie* at five for a couple of hours of cheese-making, then back to the house to get Thibaud and Margot ready for school. It's almost light by then in winter! Or then again, you could come in the evening.' She winks, as she changes her shoes outside her front door. 'We rent this from the Mairie.'

I tiptoe in to try to keep the floor-tiles free of goat-droppings. The room is small and awkwardly shaped, with one side dominated by a desk and computer screen, in front of which a silent man in overalls – presumably Bernard – nods a wordless hello. Space has been found on the other side of the room for an enormous old sideboard and matching grandfather clock, evoking more spacious living conditions enjoyed by some earlier generation. In the centre, under a pile of children's games, is a long kitchen table, surrounded by half a dozen hard wooden chairs. The only comfortable piece of furniture in the room, confirming the limited leisure-time in this household, is a small sofa – perhaps a sofa bed – in front of a huge television, watched by two catatonic five-year-old boys.

'Thibaud, say *bonjour* to the gentleman,' Rens admonishes the marginally more alert of the pair.

'So much for closing the schools on Wednesdays,' she grumbles, as the man at the computer screen gets up to leave without a word. 'Cutting the hay?' she asks and he nods a silent affirmative.

'Let's see,' says Rens, loading the computer with a CD of photographs for a virtual tour of the cheese-making process. 'Yes, here's the *salle de fabrication*. You can just see the air-conditioning machine in the corner, keeping the temperature at a constant 20°. And here's some new milk cooling . . .'

I draw up a second chair to see better.

'There are three principal stages,' she emphasizes. 'Curdling, straining and ripening. But first, while the milk's cooling, I mix in the whey, run off from yesterday's curds. That starts the so-called lactic fermentation, turning the milk sour. When it hits the target 20°, I add the rennet, which causes the curdling. Then I leave it in buckets for twenty-four hours.' The computer displays a row of curd-filled buckets. 'The next day, the curds are separated from the whey and moulded – always by hand for Pélardon.' The screen obligingly offers an image of a tray of freshly moulded, small, flat, circular cheeses. 'They ripen like that, being turned every day, for a minimum of eleven days.'

'Quite a tie,' I call after her, as she disappears to an adjoining room.

'Tell me about it!' she laughs, bustling back with a pair of cheeses on a plate. 'We can never take the kids away on holiday. Even if we could afford it,' she adds in a whisper, between television gunshots. 'Come, have a taste. The paler one's the eleven-day.'

After a week and a half of ripening, the cheese is soft, moist and creamy (but never runny, she stresses). The flavour is clean and fresh, delicately salty, slightly nutty perhaps. 'Melting in the mouth' seems to be the judgement that Rens was hoping for.

'The other one's the mature variety, the *pélardon affiné*,' she explains, encouraging me to compare. 'Turned for an extra ten days.'

The twenty-one-day cheese has acquired a light, ivory-coloured crust with a fine layer of mould, just gently flecked with blue. The texture is slightly drier, the flavour still delicate but more pronouncedly 'goaty'.

'They don't have these at the restaurant, do they?' I ask her.

'At Le Temps de Vivre? No. We haven't been, but I've heard they buy from Cédric, in the Saturday market.'

'But you're practically neighbours, you and Laurent. And yours are so much better.'

'They both won bronze medals,' she says in a way that suggests that she has been bursting to say this all morning. 'Two out of only three for Pélardon in the *département*,' she emphasizes, in case I am under-impressed. 'And no gold or silver,' she adds to make her triumph unambiguous.

I congratulate her and make a mental note not to return to the weekend market stall.

*

'Have you been to the new place?' asks Babette, the village café's *patronne*.

'Le Temps de Vivre?' I ask, still recovering from shock. For once her *plat du jour* is something other than *coq aux olives*. I can't decide exactly what, but it certainly isn't the 'signature dish' that was hardly ever *not* the dish of the day in the old days. A fishy-tasting piece of pork? An over-meaty tuna steak? It is better not to speculate.

'Don't be ridiculous,' she says, as if I'd mentioned Le Jardin des Sens or The Ritz in Paris. 'I mean, the Restaurant à Vin . . .' She sneers the words, as if she considers them pretentious beyond forgiveness 'On the corner, where the butcher's used to be. Competition!' She laughs defiantly, and I see at once why the menu has so unexpectedly diversified.

'I haven't even noticed it,' I confess. 'Your cousin Manu's had me hard at work on the vegetable patch.'

'Talked you into it, did he?' Babette laughs her all-knowing laugh. 'The new motor cultivator he's had his eye on?'

'I'm going back to try it now,' I explain, leaving most of her over-burnt *crème brulée* untouched. 'I've never used one, so Manu thought it was best for him to run it in first.'

Manu had obligingly left my mud-caked new toy in the middle of the terrace to be ploughed. The vicious-looking rotary blades were tangled with vegetation and one of the handlebars was slightly buckled, but otherwise it seemed to have come through the commissioning process intact.

My neighbour had, however, let the instruction manual blow away; and the man himself was unavailable for personal tuition. He was taking Mme Gros to the optician's for the vital six-monthly check on her spectacles, to ensure that, as always, nothing escaped her notice. I would have to experiment alone.

The lightest touch on the starter handle sent the cultivator rattling violently towards the edge of the terrace, dragging me along behind it, as I struggled not to let go. There were two possible speed settings, represented on the handle by a tortoise and a hare. These, I quickly learned, stood for fast and extremely fast. It wouldn't have been so bad if I hadn't kept tripping over a metal bar pointing diagonally down at my feet. It was useful enough to prop the machine upright when it was stationary, but in motion it was an absurdly awkward piece of design. It would have to go.

I was just working out how to detach it when a pair of quavering voices tried to stop me. 'That's the brake you're unscrewing!' called the Vargases, who had hobbled up from their olive grove to see how I was settling in.

As usual, they addressed me in their curious unison: both a reflection of over sixty years of unremitting matrimonial

harmony and a long-practised means of making two individually feeble voices stronger. Their terraces were not far away –
roughly halfway down the lane to the village – but they sounded
much more breathless after the gradient than I remembered.

'You're supposed to stick the spike in the ground,' they coun-
selled. 'The deeper you stick it, the slower you go.' Thanks to
their timely advice, I completed the ploughing by the time they
were sufficiently recovered to decline my offer of a lift back
home.

'I should think at least three rows of tomatoes,' says Manu,
having approved my results this morning. He delivers a little
homily on the pricking out of side shoots and the need to buy
my stakes (renewed promises of discounts from cousins); then
he passes swiftly on to other favourite vegetables; and, of course,
time really is getting tight if I am planning to get some more fruit
trees in. Rotten luck, he commiserates, having half the apple
trees chose this year of all years to die of old age.

Then he notices six new cypresses in the back of my Renault,
waiting to be planted. There are four well-established specimens
beside the drive, planted by my uncle twenty years ago, but I
like the thought of more of their strong, vertical accents in the
landscape.

Manu frowns disbelievingly. Perhaps he has been wrong all
these years: maybe cypress cones are edible after all.

'Ridiculous!' barks Mme Gros from across the stream, proving
the continuing power of her stern, black bifocals. 'Proper place
for those is the cemetery,' she adds, making it plain that her
husband is to play no further part in such frivolities.

*

At first I thought the man advertising himself as a trout seller in
the Clermont l'Hérault market had sold out. There was nothing
on his stall. I would just have to buy something different from
the general fishmonger at the other end of the square. But then I
saw the tank in the back of his van. The stock was all alive.

An elderly woman ahead of me was taking her time to identify a pair which conformed precisely to the dimensions that she had in mind. '*Trop petite,*' she said of one that was fished out for scrutiny. '*Trop grosse,*' of another, almost undetectably larger. The surly-looking salesman was losing patience. Finally one passed the test and was duly rewarded with a sharp blow to its head with a big stick.

'The *truites de Labeil* not good enough?' said a familiar voice behind me. It was Laurent – surprisingly far from Pégairolles for a Wednesday morning. 'It's quiet,' he said by way of explanation. 'And I'm always on the look-out for new ingredients,' he added by way of further justification.

'Do you mean I shouldn't buy from here?' I asked, aware that the woman in front had at last issued her second death warrant and that it was about to be my turn.

'The ones from Labeil are unbeatable,' he said. 'And much nearer home for you – just up near the Grotte de Labeil. But you're here now.' I made a selection at random. The trout man was visibly in no mood for further indecision.

'So when are you coming over for a service?' Laurent continued, as the stick dispatched its next victim. 'There's more to running a restaurant than just shopping, you know.'

'Sorry, I don't know where these first few weeks have gone.'

'You didn't let Jean-Pierre put you off?' he asked with a grin.

'No, I'm just so far behind on the gardening.'

'How about tomorrow lunchtime? We've got three or four bookings.'

'I've got to go salad-picking.'

'That can't take all day,' he exclaimed incredulously. He hadn't met Garance.

'Call that a salad?' she had asked me woundingly the day before, when presented with a mix of the first of my lettuces to sprout more than six small leaves. I had flattered myself that some of the varieties were quite unusual but to Garance they might as well have come from Super U. 'It's time you learned about wild salads,' she informed me.

'And I don't just mean dandelions,' she adds crisply this morning, as we set off on our hike. She explains that we're going to start in the hills with the plants that thrive in the stonier scrubland of the *garrigue*, then explore the more succulent specimens of the plain and finally tackle those that prefer the river's edge. A day should be enough, she assures me.

I hadn't really thought of Garance as the outdoor type but, freed from her migraine and blessed with a cloudy sky, she proves to be an indefatigable walker – especially when imbued with a mission. She brushes aside the suggestion that we try to build in a lunch stop as irredeemably self-indulgent, insisting that our bottles of water from my spring are all the sustenance we need. Indeed, such is her punishing pace that by mid-afternoon, we have already covered the intended territory and our baskets are brimming with greenery.

Our fifteen-kilometre harvest includes two types of wild rocket, a wild form of cress, at least three wild varieties of chicory and some salsify. It also embraces countless other assorted leaves whose names I have never heard of but which mostly look irritatingly familiar from my own rather more accessible terraces, whence we departed seven hungry hours ago.

Garance is particularly excited about the culinary uses of something which she calls *pourpier* but which my dictionary translates as Golden Purslane or, less prettily, Pigweed. I know it better as the most persistent of the weeds beside my swimming pool but I doubt that I shall be mentioning this. For the moment, I am more concerned with the chances of a four o'clock serving of *coq aux olives* with double chips at Babette's.

'Makes me feel quite peckish,' says Garance, surveying her basket and nibbling half a poppy leaf.

*

'Come and see my office,' calls Virgile from the window above his *cave*.

He continues to live in the rented flat around the corner, but the most habitable of the still essentially uninhabitable rooms above the *cave* now contains a desk – or rather a wide wooden plank balanced between two piles of empty wooden wine cases. White plastic garden chairs for the winemaker and up to two favoured guests contrast oddly with the flowery 1940s wallpaper. The only other piece of furniture is a battered shelving unit, divided into several dozen pigeon holes, where happily the one marked 'bills' seems to contain the smallest pile of papers.

My inspection complete, we go in search of Magda and supper, but supper seems less than imminent. The flat is now, in many ways, more domesticated than it was in Virgile's bachelor days – a vase of flowers, a new set of display shelves where artefacts of Polish-looking provenance mingle with the more familiar Joly collection. But Magda is busy with what appears to be several days' worth of dirty dishes before food preparations can begin, so Virgile proposes an aperitif downstairs and round another corner, in his *chai d'élévage*.

This is what I used to know as a humble tractor garage, but now it is a beautifully lit, immaculately plastered, air-conditioned space where the wines needing barrel-ageing enjoy greater cool and comfort than Virgile and Magda in their flat. It also doubles as a tasting room, with an upturned barrel pressed into service as a table and some glasses already awaiting us.

'Tell me what you think of this,' says Virgile, filling a large pipette with delicately straw-coloured wine from the nearest barrel and dividing the contents between two of the glasses.

The wine is mouth-wateringly crisp and fresh; straightforward perhaps but intense.

'And this?' he asks, repeating the operation from the neighbouring barrel.

The second wine is heavier, richer, more serious; every bit as delicious but totally different.

'Now this?' he asks, holding a pouring of each up at eye level to check that the quantities are equal and then mixing them thoroughly together by tipping the liquid repeatedly from glass to glass.

The resulting blend is a revelation, the complex interplay of freshness and richness making each of the two separate elements now seem crudely one-dimensional.

'Which is the Grenache Blanc?' I ask admiringly. I have a personal interest in knowing because it was a bottle of mine – a Grenache Blanc from a grower in the Roussillon, served 'blind' at dinner one night – which first persuaded Virgile to experiment with a white wine from this single grape variety.

'They both are,' he answers with a grin. 'From the same *parcelle*. I divided it in half and harvested the two parts fifteen days apart, so that one half was barely ripe and the other super-ripe. I'll be blending it all tomorrow, for bottling in June.'

'It's brilliant. The wine, I mean. Well, the idea too . . .'

'It's thanks to you that I made it. Otherwise, I'd still be selling these grapes to the co-op.'

'Then, you'd better call it "Cuvée Patrick",' I tell him.

'It would never sell,' he laughs, and we return to Magda's supper.

*

One of the few things that Garance and I have in common is a sense of vertigo.

'It's not so very high,' she pleaded, having failed to negotiate Manu's release for her roof restoration project. 'It's just that if I go more than one step up a ladder, I black out.'

I started to explain that I was nearly as bad, scarcely able to harvest the upper branches of my cherry trees; but Garance was already trying another tack: 'They're forecasting storms and the ceiling plaster might not survive another wetting . . .' Then a more desperate ploy: 'I'll buy you lunch at the new restaurant. I've heard they do a lovely *salade de lentilles* and an excellent *vin du patron* . . .'

It wasn't the house red that made me give in, nor even the promise of pulses; it was the way that her beseeching jumped an octave higher with each new argument. However, with hindsight, I would have preferred the labour without the lunch.

The Restaurant à Vin is run by a former Parisian stockbroker-turned Languedoc wine evangelist. Doubtless he has many fine qualities, but culinary competence is not among them. Babette has little to fear from either the watery lentils served to Garance or the overcooked trout ordered by me. It was hard to believe that the unfortunate creature derived from the same Pisciculture de Labeil as Laurent's firm-fleshed specimens, which was all the more unfortunate as it had required some considerable negotiation. As soon as we sat down, Garance declared herself a vegetarian, with convictions extending to food that she paid for, as well as food that she ate; except, of course, that on this occasion she had a leaking roof. If only I had not been so persuasive. Hervé the stockbroker's desiccated *truite aux amandes* was enough to drive anyone to lentils. A charred plastic label, still hooked on to one of the gills, confirmed that the fish had once been organic but my companion remained mutely censorious.

I tried to coax her into conversation. 'Laurent says the farm is up near the Grotte de Labeil. We could visit the caves after lunch.'

'We're busy after lunch,' she reminded me sternly, adding that, anyway, her fear of heights was equalled by a dread of underground depths. 'And you haven't finished your wine.' She was clearly impatient to leave.

'I thought it best to keep a clear head for the ladder,' I excused myself, although really what I thought was, 'One sip's enough.' Perhaps if I hadn't seen the funnel in the magnum behind the bar, or the assortment of half-finished wines that Hervé was discreetly pouring into it . . .

*

I must have been climbing the narrow road for about five kilometres when I see a sign promising eight more that will be 'narrow and dangerous'. In this stretch, someone with a sense of humour has painted a white line down the middle. This is doubtless invaluable whenever two bicycles are pedalling in opposite directions, but there is scarcely room for a little Renault to pass a pedestrian, let alone the fish-farm delivery van that may be hurtling towards me.

But you're expected, I tell myself. When Laurent made the appointment, the owner said he'd be back from his rounds by ten, and that was half an hour ago. Except there might still be customers, racing home to their fridges with carloads of fish.

Just as my nerve is starting to crack, a sign to the Pisciculture de Labeil points down a side lane, which is narrower still. It has been cut into the side of the hill, with a rock face on one side and a deep ditch, dropping vertiginously down to a river, on the other. For at least a further kilometre, anxieties over oncoming traffic give way to more fundamental concerns about simply keeping the wheels on the slim strip of tarmac. I have never been more relieved to see a pair of rusty gates and a waiting fish farmer.

'Let's start at the top,' says Yves Jouvigné, climbing the dilapidated concrete steps between his only slightly less dilapidated concrete fish tanks. He is, I would guess, in his late sixties and old enough to have mixed the ubiquitous concrete himself, but he bounds up the hillside with the agility of a much younger man.

There must be several dozen tanks, each the size of a small swimming pool, banked steeply against the hillside like a sports stadium. Or rather, like a sports stadium impersonating a waterfall, because everywhere I look, spectacular volumes of water are cascading down through pipes, from tank to tank.

'Where does it all come from?' I shout, hardly audible above the gushing water.

'It's the River Laurounet,' he calls from several paces ahead. 'Half of it, anyway. The source is just five hundred metres away, up in the Labeil caves. That's why it's exceptionally pure. There's no time for it to get polluted.'

He presses on up towards a small concrete shed, next to the battery of pipes where the water first crashes into the system.

It looks inaccessible, cut off from us by one of the deeper tanks; but then I notice a wobbly wooden plank. First Garance's roof, now this, I think to myself, as M. Jouvigné springs across the makeshift bridge like a teenager.

'Have you always done this?' I ask, as I cautiously walk the plank myself.

'No,' he laughs. 'I bought this place in 1995. I'll tell you my story later.'

Our priority is the contents of the shed: half a dozen plastic troughs, teeming with hundreds of baby fish, only four or five centimetres in length.

'How old are these?' I ask, expecting an answer in weeks or even days.

'Six months,' he tells me. 'We buy the eggs at various times during the year.'

'They don't breed here?'

'We mainly farm rainbow trout – an American variety which doesn't lay easily without human assistance, which is a specialist business in itself. Normally, they'd lay their eggs in the winter months but with changes of light and temperature, you can fool them into thinking it's winter at any time of year.' He points to the fish in one of the troughs. 'You see these slightly bigger ones? They're the same age as the others but they've grown faster. It's very important to keep sorting the fish by size; otherwise the big ones would eat the smaller ones.'

Outside, there are several next largest sizes in a subdivided tank at the top of the stadium. Then, as they grow bigger, the fish move steadily down the levels. 'It takes eighteen months for ours to reach maturity,' he tells me. 'Many people do it in nine, but the flesh is much less firm.'

He is walking effortlessly along the narrow wall dividing the top tank from the one below. On one side there is water; on the other, a sharp drop and then water again. It is clear that I have to follow him.

'How do you slow yours down?' I ask, putting one tentative foot on the tightrope.

'We starve them for one day a week,' he explains, as I inch my way forward. 'We also put much less fat in their food – a mixture of vegetable flour and fish flour.'

'And er ... (*Don't look down!*) ... How many fish do you produce?' I ask. Only by grasping an overhead wire at the halfway point can I steady myself sufficiently for articulate speech.

'Twenty tonnes a year. That's eighty to ninety thousand fish,' he says, springing nimbly down on to an unstable metal platform, more than a metre below us, on the other side of a fast-flowing canal, whither once again I must follow him.

'Would you like a coffee?' he asks, when I am finally on terra firma at the bottom

For once I could do with something stronger, but I follow him gratefully into a huge, long room in the building beside us, where a puzzling amount of furniture, around a dozen tables and fifty chairs, has been pushed back against one wall. Perhaps, being this far from civilization, he provides his staff with lunch; but surely they cannot be so numerous? Then I see the shelves lined with scores of upturned glasses. A glass-fronted cabinet holds nearly as many champagne flutes, suggesting quite extraordinarily festive workers' catering. And they must be all the merrier for the row of dusty bottles on top, containing most of the popular aperitifs and *digestifs*.

But the clue is in the dust.

'This used to be a restaurant,' M. Jouvigné enlightens me, as we sit at the only table not in the pile by the wall. 'Until last year. I kept it going when we first bought the place, but then it reached the point where it needed too much money spent on it to be profitable.'

'Is the fish farming ...' – I pause to make the question seem less impertinent – '... reasonably profitable?'

'Now that we're organic, yes. It justifies a higher price. There are only four or five of us in the whole of France, you know. The great advantage for us is the water. Not just the quality but the quantity. We work on a maximum of eleven fish per cubic metre, whereas the official organic limit is thirty-five. Another coffee?'

'I ought to be going.' I can see M. Jouvigné's workers gathering near the window, wondering who is monopolizing their lunch table. 'But you were going to tell me your story.'

'Oh yes, well, it was quite different from this. I trained at hotel and catering college, after school – that's why I could cope with the restaurant – but after my military service, I went into banking. Thirty years with Crédit Lyonnais, ending up as manager of their branch in Beaune. Then the bank had its crisis in the 1990s and I decided to do something different. I'd always loved rod fishing, so buying this seemed logical – using my half-forgotten catering skills as well. My wife and I managed twenty covers on our own, preparing everything to order.'

As everything will have to be today, I think to myself, watching four hungry-looking men hover outside; but M. Jouvigné seems in no great hurry.

'I'm thinking about retiring altogether,' he says, settling back in his chair, while the four shuffle restlessly. 'Leaving it all to my sons.'

'They live locally?'

'No, they're in Paris. They'll manage the business from there.'

'And you've what . . . just the four assistants?'

'Only two. That's all it needs,' he says and I wonder whether I should mention that there are four expecting lunch today.

*

'I'm sure my half only *looks* bigger,' insisted Manu. I had invited him to compare the disappointing pile of horse manure at the top of my drive with his own, apparently more imposing delivery. 'Just that my heap's on a slope and yours is on the flat,' he explained. 'Trick of perspective, perhaps . . . I certainly told the wife's cousin to divide it equally.' Yet he had no theory as to why the consignment on his side of the stream should look so much better-rotted, so much less diluted with straw than mine.

'Trick of the light?' I suggested, as I trudged away with a barrowload to fertilize the fruit trees.

The top priority was the cherries. They would be ready for picking in a couple of weeks, so it was probably too late to make any useful impact on this year's crop; but I still felt I had to try.

In any event, there was good news on the cherry front: I now had three big trees, not two. Uncle Milo had fenced off the land at the end of the kitchen terraces, presumably to protect the more cultivated areas near the house from his indiscriminately destructive half-dozen sheep. Throughout my first year, everything beyond the fence remained badly overgrown but now the strimmer had uncovered a supplementary fruit supply – unknown, it seemed, even to Manu – and it could hardly be more welcome.

The principal tree, outside the kitchen, had an enormous twelve-metre span supported by three stout trunks dividing just above the ground, but the table beneath was all but hidden by fallen stems. The wind and the rain had been competing to discover which could knock down the most. The crop would be much reduced, and I knew just how early my neighbour could be persuaded to leave his bed to satisfy his spouse's penchant for cherry jam. With the newly discovered tree, the three of us might get by.

'You could do with a little tractor and trailer for that manure,' observed Manu, no doubt thinking how much less strenuous some of his own exertions might be if my machinery budget were less miserly. 'You can't afford to hang about,' he nagged, as I shovelled the olive trees' quota into the barrow.

With at least five months to go before the olive crop, I felt entirely relaxed about a late dose of fertilizer. My worry was that I had done nothing about pruning. I needed some advice from the Vargases but they hadn't been seen on their terraces for several days. I decided to call at their home in the village.

Like almost all the village houses, the Vargases', just inside the gateway, is tall and narrow, with three storeys. A few, farther up the hill, have four, but they all follow similar conventions: the ground floors originally conceived as workshops, stables, sheep pens or occasionally shops, depending on the original owners' businesses; the middle floors (singular or plural) providing the living space; and the top ones, formerly granaries for stocking dry goods, even hay for the animals below. In most cases, the living-rooms have tiny balconies overlooking the street and today, like many of her neighbours, Mme Vargas is taking advantage of the end of the rains and pegging out some historic-looking underwear on a washing-line between the railings.

She calls to me to let myself in through the cluttered chaos of the lower storey – in this case, part tool shed, part olive-processing centre, part furniture store for items older and uglier than those which already fill the floor above but which might yet, one day, serve a turn.

'Albert's doing the rubbish sorting,' explains Mme Vargas. 'He'll be back soon.'

Then we both laugh in acknowledgement of the incompatibility of these two propositions because, while I was away, the authorities devised an ingenious way to fill the extra leisure hours created by the thirty-five-hour week.

The old, undiscriminating, communal waste bins on wheels have rolled away for the last time and the so-called *tri sélectif* now requires every household to sift its refuse into five separate classifications:

- biodegradables (anything from potato peelings to tea bags);
- paper (but not kitchen paper, because that is biodegradable);
- glass (including bottles but not, for some reason, drinking glasses);
- packaging (including tins and plastic bottles but not, for some reason, plastic olive oil bottles or plastic bags); and finally
- whatever has managed to slip through all of these nets (for which a deliberately diminutive receptacle has been issued to each home).

Bizarrely, each of these personalized residual bins has a lock, with a key, but everyone's key is the same. 'What will happen when the tourists arrive?' I asked the telephone information line. 'We're thinking of installing unlocked bins on picnic sites,' they assured me. I wanted to ask about visitors impudent enough to picnic outside the sites, but I didn't think they would understand. Meanwhile, rumour has it that the Rubbish Police are out there, doggedly amassing evidence of non-compliance.

Virgile thinks it's hilarious, but that's because Saint Saturnin hasn't yet had to submit to the system. He doesn't have to spend hours in front of the various centralized collection bins, agonizing over whether a cardboard box counts as paper or packaging, or what we are supposed to do with the plastic bags that we use to carry down our wine bottles. At least they have issued compost-makers to those of us with gardens. The Vargases had to find space in the house for a special green wheelie-bin, which they struggle to push into the street once a week.

'Have you read what they're going to do with the plastic bottles?' asks Mme Vargas.

I know there was something in the promotional literature that was supposed to make us feel good about the recycling, but I have managed to blank it out.

'Make pullovers!' she reminds me disgustedly. Then, suddenly anxious, she asks, 'Do you think we'll be made to wear them?'

'Only if we put something in the wrong bin,' I reassure her.

'How was the olive pruning?' asks M. Vargas, returning from his *tri sélectif* with a handful of empty plastic bags, which he starts to fold methodically.

'That's why I'm here,' I explain. 'I haven't managed to start and I'm wondering if I've left it too late.'

'It's the middle of May.' They revert to the usual unison. 'The trees will be flowering in two or three weeks.'

'But there's so much dead wood. After only one year away!'

'Best to cut that out and leave the rest till next year,' they advise me, as ever in agreement.

'That'll give you more time for rubbish-sorting,' laughs M. Vargas, while his wife gathers up the neatly folded bags.

'I'll put these under the mattress,' she whispers, ever mindful of the threat of plastic pullovers.

*

'*C'est toujours calme*,' said Laurent, when I asked him whether they were busy, adding this time, '*dramatiquement calme*. Not a single reservation.'

He explained that no one was going out this week because it was Mother's Day on the coming Sunday and everyone in France who had the most tenuous connection with a mother went out to eat on Mother's Day. They had been fully booked for Sunday for two weeks and had already had to turn ten tables away. In fact, they were going to serve forty-four covers – really stretching themselves – to try to make up for the lack of bookings during the week.

'There's another public holiday, Ascension Day, next Thursday; then Whitsun ten days later. It's catastrophic for business on every other day of the week. And this doesn't help,' he sighed, as I followed him through to the glazed veranda.

A dramatic brown scar had appeared on the opposite hillside. The motorway diggers were raising huge clouds of dust as they cut into slopes that had once been vineyards to widen the carriageways; and the wind was blowing much of the dust across the valley towards us. The tables in the main room behind us must be coming into their own.

'*Tant pis*.' He shrugged, turning resolutely back to the kitchen. 'There's always preparation to be done. Georges will get you started. Here, you'd better wear this,' he said, tossing a rolled-up white apron from the other side of the central wooden worktop. Then, seeing me hesitate, he added, 'I told you, the washing-machine never stops.'

'We could still get some *tables de passage*,' said Georges the optimist. 'We always have to be ready.' And this, I am rapidly learning, means ready in particular with vast amounts of *caviar d'aubergines*.

There are three deep trays on the worktop, each stacked with alarming quantities of droopy, sweaty-looking, surely overcooked aubergines, which I have to turn into something fit to eat. Georges explains that they have been roasted slowly in the oven to get rid of most of the liquid and concentrate the flavour. What I now have to do is cut them open and scrape out the innards – an easy enough assignment but one that soon proves both tedious and mildly repellent. The outside of a slow-baked aubergine is an item of beauty compared to the inside. The mushy, grey-brown pulp that my labours are generating bears no discernible relationship to the finished *tarte friande* that Virgile and I enjoyed before Easter. The trans-formation, Georges assures me, will come with the addition of olive oil, some sweated onions and garlic, a few herbs and a little tomato purée; but all of that seems impossibly far in the future, as I finish the first of my trays.

There are two large rubbish sacks in the kitchen, one beside the worktop, one near an all-purpose sink in the corner and both suspended from the kind of hoops found in public parks. Laurent sees me hesitating with my debris.

'It's all the same,' he assures me. 'Meat, aubergines, paper, tins, everything.'

'What, no *tri sélectif*?'

'Come.' He beckons me out into the wind and around to the back of the building, where he still has two of the giant bins on wheels such as used to serve whole sections of the village. 'Imagine,' he says. 'They empty these once a week and yet they expected me to sort the kitchen waste into biodegradable and otherwise, then throw it into these unbagged! I said to them, "Are you *malade*?" I mean, what did they think my lobster shells and meat bones were going to smell like after a week in summer? "Do you really think anyone would eat here?" I asked them.'

'So they let you off?' I ask, as Laurent returns me to my auber-gines.

'He ignored them,' laughs Georges, who is quietly chopping, slicing and stirring his way through a variety of assignments, needing little if any apparent direction.

'We knew each other at the Jardin,' says Laurent, as if to explain the high degree of trust between them. 'What are we doing for today's *amuse*?' he asks of Georges, as if to confirm it.

Lest I underestimate his pedigree, Jean-Pierre explains that he too is an alumnus of Le Jardin des Sens. 'Not the real Jardin', whispers Georges mischievously, only the sister restaurant called La Compagnie des Comptoirs across the road, which Georges disparagingly brands the 'annexe'. But annexe or no, Jean-Pierre's glazed expression suggests that he wishes he were back there.

He has been polishing cutlery again, but by the time I reach my third tray of aubergines, he is breaking new ground and polishing plates. Looking studiedly casual today, in designer-faded jeans and sweat-shirt, he is standing at the table in the middle room, working his way through an intimidating pile of the outsized 'presentation plates' which fill each place setting until the arrival of the first course.

'Get back to your aubergines,' he says as I peer over his shoulder, pretending to supervise.

In doing so, I notice something that I had forgotten from my dinner here. As well as bearing the name 'Le Temps de Vivre' on the rim, the plates have a tiny, exquisitely painted feather in the centre.

'*Bécasse*,' says Laurent, when I ask him. 'But not because woodcock is something you're likely to see on my menus.'

'It's because he's obsessed with hunting,' jokes Georges.

'Not even that,' laughs Laurent, producing an actual *bécasse* feather from his desk, as tiny as the picture on the plates. 'It's what artists use to paint the very finest of details,' he explains.

I get the point and so, apparently, does Jean-Pierre who goes off to check on the details of the place settings.

'Each service has to be like a theatrical performance,' explains Laurent. 'No mistakes, everything precisely timed. We've started building up a loyal clientele but it only takes one little thing to stop them coming back. *N'est-ce pas*, Eric?'

The *plongeur* has been doing his best to keep a low profile, as if he, more than anyone, is likely to perpetrate the 'one little thing'; but Laurent stops him as he is about to scuttle downstairs to the basement with a polystyrene box.

'It doesn't smell,' he protests, having already washed it a second time. He sniffs nervously inside and slowly, almost reluctantly, Laurent concedes that he might be right.

Eric, now the happiest man in the kitchen, skips on down the stairs and almost trips over a two- or three-year-old girl who is clambering up from whatever accommodation the Arrazats have in the basement.

'*Bonjour*, Geo-geo,' she says, running straight to Georges.

'*Bonjour*, Leah,' he replies, opening the nearest half of the double-doored fridge. 'You know what this is?'

He takes out a bundle of damp tea towel, inside which is a metal platter. On the platter lies a glistening, dark-shelled, living lobster. Its claws are securely restrained by rubber bands but even so Leah shivers with apprehension. Laurent warns her of the many ways in which she could hurt herself (apparently, the only safe place to hold a lobster is the middle of its back) but she rapidly proves herself her father's daughter by trying to force the wriggling crustacean into a child-sized frying-pan. She giggles delightedly but there are tears when 'Geo-geo' – understandably reluctant to cause the boss's daughter injury – returns the new pet to the fridge.

'That's really why I chose this location,' laughs Laurent, dispatching his daughter downstairs after a cuddle. 'On all the busier services, when Laurence is in the dining-room, Leah can stay with my mother and stepfather in Lodève. They spoil her more than Georges.'

Leah's lobster adventure has given me time to finish the last of the aubergines but now Laurent puts two large crates of uncooked beef tomatoes in front of me. However, I never learn what he has in mind for them.

'In a moment,' he calls to Leah. 'We'll play when I've explained this to Patrick. No, don't climb the stairs. *C'est dangereuse, la cuisine. Reste là . . .*'

Then tears.

A tantrum, I assume, but Laurent, more skilled at decoding the language of tears, drops the tomato boxes like a scalding dish and rushes to the staircase. It seems that the basement is equally dangerous because seconds later he runs back up with his daughter cradled in his arms. She is bleeding from just above one eye.

'Georges, you may be on your own,' he warns, as he picks up his car keys. 'Sorry, Patrick. I'm sure the hospital in Lodève can deal with this but it may take a while. We'll phone each other, yes?' And he rushes back down to the Subaru.

'Perhaps I'd better leave it there,' I suggest to Jean-Pierre after a brief, embarrassed pause.

'Oh, so you're not interested in *my* work,' says the maître d'hôtel, sounding genuinely hurt. 'I suppose you think looking after the cheeses is just a matter of taking off the wrappers. And managing the wine stocks . . .'

'No, no.' I try to soothe him. 'Now this, for instance . . .' I turn with exaggerated curiosity to the tall, glass-fronted cabinet filled with bottles, in the middle room. 'Is this where you chill the white wines?'

Jean-Pierre looks at me warily, wondering whether this is a send-up, but gives me the benefit of the doubt. 'It's for keeping the reds cool. Not iced, but not summer-in-the-south tempera-ture either. You'll understand in July! There's a couple of every-thing under thirty Euros in there. We keep the more expensive bottles in the cellar, so the chef's never happier than when he sees me going downstairs.'

A colder, waist-high fridge fills the rest of the wall beneath the farmhouse-kitchen cupboards. It holds a representative selection of whites and rosés, aperitifs and mineral waters and, near it, is a machine that is noisily spitting ice cubes into a refrigerated drawer. Hot times ahead, appears to be the message.

The wine cellar is by no means enormous, especially since an air-conditioned cold room has been carved out of one corner to accommodate the cheeses and other supplies that would be over-chilled in the fridges. Nonetheless, allowing for the office beyond the cellar, which I glimpsed from the outside, there can be very little basement space for a family of three at the far end. No wonder Leah wants to play in the kitchen.

Another corner of the wine cellar is taken up with washing and drying machines. A third doubles as Jean-Pierre's changing-room, with a dress-shop coatrail on castors holding a week's worth of colourful shirts and ties, with a choice of two suits. Wheeling this aside, the maître d'hôtel shows me the system of racking that he installed for the costlier, below-stairs beverages, and I express what I hope is convincing admiration.

'We normally stock just a few of each,' he explains. 'We work with two Montpellier wine merchants. They deliver whatever we need to reorder every Thursday. We also take a few things from Virgile's *négociant*, but he makes us buy in larger quantities.'

'Do you sell much of Virgile's wine?' I ask.

'We've got twelve of his Coteaux du Languedoc 2000,' says Jean-Pierre. 'But we haven't sold any yet. Puech, the middleman, fixed the price so high. We've finally persuaded him and Virgile to lower it a bit. It was working out more expensive than a lot of the better-established names. Great for Virgile's ego but not so good for his bank balance.'

He pauses with extra reverence at a section holding six bottles, explaining that these are all from the illustrious Domaine de la Grange des Pères. (It was the red from this property that first ignited my enthusiasm for the wines of this region but I have only been able to afford one bottle since, and that was in the safety of my home, away from restaurant mark-ups.) Just these half dozen bottles – spread between three different years, 1996, 1998 and 1999 – represent a significant investment for Laurent, especially as he had to buy the first two vintages at a time when they were already mature. But no serious wine list in the region can afford to be without them, and he has several dozen more reserved in Montpellier.

'What if you get six rich customers in the same week?' I ask, as we go back upstairs.

'If only!' laughs Jean-Pierre, looking at last as though he might be feeling appreciated. 'Imagine this in the old days.' He pauses halfway towards the main door. 'A hundred and twenty covers, elbow to elbow. Happy campers.'

'And remind me, the maximum's how many now?'

'Thirty to forty. It depends on the size of the parties.'

'You can't give all of them the view, of course.'

'No, that's one of our biggest problems. The people who arrive at half past one on a busy Sunday, without a reservation, expecting one of the best tables on the veranda.'

'And today?' I ask on the doorstep, as a gust of wind nearly blows me back inside.

'Still no one. But you always have to be ready.'

Returning home, I find Manu crawling on his hands and knees amongst the weeds at the foot of the principal cherry tree.

'You always have to be ready,' he wheezes reproachfully.

In my rush to the restaurant, I failed to notice that the cherries were ripe. It was the ideal moment for picking. They would never again be so perfect. Now, less than three hours later, a distressing percentage lies at my feet.

'They forecast this wind for tomorrow,' puffs Manu, as the tree bombards us with a further shower of fruit. 'But you always . . .'

'. . . have to be ready,' I acknowledge, scrambling on the ground beside him. There will be no lunch for either of us, if we are to salvage the windfalls before the birds or insects or animals find them.

*

No rain for three weeks. Already the landscape has turned from green to yellow, and even with Uncle Milo's watering system, I am starting to regret the late-planted fruit trees.

Apparently, my benefactor's life here began as an experiment to see how far it was possible to manage without all the conventional gadgetry of late-twentieth-century life. Even electricity arrived relatively late, which explains the eccentric shape and irregular depth of the swimming pool. Excavation simply stopped wherever the underlying rock was too hard to be dug with spades and pickaxes. However, when he finally did give in, my uncle also succumbed to two different water pumps: one to improve the water pressure in the house and one to irrigate the land.

Along with a bewildering network of pipes and sprinklers, the second of these delivers water from the pool to most of the cultivated corners of the land. Theoretically, my extra apricot and plum trees are all within its scope. However, the pump appears to be nearing the end of its natural life and, with Manu still harping on about a tractor purchase, I am reluctant to replace it. In any event, the apple orchard down by the stream is beyond the reach of the plumbing (presumably because the original trees – predating even Uncle Milo – never needed watering).

I have been trying to manage, hooking water out from the brook with a bucket, but with each dry day the water level seems to fall, making this an increasingly unrewarding solution. Today, however, it occurs to me that the two main pipes from the *source* (the one supplying the house and the one directing the surplus into the pool) run conveniently down the edge of the orchard. All I need to do is make a cut in the second of these and insert a joint with a tap to attach a hose. It will still take twenty minutes a day, but anything is better than the bucket.

As I am returning to the house for a hacksaw, I hear the angry rasp of a more disquieting sawing. It sounds like multiple chainsaws, intent on a significant act of deforestation; and it is coming from the direction of the lane.

I run to the scene of the action to find Garance there before me, attempting to act as a human shield to protect the line of trees along the southern side of the lane; but there are simply too many trees and too many chainsaws.

I never realized how close our lane was to the old dual carriageway, because it was sufficiently far above for a single line of trees and bushes to screen it. But not any more. We shall never in future doubt our proximity. The trees are falling one by one.

Summer

'Are those supposed to be vines?' laughed Laurent, less charitably than I might have hoped from a lunch guest, even if I had undercooked the red mullet.

'They've had a lot to put up with,' I explained defensively, enumerating the successive ravages of the rabbits, the wild boar and the goats, as we walked up the slope towards my infant vineyard. 'For most of them, it's effectively still their first year.'

'Well, I see you've got some flowers already,' said Laurent to my surprise. I had been too busy watering, weeding and spraying to notice the formation of the buds but now I could see there were small clusters of flowers on perhaps fifteen out of forty plants, spread between three out of five varieties. Fortunately, Laurent didn't ask about the varieties, so I didn't have to retell the tale of the rain and the labels.

'Just a pity about the flowers being trapped in the rabbit netting,' Laurent chuckled again, and I saw that he was right. Most of the bunches were poking halfway through the wire mesh, but it was too late to disentangle them now.

Laurent was enjoying his last free Tuesday. As from the following week, he would be opening twice a day, six days a week, for the whole of the summer. As Leah was unwell, he had come on his own and we had sat at the little round table under the cherry tree, listening to summer make itself more audible, as successive cicadas shed their old winter skins on the branches immediately above us, bursting instantly into noisy, celebratory chirruping as they did so. 'Can we go for a walk for some peace?' my guest had chuckled at the end of the cherry course.

'I never realized you had so many hectares,' he remarked, as we continued on up towards the *source* and the back gate. It was good to see him so relaxed, so thoroughly in his element in the open air.

'Between four and five, I think the *notaire* said. I'm not very good at these things.'

'No wonder you've had so little time for us,' he teased. 'I thought it was because you couldn't face any more aubergines! But don't tell me those are supposed to be vines as well?' he asked, this time sounding genuinely shocked, as our walk took us round the back of Manu's land.

'My neighbour doesn't really go in for pruning,' I said, trying to explain the chaos on the other side of the bramble-tangled fence marking our boundary, although privately I recognized that Manu's theories of viticulture were, like his wine, beyond understanding.

'Pssst,' said a voice suddenly from the other side of the brambles, while Laurent looked at me disbelievingly.

'It's my birthday,' the voice informed me in a whisper.

'Sorry, Manu, I had no idea. *Bon anniversaire*! . . . But why are we whispering?'

'You know the wife,' continued Manu, still *sotto voce*. 'Never much of a one for a party. But I was thinking, if you could slip out for a bottle of you-know-what . . .'

'Of Noilly Prat?' I asked, still addressing the invisible Manu in an undertone.

It has always amazed me that this one particular herb-infused aperitif, made down on the coast at Marseillan, should have been singled out as the unique exception to Mme Gros's otherwise unbending alcoholic abstinence. Admittedly, even this is strictly reserved for occasions of special festivity but, on some of the more notable, she has even been observed to accept a second glass.

'I thought if you could bring a bottle over, we might get a bit of a shindig going.'

I was too dumbfounded by the man's optimism to answer.

'Come over at six,' he hissed and, without waiting for a reply, he rustled away through the undergrowth.

'Now I see the real reason you've so little time,' laughed Laurent.

*

I told myself: not till the temperature reaches 35°. Only then will you allow yourself an afternoon by the pool, instead of by the melons.

That was nearly a week ago, since when the courtyard thermometer has never been so assiduously watched. But there I remained: bent double over the potager, pricking out side shoots on the cantaloupes, tying tomato stems to stakes, wishing I hadn't put the plants needing lots of water next to those needing virtually none . . . And all under an obstinate 34° sun.

Then finally, the day before yesterday, the mercury hit the target. I wheeled a plastic sunbed into a prime position, hardly pausing to put some rosé in a tumbler. I knew I ought to fetch some sun cream but too many days had been devoted to earning this moment to leave the poolside now. There might be some in the little storage box behind the sunbed's backrest, something left over from last year. I'd look in moment, I told myself, as I drifted peacefully into sleep. Seconds later (or so it felt – perhaps I had slept for an hour) I woke with a sharp stab of pain. Something had stung my upper lip and, to judge by the buzz of activity round the storage box, it was a wasp. A tentative lifting of the lid confirmed that scores of them were busy establishing a nest on top of my abandoned Ambre Solaire.

'You'd have been safer tidying the courgettes,' said Mme Gros, at the sight of my lopsidedly puffed-up mouth, '35° is nothing.'

'57° at the *bergerie*,' claimed Rens in yesterday's market. She was squeezing into an inadequate patch of shade beneath a child-sized parasol, while a neighbouring fruit and vegetable seller stood more comfortably in the generous shadows cast by the buildings behind her. Perhaps when Rens has had her stall for the same twenty years . . . '42° in the shade,' she added, trying unsuccessfully to look nonchalant as she sealed my assortment of Pélardons with a sticker attesting to the winning of her medals. 'I headed straight for the cheese-making room. I'd done all the work in the morning but it's the only place that's air-conditioned.'

'How do the goats like the heat?' I mumbled through my still-swollen lip.

'Eating less and producing less milk,' she said. 'We're keeping them inside most afternoons. *C'est vraiment exceptionnel!*'

'Exceptionnel' was the general stall-holder consensus at this, the first of the season's Marchés du Terroir. Exceptional for the middle of June, that is. And still no rain.

It was so exceptional that Garance had tried to persuade me to do her shopping for her. Even at five in the evening, she was worried about the risk of sunburn, and it was only after much persuasion that she agreed to brave the daylight beneath a big black umbrella. Yet half-invisible as she was, she still saw me hesitate as we passed the forbidden goat's cheese stall.

'I need some honey,' I explained defensively. 'I've stopped buying the *chèvre* but his Milles Fleurs is always lovely and clear. It doesn't matter how long you keep it.'

'You can't,' said Garance crisply. 'It isn't organic. I'll introduce you to the Andrés.'

'Miel non-chauffé,' proclaimed the labels on the nearby stall. Unheated honey: an improbable claim in these temperatures, so I asked what they meant.

'Most people heat their honey to stop it solidifying,' Dominique André explained, between puffs on his pipe. 'We're the only professionals in the Lodève region who don't.'

'Is heating a problem?'

'It changes the sugars. One of the reasons I went into this business was a diabetic mother. Diabetics are fine with natural honeys but they can't eat heated ones. Until 1999 I was in computers,' he added, as if to explain his other reasons.

'Have a taste,' encouraged Garance proprietorially. 'They're organic.'

'Natural more than organic,' Dominique laughed, without

releasing the teeth clenched firmly on the pipe. 'Bees cover up to three kilometres around their hives – the equivalent of once round the world to make a kilo of honey. You can't control all the plants they land on, although we've stopped making the lavender honey this year. We didn't like the chemicals they were using on the Carpentras farm, where we used to put our hives.'

'Carpentras? That's right over in the Rhône, isn't it?' I had always imagined beekeepers' hives at the bottom of their gardens.

'Absolutely. Most of the hives are nearer Soumont, where we live.' He gestured vaguely to the east with his pipe. 'Some are up on the Larzac, some down by the Lac de Salagou – all in groups of thirty or forty. Everything depends on the siting of the hives. That's the skilled bit. They have to be in the right place, at the right time for the chosen flowers. We move them around, maybe two or three times in a year. The transhumance, it's called.'

'So you don't own the land?'

'No, we pay the landowners in kind. The rate's been established since Napoleon: a kilo of honey for every five hives.'

'They've got three hundred and twenty hives,' said Garance, as proudly as if they were her own.

'Making how much honey?' I asked Dominique.

'Four thousand kilos,' answered Garance, still determined to identify with his every achievement.

'It depends,' said Dominique. 'If the weather stays hot and dry, we shan't have an easy year. Tomorrow we're bottling what we've managed on the Causses, if you want to come up and see. Our *mielerie*'s up at Soumont too.'

'I wouldn't miss it for the world,' said Garance; but in the end, she misses it for a darkened room.

'You should never have made me go to the market,' she whines accusingly from inside the *maset*. 'No, wait,' she calls, as I prepare to leave without her. 'Could you just take some rubbish? I nearly fell off my bike the last time I tried, and Manu's always got some excuse. It won't take a minute to sort it. I just need to get the staples out of this cardboard and . . . Stop! You can't take the jam jars like that. We need to steam the labels off and put them in with the newspapers.'

I am accordingly an hour late when I start the ascent to Soumont.

It sounds as if it ought to be under a mountain (*sous mont*), but in fact it is very much on top. Perched high above Lodève, the approach road commands a magnificent view of the Lac de Salagou and much of the plain stretching down to Saint Saturnin. The village, however, feels inward-looking, huddled tightly around the tiny central square, where a battered stone cross in the middle makes considerate parking impossible. Best to block what must be Dominique's van, I decide, having spotted a bee-sign above the door to the narrowest of the various narrow buildings; but there is no sign of Dominique when I push it open.

'*Il n'est pas là*,' confirms a stranger inside. 'But Claudette's up above.' He indicates a flimsy wooden staircase, leading to an equally insubstantial boarded platform which divides the tall, tight space into two usable parts. 'She's expecting you.'

'Gérard's come to borrow some frames,' says the woman who welcomes me to the awkward, makeshift loft. She is putting the finishing touches to the cleaning of what looks like an electrified stainless steel dustbin: a centrifuge, she explains. Beside it is a pile of comb-covered wooden frames, taken from the Causses du Larzac hives; but thanks to Garance's *tri sélectif*, I have missed the spinning-out of the all-important product.

'The honey's in a tank downstairs,' says Claudette, explaining how they try to avoid pumping it, doing everything possible by gravity, hence our risking our combined weight on these wobbly floorboards. 'The absolute minimum of intervention,' she emphasizes, as she leads the way downstairs to the bottling machine.

'I used to be afraid of bees,' she confesses. 'I wasn't at all amused when Dominique suggested this.' (Entirely reasonably, I can't help feeling, with the swimming-pool wasp experience still uncomfortably vivid.) 'But now they're a passion,' she continues less explicably. 'Right down to tending them when they're sick.'

'No vets for bees,' says Gérard with a chuckle.

'How many do you have?' I ask, imagining a hundred or two per hive.

'Depends on the time of year,' says Claudette, weighing the first jar of honey to see whether her sophisticated, gravity-powered machine has delivered exactly the intended half kilo. 'Say, eighty thousand per hive at this time of year; something closer to ten thousand in winter. It's all a matter of daylight. The closer you get to 21 June, the more eggs a queen lays.'

'Up to two thousand a day,' emphasizes Gérard, lest I under-estimate the queens' fecundity.

'I'll lend you this,' says Claudette, producing a lavishly illustrated bee book. The full frontal close-ups of apparently monster-sized bees would give anyone of average sensibilities nightmares; but for me, after the wasp incident . . . 'We mainly use the Buckfast bee,' she continues, unaware of my trauma, 'developed at your English abbey. Gérard uses the more tradi-tional black bees.'

'More aggressive,' he laughs.

'Are they more productive?' I ask, puzzled by this ostensibly reckless choice.

'Less,' he laughs again.

'Gérard's a real *amateur* of bees,' says Claudette, enjoying the banter.

'No one loves bees,' Gérard corrects her solemnly.

'One person does,' she chuckles. 'You!'

A waft of pipe tobacco signals Dominique's arrival. 'I've got a bone to pick with you about yesterday,' he says sternly.

'I really meant to buy some,' I begin. 'But then my neighbour had one of her turns . . .'

'Never mind buying.' He grins behind a puff of smoke. 'You didn't taste any!'

Obediently, I perch on a stool in a low-vaulted niche at the back of the room. The whole of the Andrés' production is piled on half a dozen shelves. There are ten or so samples, with a supply of plastic ice-cream spoons.

Even before I taste, I am struck by the wide range of colours, from the deepest brown of the chestnut to the almost white of the rosemary. On the palate, some are citric, some toffee-like, some astringently woody. Some even I can identify, like the lavender and the rosemary; others are less specific, more evocative of different landscapes, here softer, there wilder.

'It's like wine-tasting,' says Dominique. 'The same variations from year to year, the same importance of *terroir* – the characteristics deriving from a particular physical site. Even the same descriptive words – sweet, spicy, full-bodied, tannic. And you need the same care in matching them with other foods.'

I decide to buy a selection and take them home to experiment.

'Tell you what,' says Dominique. 'You're up near Le Temps de Vivre, aren't you? I'll give you these if you'll drop a second set off to the chef. I've been meaning to get him to taste them.'

*

I have worried since March about the unpruned Carignan beside the lane leading down to the village.

It is not the welfare of the vines over which I am losing sleep, although it is undeniably sad to see their ancient, twisting root-stocks so raggedly neglected. My concern is more that the vineyard, perched on the corner of the hillside, is the last surviving buffer between our quiet little track and the soon-to-be motorway down below. The *vigneron* is plainly not expecting the vines to be there at harvest time.

'They've ripped them up!' wailed Garance, as she sprinted up my drive to find me still at my breakfast in the courtyard.

'Maybe the grower's got a grant,' I suggested without conviction. 'Taking the EC subsidy to replant with superior varieties.' But as I went down to look, I knew I was deceiving myself. Having demolished the vines, the workmen were bulldozing the hillside.

It had to happen, I told myself. We knew they were widening all the way up. Maybe they'd just shave the edge off the field. But then Garance shrieked and tugged at my arm.

I turned to see what had caught her eye: a double line of wooden marker posts, daubed with particularly disquieting, bright pink paint and leading straight up through somebody's cherry orchard behind us, in the direction of our homes.

'It's the access road to the new service station,' said Manu, appearing at our side.

'He was only joking.' I was still trying to persuade Garance more than half an hour later; but leaving late again for Le Temps de Vivre, I cannot entirely dismiss the image of a petrol forecourt next to the swimming pool.

'I've brought you a present,' I announce, handing Laurent the box of honeys.

'I suppose they're hoping I'll create a dish around one of them,' he says, eyeing the handwritten inscriptions doubtfully.

'Preferably a whole menu.'

He laughs obligingly but confesses that he is not really much of a honey fan. I tell him there was a time when a jar of honey went a long way in my house. Certainly, the same variety served perfectly well for every use: a spoonful with some yoghurt, an occasional spreading on toast, a nod to fashion with a dollop on a grilled goat's cheese. But not since Soumont. Now it has to be fresh, liquid Causses du Larzac drizzled on the breakfast yoghurt; herby Garrigue on a slice of dark wholemeal bread; and, my favourite discovery, the stiff, white Rosemary served beside Rens's soft, creamy Pélardon. But the chef shakes his head with a smile. Maybe André should work on Jean-Pierre for the cheese course.

Laurent puts the jars to one side and hands me an apron. My heart immediately sinks as Georges comes up from the basement, panting slightly with the weight of a huge tray of slow-roasted aubergines; but stoically he takes charge of these himself. For my own entertainment, Laurent heaves a crate of beef tomatoes on to the central workspace, quickly plunging a third of these into a saucepan of boiling water. Then he takes a plastic tub and dashes to the middle room, where I hear him shovelling ice. Within a minute, he is ladling the hot tomatoes into icy water. It is my job to peel them, while he organizes two more saucepan-loads for himself.

The heating and cooling have successfully cracked the skins, but the tomatoes are simply not ripe enough for the skins to fall away. They will, he assures me, if I stick the course until later in the summer but, for the moment, I need a sharply pointed knife to ease them free.

'Try not to tear the flesh.' Laurent leans across to inspect the extent of the damage.

My problem is that, on the rare occasions when I get the skin off cleanly, the flesh looks so beautifully smooth that I mistake it for skin and continue hacking away. I manage only one to every six of Laurent's, despite the time that he needs to spend stirring stocks and sauces, taking telephone calls and generally dissenting from Eric's notions of cleanliness.

As I finally peel my last, I learn that my second task is to sculpt four or five approximately petal-shaped slivers of flesh from each fruit, laying them (outside up, Laurent stresses) on a pair of lightly oiled trays, where he sprinkles them with salt and thyme and splashes on some extra olive oil. He then opens an oven to remove a batch that was started by Georges while I was still in bed. Baking ultra-gently at 100°, they have shrunk to what Laurent describes as *tomates confites* – a fresher-tasting, more succulent cousin of the aggressively sun-dried specimens with which I am more familiar.

'This is roughly two crates' worth,' he announces, emptying the last of four trays into one depressingly small plastic tub.

'Back aching yet?' calls Jean-Pierre from the middle room, which I am beginning to understand is largely his territory. He is no longer polishing cutlery or even plates today. He is doing something even more mind-numbingly tedious. He has emptied an enormous packet of Métro-purchased caramelized nuts – the sort that Laurent serves with coffee – on to the long, low wine fridge, where he is methodically eliminating any that he judges insufficiently toffee-coated.

Jean-Pierre is right, however: tomato-petal production is proving unexpectedly punishing. Perhaps it is just the concentration required to avoid having to start all over again, as Eric has just been instructed to do with an under-scrubbed roasting pan.

'Look,' says Laurent patiently, 'this is a clean pan and this is a dirty one; you see the difference?' Eric giggles affirmatively.

'Have you heard about Le Jardin des Sens's new venture?' asks Laurent, as the petal production grinds on.

'You don't mean the beach restaurant?' I remember reading that a second, coastal branch of the Pourcels' 'annexe', La Compagnie des Comptoirs, had become THE fashionable place to be seen having lunch.

'That was one of last year's innovations,' laughs Laurent. 'That and the Tokyo restaurant and the cookery school. No, I mean the sandwich bar in Montpellier. Sens Eat NoMad, it's called.'

'You're kidding.'

'Not at all. People's lunch habits are changing. And these are *sandwiches gastronomiques*. You should try them.'

'But for a restaurant with three Michelin stars . . .'

'Three-star restaurants don't make money. They need so many staff and there's a limit to what you can charge, even at that level. It's the satellites that subsidize the prestige operation. But even so, the Jardin's cut its staff dramatically since I was there – a hundred and twenty down to eighty. And mainly because of our old friend, the thirty-five-hour week. It's like I told you, if you can't increase your prices, you're forced to close more – three lunchtimes a week, in the Jardin's case – which then reduces turnover, so you end up economizing on staff, instead of recruiting more.'

'The opposite effect of what was intended?'

'Yes, and what's worse, it's changing the way people think about work. I mean the French don't really want to work at the best of times, but now that there are people patrolling office car parks, on the lookout for anyone illegally working overtime, anyone crazy enough to enjoy his job, how can you not end up thinking that it's something you're supposed to hate?'

Laurent checks himself and gives a little sheepish laugh, as if to say, 'glad I got that off my chest'. Then he comes to inspect my petals, the last of which are finally ready for the oven.

It has just gone eleven o'clock, nearly lunchtime for the workers, but Georges suggests that first I set up enough *tartes friandes* for today's reservations: just two tables of three and four respectively. Perhaps three extras for any unexpected *clients de passage* – it's the most popular dish on the most popular menu, he explains, and he slides a freshly made tub of aubergine caviar in my direction.

Handing me ten circular tins, a couple of centimetres deep and ten or so wide, he shows me how to line the bottoms with ready-roasted petals ('Try not to leave any gaps,' comes his almost impossible demand); then he demonstrates how to fill them with the aubergine mixture ('Try not to let it touch the sides,' the utterly impossible follow-up); but as these first two ingredients meet in their mould, I almost feel like a chef.

All I need now are customers but none of us can be expected to cook on an empty stomach, so we gather at the farmhouse table in the middle room for the grilled tomatoes and steak that Georges has been preparing, alongside everything else. A wine delivered as a sample by a hopeful *vigneron* is given a trial by all except Eric, but it fails to win a place on the list.

There is no sign of Laurence (Jean-Pierre can easily manage seven on his own) so it is Laurent, not her, whom I ask whether his wife has always done this kind of work.

'We met at La Tamarissière,' he explains. 'She was working in the kitchen but she found it difficult being a woman. Too macho. So she switched to working *en salle*.'

'Difficult for a man *en salle*,' mutters Georges, with a mischievous nod towards the maître d'hôtel.

'What was that?' Jean-Pierre bridles.

'I said, difficult for a man *en salle*.'

'What's that supposed to mean?' demands Jean-Pierre, his face quickly colouring. 'You think all men in the dining-room . . .'

'You see what I have to put up with?' laughs Laurent, interrupting. 'I call them my two old women.'

Fortunately, it is time for Jean-Pierre to go and change. The customers could be here in five minutes. Georges puts some tapenade- and sesame-coated pastries into the oven to accompany their aperitifs; Eric clears the table; Laurent has a hasty cigarette outside the back door; and my *tartes friandes* wait breathlessly in the fridge.

Jean-Pierre reappears (in rakish pale green suit, matched daringly with a bright yellow shirt) only minutes before the arrival of the three and, in no time, he is breaking the news of their order to the expectant kitchen: a single, expensive dish à la carte for each of them – lobster, pigeon and *foie gras*; perhaps a dessert to follow but not a flicker of interest in the *tarte friande* or the value-for-money, four-course menu built around it. More cash than sense, I can only conclude. The next customers quickly follow with an equally hurtful order for the middle menu: gluttonously seduced by the extra fifth course; bedazzled by the shallower pleasures of Laurent's fillet of beef; too full of themselves to appreciate an honest *tarte friande*.

'They'll keep for a day or two,' Georges consoles me, as he and Laurent apply themselves with total concentration to four or five different recipes. With my 'signature dish' so cruelly spurned, there is no time now for them to teach me further tricks. I can only keep out of the way and watch.

'The *foie gras* is becoming a bit of a "fetish",' Laurent tells me, while he works. 'I've had people from Montpellier ask whether it's still on the *carte* before they book!'

His approach is certainly distinctive: *Le foie gras poêlé, saumon fumé et oignons caramélisés au balsamique*. The juxtaposition of the chunky, pan-fried duck liver with thin-cut strips of uncooked smoked salmon is one of several combinations of meat and fish in his repertoire: one of his trademarks almost. But it's the rich, syrupy onions in their caramelized balsamic vinegar sauce that tie the two contrasting elements together. 'You must have it one day, when you're feeling rich,' he teases me.

Jean-Pierre returns from another visit to the dining-room to report on the wine selection for the three. 'Viognier!' he announces scornfully. 'How do they imagine a white wine will stand up to pigeon? It must be the lobster woman who's paying!'

'He was just as bad when you came,' laughs Laurent, dissecting a previously part-cooked crustacean in readiness.

It is Jean-Pierre, I notice, more than Laurent who sets the pace of the kitchen. Or more accurately, I suppose, it is the diners, with whom Jean-Pierre alone is in contact. '*Ça marche: un homard, un pigeon, un foie gras,*' he shouts to activate the à la carte main courses. A commanding '*Ça marche: quatre ravioles*', in impossibly quick succession, fires the starting-pistol for the foursome's menu and a bewildering selection of ingredients starts converging from different directions: some from the fridge, some from the basement cold store. Many find their way to pans that are sizzling or simmering on the stove; others are consigned to the oven. A few are simply chopped or sliced and kept on one side.

The à la carte selections take priority, partly because they were ordered a fraction earlier and partly because they represent the bigger challenge. Remarkably, the two men hardly ever confer on the division of labour, working almost like a single individual with two pairs of hands. If Georges registers Laurent performing step two on the lobster, he simply moves quietly on to step three for the *foie gras*, leaving Laurent in turn to start the pigeon pieces roasting at the *moment juste*. They must each have a clear mental route map to the finished dishes, an almost instinctive sense of when to apply the brake and when the accelerator to ensure a simultaneous end to the separate journeys.

Laurent told me earlier how most restaurants, certainly ones like Le Jardin des Sens, have a kind of serving counter on the dining-room side of the kitchen. It is known as the 'pass' and everything destined for the dining-room converges there for inspection by the head chef, before it is whisked away by the waiters. In many establishments, the elements of a dish are directly assembled on the pass; but there is no room for such luxury here. Laurent and Georges must make do with whatever space can be spared (and wiped clean) at the end of the central work table. The three à la carte main courses, on their extra-large à la carte plates, will have to go before there is any hope of anyone composing the four *ravioles ouvertes.*

'*Service!*' shouts Laurent, when the final details are meticu-lously in place, the pieces of lobster shell adjusted to precisely the right angle, the pattern of cayenne pepper on the big square platter tidied for the second time. '*Service!*' he repeats, as if there were queues of waiters standing ready to ferry plates to the dining-room, instead of Jean-Pierre alone and he, at this moment, unable to escape from a garrulous customer.

The so-called 'open ravioli' have nothing to do with pasta and everything to do with Laurent's devotion to his native soil and its specialities. The menu says *raviole ouverte de galabar, fricassée des hauts cantons*, but few would be any the wiser without advice from Jean-Pierre. The *galabar* proves to be an obscure mountain variant of black pudding, as discovered by Laurent one morning in the Lodève market; the *fricassée*, served ravioli-like between the *galabar* slices, a sautéed mixture of lamb's sweetbreads, crayfish, so-called *petit gris* snails and special sweet local onions called *cébettes* – a combination almost defiantly rooted in this *terroir*.

'I know there are easier locations,' admits Laurent, as if reading my thoughts. 'But it was here or nowhere.' He smiles to excuse the brief, unguarded note of passion, then bellows another impatient '*Service!*' to the distant Jean-Pierre.

It is three o'clock when I finally stagger out into the hottest part of the afternoon. I have been here for just five hours, and yet it feels like Friday night at the end of a long week's work. Everyone else arrived an hour or two before me and I have been mainly spectating. What's more, they all have a second service to complete this evening. But then again, they don't have late-planted fruit trees to keep alive at home.

I have been running the watering system for barely fifteen minutes when the pump splutters and stops.

'Too old to be repairable,' says Manu, arriving on the scene an hour later. His wife is, in his words, 'attending her coven' in the village and he came straight over with a litre of *rouge*, only to find me fiddling ineffectually with a screwdriver. 'You're wasting your time. You'll find they don't make the parts any more. But if you play your cards right . . .' He indicates the unopened bottle. 'I'll speak to my cousin tomorrow. After all, it's not just the fruit trees. The vegetables are going to shrivel up in no time.'

Card-playing completed, it is very late when I start the watering by hand and nearly eleven o'clock when I finish. Yet even at such a late hour, the air is hardly cooler than it was when I left the restaurant. The pool seems the only solution.

Sitting in the shallow end with the water lapping round my neck and a sandwich in my hand, both the pump and the *tartes friandes* seem far away. It must be nearly the longest day, still light enough to see the bats swooping low over the shallow end. The tinkling of goat bells from the lane behind the house tells me that the goatherd is not yet home. Only the irregular rumbling of a motorway bulldozer working overtime spoils the idyll.

*

I can never remember wishing so vehemently that it would rain. English friends who telephone think I'm joking, or striking some sort of pose. But there has been not so much as a sprinkling since May and everyone, apart from the early tourists, is longing for respite.

It doesn't help that the local newspaper keeps changing its promises. The Sunday forecast was quite emphatic: there would be storms on Monday, so I called a confident halt to anything beyond what the automated system could cover with the new pump. But then Monday proved scorchingly cloudless so, indignantly, I bought the Tuesday edition, only to find that any hope of wetness had slipped to Thursday. Which is why I ended up watering the apple trees by torchlight.

'Will the weather mean an early harvest?' I asked Virgile, when he and Magda came to lunch the next day.

'It all depends,' he said. 'As long as we get a little rain, the heat will make the grapes ripen faster. But if there's none what-soever, the vines may simply stop photosynthesizing till some rain falls. And that would mean a late *vendange*.'

'So how do you know when to book your picking team?'

'We don't,' sighed Magda – the simple 'we' showing in a second how completely she now identifies with the business.

'And there's my partnership.' It was Virgile's turn to sigh. 'I told you about that, didn't I?' Obviously not, he deduced from my blank look. 'It's been a month or two now. Some wealthy market gardeners down on the coast who've bought some vineyards in Aniane. Money no object, state-of-the-art equipment but not much know-how. The idea was to combine their resources with my expertise; but already I'm wondering if we can make it work. It's so time-consuming.'

'At least there's three of us,' said Magda, and again I looked blank. 'My sister Martha from Poland,' she explained. 'She was originally coming just for the *vendange*.'

'But then she read the weather forecast,' I laughed.

'I suppose we should be grateful,' concluded Virgile, as they said goodbye. 'The first real summer for years. After the first real winter.'

'Well, the apple trees and I were hoping for an unreal summer,' I grumble, as I prepare for another round of evening watering.

*

'It can't be mice,' said Garance irritably, as she shaded her eyes against the sunshine after the gloom inside her *maset*. 'Not in July, when there's plenty of food for them outside. And you haven't had a problem before.'

'Maybe they just appreciate good tomatoes,' I suggested,

trying to jolly her into a better mood but, all the time, looking sorrowfully at the dish containing my first crop. They were supposed to be my contribution to lunch but almost every one of them had a mouse-sized bite in it.

'Traps,' I had written on my shopping list, without telling Garance. (The ant arsenic had earned me sufficient opprobrium already.)

'They're only ordinary tomatoes,' she grumbled, adding insult to injury. She seemed unusually grumpy this morning, having been kept awake, so she said, by nocturnal work on the road. Nothing had interrupted my own sleep but I knew from experience that it would be counter-productive to say so. Instead, I started mentally counting, wondering how long it would be before she revealed the identity of her preferred supplier. 'You should have gone to Pascal,' she rewarded me, before I had even reached three. 'Up at Olmet.'

'Want to come?' I asked half-heartedly, hoping she'd be busy with the lunch preparations.

'The sun's too bright.' She retreated to the shadows, as soon as she had given me directions.

The Conservatoire de Tomates is located high in the hills to the south of Lodève, at the altitude where vines and olives give way to chestnut trees. A hand-painted, lopsided, plywood sign, just after Olmet, tells me I must hazard one of the stoniest lanes in the Languedoc if I am determined to visit it. Several hundred metres of damage to my suspension later, a second sign of similar constitution suggests that the seat of the Academy is a small stone *maset* – smaller even than Garance's – and a couple of elderly caravans, parked alongside. It promises, however, more than two hundred old tomato varieties, along with numerous other vanished vegetables.

The sound of the Renault's hesitant approach has summoned the curator, a wiry figure of indeterminate age, his muddy shirt hanging loosely over muddy trousers. The tangled, shoulder-length hair, which pushes here and there through the holes in his battered straw hat, perhaps makes him look younger than he is.

He smiles from behind a beard that was probably last trimmed when the signs were painted.

'Pascal Poot,' he introduces himself, losing no time at all in escorting me to the nearest tomato patch. 'No, we haven't been here long,' he answers to the first of my questions. 'Only since 2000. But I was doing the same thing before, only further north, in the Lot. I've had at least a corner of a garden somewhere ever since I was a small boy. I must have been eight or nine when I started collecting and exchanging seeds.'

As he talks, I register the fact that his tomato plants are quite unlike any that I have seen. For one thing, relatively few of the fruits seem bothered by conventional expectations of redness or even roundness. Even this early in the season, there are pink ones, yellow ones, green ones, black ones, even multi-tinted striped ones; and the contours are often as eccentric as the colour schemes: pear-shaped, pepper-shaped, courgette-shaped . . . Pascal picks me one to taste. It is perfectly ripe yet defiantly, outlandishly green; it also has a wonderful, almost citric acidity; but at least it has the decency to be round.

The other nonconformist thing about the Poot plants is that they grow completely unsupported, at ground level, simply trailing across the soil, the tomatoes warming themselves on the stones, with never a stake in sight.

'All the botany professors say the same thing,' remarks Pascal. Prick out the side shoots and grow them high to produce the fruit faster and in larger quantities. But in fact it's the opposite. I know because I seem to be the only person who's done a test. Twenty years ago, I planted two rows side by side, at exactly the same time, so that no one could blame it on the moon or the stars or anything else.'

'And the ones like this came out best?'

'Ten times the fruit, with a tenth of the work – and earlier too,' he insists, as I joyfully resolve to do things differently from tomorrow morning. 'Growing them high is all very well, if you've got limited space in a greenhouse. But otherwise, the only reason to do it that way is to make sure your neighbours can see them over the garden wall.' He smiles in a way that suggests he has little time for either garden walls or neighbours. 'But you mustn't touch any of the side shoots. They stabilize and balance the plant. Too late now, if you're already pricking out.' He smiles again, having glimpsed my short-lived resolution, now despondently postponed.

He proposes a coffee and I follow him inside the *maset*, which proves indeed to be both smaller and darker than Garance's. As far as I can make out, it is just a single modest room, with a tiny, passage-like kitchen leading off from one corner. The only visible concession to twentieth-, let alone twenty-first-century living is a portable television, glued to which is a gangly, bristly faced youth, prompting a further upward revision of his father's minimum age. The son mumbles that there may be enough coffee for two in the pot, and Pascal rummages in the gloom for a couple of thick-rimmed beakers.

'You do everything yourself?' I ask, meaning the tomatoes rather than the coffee.

'Me and Jocelyn, yes,' he answers, with a nod towards the kitchen. 'The boys prefer television. I'm usually on the go from seven till half past ten. There's less to do in winter, of course, but fewer daylight hours to do it in.'

'What do you do for water?' I ask, seeing no sign of hoses or sprinklers, as we carry our glasses back into the sunshine.

'Nothing,' he says bluntly, as if that were perfectly natural. 'There isn't any.'

'How do you manage in the house?' I query, regarding the coffee with greater circumspection.

'Oh, the village fixed us up with a meter,' he says dismissively. 'Down at the end of the lane. I connected up a pipe for the house . . . *Mais, c'est très cher,*' he explains, confirming the impossibility of metered water going anywhere near his tomatoes.

'You mean you never water anything?'

'Just once, when I plant the seeds. Just the first day. I fetch a little on my lorry from the stream behind that hill.' He points to a faraway crest. 'But nothing after that. If I watered the way the professors would have me do, I'd need a lorry-load for an area the size of those two caravans and I couldn't manage more than two trips a day.'

'So do you get a lot of rain?'

'None at all,' he says, as if this were equally natural. 'Nothing in July and August and much less than you the rest of the year. You see that village over there?' He points to a distant blur between the hills. 'That's Gignac. If there's ever a storm, it goes up from there, round the back of that ridge, and on past Lodève and Pégairolles towards the Larzac plateau, missing us out completely.' He pauses beside some desiccated *petits pois* that seem a less than perfect advertisement for water-free gardening. 'It normally rains in June,' he adds by way of excuse. 'And you can see these potatoes aren't very happy,' he acknowledges as we descend to a lower level, where only a few square metres shaded by a chestnut tree have sprouted any significant greenery. 'They'll take off again in October . . . Oh look, a wild boar's been at these,' he adds, with an 'all in a day's work' kind of shrug, on finding some aubergine-like, purple tomatoes rudely uprooted.

Even the most orderly of Pascal's plots have an accidental, 'if it survives, it survives' air about them but the landscape changes as we clamber down to a terrace that has only barely been reclaimed from decades, maybe centuries of abandonment. Stumps of half-felled trees and broken bushes are everywhere. 'This is how I spend my winters,' he explains. 'Clearing more land.' Looking closer, I see that wherever his low-season labours have achieved as much as a few square centimetres of remotely unobstructed earth, a tomato seed has been sown and a hand-written label planted beside it.

'Look how little soil there is.' He kicks the surface to show me solid rock no more than ten centimetres below. 'But they manage.'

'What about manure?' I ask, wondering whether even this much intervention is permitted.

'Sheep and goat,' he says. 'Helps retain moisture, as well as feeding the plants.'

'You buy from a local farmer?'

'I never buy,' he says, leaving the fact that there is dung round each plant unexplained.

'And selling?' I ask, thinking something must pay for the television and the metered water.

'I do a couple of markets,' he says. 'But a lot of people come to me. Usually when I've got the biggest amount of work to do.'

He glances furtively in the direction of the woman, now busy at a washing-line slung loosely between one of the caravans and a rusty pole; then he tiptoes into a nearby shelter, crudely hammered together from ancient oddments of wood, and emerges with a packet of tobacco and some papers. 'Less tempting, if I keep them here,' he explains. 'And Jocelyn doesn't know,' he adds with another check on the progress of the laundry.

'So, where could I get seeds for these kinds of tomatoes?' I ask, when the cigarette is lit.

'From here.'

'You sell seeds as well?'

'I *produce* seeds as well.'

'How do you produce a tomato seed?' I ask, thinking this way lies total self-sufficiency.

'Well, I scoop them out, obviously. Then I ferment them. That's what would happen inside a rotting tomato, if nature took its course. After twenty-four hours, I sieve them in a tea-strainer and dry them. Then I keep them all in envelopes in metal boxes. Otherwise the mice would have them.'

'You make it sound easy.'

'It is. But don't believe what the botanists tell you. Tomatoes are self-pollinating so, according to them, all you need do is collect the seeds from a particular variety to grow the same one next year. But the trouble is they're not exclusively self-pollinating. They can be hybridized by other varieties growing up to three hundred metres away. I've done experiments to prove it. You see this tomato here?' He shows me one with two tiny points at the base. 'That's probably been hybridized.

But this one . . .' He shows me one with just a single point. 'This will be self-pollinated.'

'You've convinced me,' I tell him. 'It's too complicated. I'll come back for some of yours in the spring.'

'You could take them now.'

'Not likely,' I laugh. 'I've got mice of my own.'

*

'That reminds me,' I said, watching attentively over Mme Vargas's shoulder. She had promised to show me how easy it was to make *confit de canard* and was rinsing away the salt in which a pile of plump-looking duck legs had been buried since the previous morning. 'The salt,' I explained, as she carefully patted the duck legs dry. 'I was on a walk the other day . . . Ridiculous in these temperatures, but what do you do with restless guests? Anyway, they had this book about the footpaths. We were slogging up that steep one, through the forest behind the village, and the book said it was part of the Salt Route.'

'Up to the Larzac, yes,' Mme Vargas agreed, cutting lumps of what she told me was duck fat into smaller pieces and putting them into a big saucepan.

'But it didn't say why it was going there. Or where it was coming from, for that matter.'

'Ah,' said Mme Vargas resignedly. 'You don't know about Camargue salt.'

For once in fact I did, up to a point. A succession of people had been giving me what seemed to be this year's fashionable coming-to-dinner present: a small cork-lidded tub, filled with delicately friable salt crystals and labelled 'Fleur de Sel de Camargue'. Each of the lids bore the signature of a different 'master salt maker' and I imagined some quaint little cottage industry, squeezed into a quiet corner between the galloping white horses and thundering black bulls with which the coastal marshlands, south of Nîmes, are more usually associated.

'They say the salt works are as big as Paris,' said Mme Vargas, crushing my illusions.

'You never cook a whole duck?' I asked, as she threw the duck legs into the bubbling fat.

She gave me a look, as if I had asked for mushy peas and ketchup with mine. The different parts needed different methods and different timings, she explained. Usually, she served the breasts rare and thinly sliced; the livers she saved for pâtés; the gizzards were fried and served in salads; the other giblets used in soups. Nothing whatsoever, it seemed, was wasted.

'I'll cook these gently for an hour and a half,' she told me, giving the legs a stir. 'After which I put them in jars and top them up with the filtered fat. Then I seal the jars and boil them for another hour in a big pan of water to sterilize them.'

'They keep indefinitely like that?'

'For at least a couple of years.' She reached down a jar from an upper shelf. 'This is one of last summer's. You see, salt's been used for centuries as a preservative – especially in the mountains, where fresh things were harder to come by.'

'Hence the Salt Route.'

Mme Vargas smiled encouragingly, acknowledging her pupil's progress, as she emptied the 'Canard 2003' into a frying pan. 'All those Auvergne hams and *saucissons*,' she elaborated. 'Cured with salt, before they're hung up to air-dry.' She discarded the melted fat and started browning the legs to crispen the skin. 'Then you've got sheep's cheeses, including Roquefort, not to mention leather tanning up in Millau.'

'You'll stay for lunch?' she asked, as her husband arrived back from the rubbish sorting that so often kept them apart these days. 'Remember, you must leave the meat in the jar for at least a month,' she emphasized, tossing a simple green salad, while Monsieur dished the finished product on to plates.

'No, stop!' they almost screamed, in more typical unison.

I thought I was being helpful, running some water into the pan as my tiny contribution; but clearly not.

'Don't waste the *fritons*,' they chorused, referring to the burnt-up bits of skin and scraps of meat left clinging to the pan. 'They're wonderful on toast with *apéros*.'

Truly, nothing whatsoever was wasted.

*

There are consolations in letting the grass grow long. In the last few weeks, the exuberant array of unidentified flowers growing wild in the olive grove and the flickering variety of butterflies drawn to feed on them have made the wobbly bench at the back of the house my favourite spot for an evening drink.

It has the great advantage of being the first outdoor seating option to benefit from shade. It also commands a view of the pine-clad hills behind my terraces, which I am beginning to love as much as the more obviously spectacular one down the valley from the courtyard at the front. Perhaps most importantly, it is invisible from across the stream, facilitating uninterrupted aperitifs.

Then last weekend, my cover was blown. Creeping stealthily up the slope from the parking area, Manu discovered me with a start.

'I was on my way to check the vines,' he stammered uncon-vincingly. 'For mildew and all that.'

Ever since May, I had been up there regularly, as Virgile taught me, spraying my vines against both mildew and oïdium; but Manu never seemed to worry much about his own vines, let alone mine. The wicker basket on his arm was more consistent with Mme Gros planning apricots for dessert.

'No, don't get up,' he insisted. 'I'll fetch a glass myself.' Then, as soon as he was settled with a tumblerful of crisp, white Picpoul: 'You really could do with a tractor for that grass, a sit-on mower thing, with a trailer. I'll speak to my cousin . . . get you an end-of-season discount.'

As usual, it seemed that the end of everyone else's season was the start of mine, but so far the machine has been mainly used around Manu's vines – even he is prepared to apply a little *bouille bordelaise* and sulphur dust with the benefit of motorized transport.

When I hear him chugging up the drive this evening, I assume that this is simply to avoid the gradient standing between him and another glass of Picpoul. However, to my surprise, he rattles gaily past the waiting bottle, speeding straight into the olive grove. 'Save some for me,' he shouts, cutting a crazy slalom course through the long grass. Clearly the tractor was never half so much fun on his own more constricted terrain. 'You could do with something to protect these tree trunks,' he yells, as a daringly tight turn round one of the younger examples shaves away some of the bark. 'I'll just see how it goes at the back here,' he calls, striking out into the rougher terrain behind the olive trees.

'No, Manu, stop!' The tractor mower is heading remorselessly towards a group of three short stakes, which he appears not to have noticed, still less the three young, spiky-leaved shrubs beside them. These are the secret truffle oaks that Virgile gave me eighteen months ago and I have been wondering whether I was wise to plant them in such stony land, until I noticed last week that they had finally grown a couple of centimetres since Easter. Yet all in vain. They are about to be flattened by Manu's inexorable advance.

'Manu, stop!' I try again but he cannot hear me. As I run towards him, there is a loud explosive bang. The tractor comes to a sudden halt, less than a metre short of the nearest sapling. The stony ground has saved it with a puncture.

'Is that anything?' asks Manu, ignoring the deflated front wheel and pointing instead at the truffle oak.

'Oh, that,' I answer vaguely, as he takes in the other two. 'I'm not very good on these things. Is it . . . one of the oaks?'

'Self-seeded?' asks Manu, looking pensive.

'What time does the garage close?' I answer.

*

'What could Patrick do?' asks Laurent, as I tie on my apron for the evening's advance preparation.

'There's always the *blettes*,' says Georges with a mischievous grin. 'What do you think, Joris?' he asks a lanky, earringed apprentice who arrived a couple of weeks ago. The boy nods shyly in agreement.

I have no idea what the *blettes* will be or what I shall be expected to do to them but something about the grins tells me that they are nobody's favourite job. Or that there are indeed 'always' *blettes* to be done, because Laurent's latest menus require such a constant supply. Or both, as proves to be the case.

'I'm serving a *gratin de blettes au parmesan* with the new lamb dish, on the first menu,' he explains.

'So this is the quantity for an evening billed as "*toujours calme*",' I think to myself, as Laurent lifts a couple of boxes of what appears to be Swiss chard on to the central working area.

He shows me how to trim away the green floppy leaves and set them aside for a later stage of the recipe; then how to cut the broad, white stalks into five-centimetre lengths, dissecting each into single-centimetre widths. Next I must take a tiny slice from the end of each piece and pull it gently, teasing away the dozens of little strings running down the side of the stem, before repeating the process on the other side. Finally, every string-free portion has to be further subdivided into the chunky matchsticks which will somehow, sometime, be combined with the discarded greenery and some parmesan.

'You never got to do a *tarte friande*,' notes Georges sympathetically, as I contemplate the dauntingly well-filled crates. 'I'm sure you'll be luckier with the new dish. Lamb's always our best-seller.'

Swiss chard has never been a favourite vegetable of mine but such little appeal as it ever exercised fades rapidly over the ensuing hour, the complications of aubergine caviar and tomato petals resembling some lost youthful paradise. Indeed, I bless the motorway for inhibiting demand.

It would be bad enough in comfortable temperatures but the

kitchen this evening feels like a steam bath. Leaving the relative cool near the swimming pool at five o'clock was torture enough; forcing myself into jeans instead of shorts still worse. But here, even with every door and window open, my sweat-soaked shirt clings heavily, like a wet towel.

Joris is the only one in the kitchen not complaining. Not that he looks any happier in the heat than the rest of us. He just looks too nervous about doing the wrong thing to risk making matters worse by saying it as well. In the *plonge*, by contrast, the temperature appears to go entirely unremarked, as Eric bounces cheerfully through the utensils that the four of us are dirtying.

'There's going to be a storm,' says Georges, who is delicately extracting the skeletons from a trayful of otherwise whole-looking Labeil trout, with Joris equally delicately tackling any last remaining side bones with tweezers.

'You promise?' I ask, feeling ready to dance in the rain, if it comes.

When Jean-Pierre arrives, looking fresh and cool in light-weight jeans, designer vest and expensive-looking sandals, he fails to find my 'working a half-day' joke even mildly amusing. *'Vous n'êtes pas entr'amateurs ici,'* he rebukes me prissily.

Switching his efforts to *caviar d'aubergines* production, Georges mimes a flouncing Jean-Pierre parody.

'I thought the *tarte friande* was off?' I ask, with a grin to acknowledge Georges's wink of solidarity.

'It is, but we're doing an *amuse* at the moment, combining the caviar with gazpacho. There's no escape,' he says resignedly.

My *blette*-trimming must have met with Laurent's approval because the last of my matchsticks is hardly consigned to a cooking pot before I am promoted to fish-filleting: in my case, some *lisettes* (smaller siblings of the mackerel) which feature in one of the starters on the new first menu.

I say 'promoted' because, with fish in one hand and knife in the other, I realize there is only so much damage that an ill-judged cut can do to a bunch of Swiss chard. With a *lisette*, on the other hand, a fillet is either mangled to the point of unservability or it isn't. The fish may be on the cheapest menu but the pieces still have to be perfect.

It doesn't help that Georges, who demonstrates, is left-handed. It all happens too quickly for me to figure out how to turn each deft little flick of the knife back to front to avoid catastrophe. So Laurent tries again with a slower mirror image. First a knick behind the gills, with the head pointing away and the back fin to the right. Then, starting from the head, trace the upper edge of the spine with the point of the knife, slicing gradually deeper into the fish, keeping the knife as close as possible to the ribs until you reach the central backbone. Then gently ease it over the backbone and on across the other side of the ribcage. And suddenly, almost magically, an immaculate fillet drops away from the skeleton, before the process is repeated from the tail end on the other side. Or at least that is what happens in Laurent's hands.

Left alone while he attends to a sauce, I try to psyche myself up for my first incision.

'Don't laugh,' I tell Jean-Pierre, who is peering sardonically over my shoulder.

'He shouldn't laugh at what he can't do himself,' says Georges.

'See, I told you,' says Laurent, 'two old women . . .'

But I risk nothing further until Jean-Pierre and Georges are both distracted. Then, to my amazement, just a few courageous cuts later, my first two fillets are lying indistinguishably beside Laurent's. '*C'est bon*,' he judges, as the silent apprentice whisks them away for the tweezer treatment, and suddenly the fact that he did the same for Georges's trout seems to elevate me to nearly Georges-like status. Thanks to the coming of Joris, I am no longer the lowest of the low.

More importantly, I now have a proprietorial interest in two out of four of the dishes on the bestselling menu: a starter and a main course. Surely, statistically, even on the quietest of nights, there must be *some* demand.

'The storm's been cancelled,' says Laurent, returning from a listen to the radio. 'No rain till next week. You'll be watering tomorrow after all,' he laughs, as we settle down to Georges's ratatouille and rump steaks.

At seven-fifteen, I feel as if I have done a full day's work, and yet this is my only service in nearly a month. For everyone else, it is one of twelve in a week, with the restaurant now opening for lunch and dinner, on every day except Mondays, until the end of the summer.

Eric isn't eating tonight. 'Don't ask,' says Jean-Pierre. 'Sometimes he does and sometimes he doesn't.' Instead, he continues bustling round behind his hatch, preposterously impervious to the heat.

'How many finally?' asks Laurence, coming up from downstairs to join us.

'Just the two and the three that booked yesterday,' says Laurent gloomily. 'And one of the three's a child. I don't know whether he'll eat.'

Laurence frowns, as if adjusting her profit forecasts, while her husband bemoans the difficult season. 'I haven't seen an American all year,' he tells me. 'Even the English with houses here don't seem to have arrived. And the French are feeling squeezed from all directions by the new government – shutting themselves indoors and hoping it'll all go away. The only time we've been full for weeks was last week's private view – the dinner for the Lodève museum. It was really someone else's turn, but the Mayor's trying to help the businesses hit by the roadworks.'

'Everyone's finding it hard,' says Laurence.

'But they haven't all got traffic jams,' grumbles Laurent. 'Of course, the police getting tougher on drinking and driving doesn't help.' He pours me a little red from a half-consumed bottle, abandoned by a cautious customer yesterday evening. 'I've started telling everyone that they're welcome to keep the cork and take any unfinished wine away with them. Otherwise, I'm really going to lose sales. But the biggest problem of all is the fact that no one, but no one wants to eat lunch in this weather.'

Everyone seems unusually subdued, though whether by the heat or the lack of business it is hard to judge. Such conversation as there is, is mainly argumentative. Laurent complains that Georges has cut the steaks in the wrong direction, slicing along the muscle instead of across, or maybe the other way round. Georges insists that it's the right cut for rump; Laurent must be thinking of *onglet*. But no, Laurent does know the difference. And so on for several irritable minutes, while Joris keeps quieter than ever.

Suddenly it is eight o'clock. Jean-Pierre, who must have discreetly withdrawn to the wine cellar to change, returns reluctantly tying a brightly patterned tie over a sober white shirt. 'Coloured ones show the sweat too much,' he explains to excuse his enforced conservatism. However, as he kicks the swing doors to give the dining-room a final check, an incongruous bare ankle below the well-pressed black of his trousers proves socks to be a degree of conventionality too far.

The two tables are occupied and their orders taken in rapid succession; and once again they spurn the first menu: two à la carte, two middle menus and a child's portion of pasta. The universal lack of interest in either my *blettes* or my *lisettes* is positively discourteous.

'What time is last orders?' I ask, assessing the chances of some more discerning, late-passing trade.

'Nine-thirty,' says Laurent, sharing none of my optimism.

Jean-Pierre at least is happy. Both of the tables have sent him downstairs for one of the list's more expensive bottles.

He looks less happy when it comes to setting up the cheeses on his trolley. The current slow turnover makes it difficult for him to maintain a respectable selection in top condition. He shows a particular *chèvre* to Laurent who shakes his head. The goat's cheeses all derive from the man in the market, and Jean-Pierre thinks the quality is declining.

'Have you tried the ones from Pégairolles?' I ask.

'No, I should,' admits Laurent. 'It's my village, after all. *Mais, c'est compliqué,*' he adds, as if some wider issue of country politics needs resolving first.

'Come and have a breath of fresh air,' he suggests, when all the main courses have left the kitchen, and I follow him out to the grassy terrace by the dustbins. 'My favourite time of day!' He sighs with pleasure, pointing up to the distant cliffs below the Larzac ridge, their white now tinged with pink. Then he sighs with regret at the scar of bare earth, cutting deeper each day along the opposite side of the valley.

'They've promised fifteen years' worth of greenery in five years,' he says. 'But you know what that means – pines, like the ones on the hills behind. All planted by man in the last fifty years. The indigenous trees, the oaks and ash, will all disappear if we're not careful. And look at this side of the valley. It was nothing but vines and olives when I was a boy, some of the fields so steep you'd have to be *malade* to work them; but so much of it's been abandoned. Then you see that nearest cliff, behind Pégairolles? There are fertile fields up there, accessible only on foot. The villagers used to take donkeys up to carry the corn down. Forty-five minutes each way. They had a different notion of time . . .'

A clarion '*Ça marche: trois tartes tatins*' brings him sharply back to modern notions of time. But it could be worse. At least the order for the first desserts means we are on the home straight.

Or we thought we were, until Jean-Pierre bursts in from the restaurant. He waits until the swing doors are safely closed behind him before giving way to the laughter that he has been struggling to suppress on the other side. '*Trois de passage*,' he manages to articulate. 'Just arrived.'

Laurent looks at his watch and nods in puzzled assent. He isn't going to turn away a party of three, even at a quarter to ten. But that doesn't make it funny.

'They've got a pig with them,' splutters Jean-Pierre, as if that explains everything.

'A pig!' exclaims Laurent. 'Where?'

'In the restaurant. On the floor beside their table . . .' He can still barely speak for laughter.

Laurent looks all set to rush through the doors to defend the purity of his dining-room – 'I mean, dogs are one thing,' his expression seems to say – but Jean-Pierre holds up a hand and forces out a few more words of explanation. 'It's frozen,' he says. 'They want to know if they can put it in your deep-freeze while they eat.'

Laurent looks relieved. 'How big is it?' he asks quickly. Even in the current business climate, one has to be practical.

Jean-Pierre mimes about two-thirds of a metre and Laurent once again nods his assent. 'I thought I'd seen everything,' he laughs, as his maître d'hôtel reappears with a grimace of theatrical disdain and a shrink-wrapped, curly-tailed sucking pig. However, just as the ice-cold carcass is about to take its place among the sorbets, Laurent grabs it and tiptoes round to the *plonge*. With a finger to his lips urging silence, he taps Eric on the shoulder, waits for him to turn and hands him the pig like a baby. Instinctively, Eric takes it like a baby, then realizes his mistake and almost jumps into the sink with fright. But he is laughing as much as anyone when Jean-Pierre calls the kitchen to order with a commanding '*Ça marche: trois amuses!*'

Another two- to three-hour cycle has just been set in motion. Main courses by eleven, if we're lucky; cheese at half past; then, if they opt for one of the cold desserts, Joris could even start the swabbing down before midnight. But can Jean-Pierre be counted on to recommend the sorbets?

I thought I was keeping these calculations to myself but my exhaustion must have been all too obvious.

'The four of us can probably cope,' says Laurent, with a sympathetic grin.

I totter gratefully down to the Renault. Anyone watching me fumble with the lock would think I was drunk. I rub my eyes before starting the engine and notice that my hands reek of baby mackerel. I am, however, much too tired to wash them.

*

'*C'est pas possible,*' squawked Garance hysterically. 'You must know all the best lawyers.'

I stopped the tractor reluctantly. The garage had taken a week to repair the tyre and this was my first opportunity to cut the hay in the olive grove. Without leaving the seat, I tried to explain that I had never had any contact with the French legal system, not even in my previous existence. Except for the *notaire*, of course, when I acquired the house . . . But Garance wasn't listening.

'You must know someone who can stop them,' she ranted. 'I mean, don't you care? With a motorway coming practically at eye level, within a hundred metres of your property? You won't get a *centime* of compensation! You only get that within fifty!'

'But they can't be coming that close to us. The old road must be five hundred metres away at the moment.'

'Five hundred and sixty-eight,' she declared with startling precision. 'That's why your postbox says five-six-eight.'

This really did seem an odd proposition. Could Manu's residence, numbered five-six-seven, be no more than one metre nearer the dual carriageway? And how would the system distinguish between two equidistant properties? Indeed, how did it manage if there were no convenient highway to determine these things? My mind filled with images of punctilious postmen traversing the countryside with tape-measures.

'I told them I'm a writer. I need peace and quiet . . .'

'Hang on.' I tried to get a grip on the issue. 'Surely they're just widening the lanes and adding a hard shoulder?'

'They were. But they've run into water problems. Unexpected springs or something, making them take a wider loop. Haven't you been out in the last twenty-four hours?'

'It was dark when I came back.'

'Then you haven't seen what they've done to the cherry orchard.'

'I saw the marker posts,' I said. I could hardly have missed them, with their luminous-looking pink paint, and I was still haunted by Manu's jest about the service station. 'Many a true word . . .' I kept thinking.

'Well, that's where they've bulldozed!' cried Garance triumphantly.

'But that's fifty metres higher than the existing road.'

'Exactly!' Her pitch had risen almost to the point of inaudibility. 'You've got to ring someone. I've tried. I've talked to the foreman. I've been to the Mairie in Lodève. But as soon as they see a woman, they just laugh in my face.'

Garance then spent half an hour telling me how she didn't have five more minutes to spend on the problem. She was overwhelmed by the heat; she had crippled her back and punctured both her tyres on the latest upheaval in the landscape; and on top of everything else, she was desperately trying to finish some pieces for the forthcoming poetry festival in Lodève: the most important week in her year.

To be fair, it would be an important week in the year for much of Lodève. They call it 'La Voix de la Méditerranée' and it features musicians and writers from all over the French-speaking world. In my first year here, there were concerts, theatre pieces and poetry readings, at all hours of day and night. A dozen or so private courtyards and gardens were opened as performing spaces, and the streets were lined with bookstalls where earnest poets gave one-to-one renditions to anyone willing to linger long enough.

My abiding memory is that of a pony-tailed ascetic intoning his stream of consciousness in an alley filled with rickety metal chairs, near the Saturday morning market. He was even equipped with a microphone but the improvised auditorium was deserted, except for an elderly lady, apparently only resting from the exertion of filling her shopping trolley. She was fiddling frantically with her hearing aid and, to this day, I ask myself whether she was trying to turn it up or switch it off.

'What does Manu say?' I tried to return to the main agenda.

'He's gone away. After promising me he'd help with my inner tubes.'

I remembered then: he was visiting his sister-in-law, the legendary teetotaller whose abhorrence of liquor was several degrees fiercer than her sister's, more ferocious even than

Manu's thirst. He would be in no mood for bicycle maintenance when he returned.

To buy some tractoring time, I persuaded Garance that it was reckless to act without the benefit of Manu's wiser counsel. He had been here so much longer than either of us, and he seemed to have so many cousins. However, I am barely halfway round the olive grove when the drone of the tractor is drowned by what sounds like a massively amplified engine and a reverberant clank of metal coming up the drive.

'Broke the exhaust on the roadworks!' shouts Manu from the window of his van, in which there is no sign of Mme Gros.

'I thought you weren't coming back till the weekend,' I call, as I go down to meet him.

'Pretended I had flu,' says Manu. 'Sister-in-law's a whatsisname. Always afraid of catching something.'

'Hypochondriac?'

'One of those. But never mind that. This exhaust . . .'

'Why don't you come in for a drink?'

'Never mind that either,' he snaps. 'More important things. I'm issuing a *procès*. Told the foreman so, just now. But damned if I'm going to that *avocat* in Lodève. Charges a fortune. No, I said to myself, you'll know someone who'd do me a favour. You must know all the best lawyers.'

*

'*Une pièce d'identité*,' demands the Salins du Midi security guard, as if I were seeking entry to a nuclear power station, instead of a salt marsh.

I slide my driving licence through an aperture in the reinforced glass and he suspiciously compares the photograph with the real thing, before copying most of the copiable details into a ledger. Then, with a second mistrustful look, he pushes a clip-on badge, with my name on it, out through the slit. I hover for a moment, thinking he has forgotten the driving licence.

'You get it back when you return the badge,' he tells me bluntly.

I check the badge. Perhaps I have indeed come to the wrong place, but no, this really is where they make the Fleur de Sel de Camargue and, to prove it, the man whom I have come to meet drives up beside me.

'Patrice Gabanou,' the managing director introduces himself, as he pushes the passenger door open. I stifle a yawn and get in beside him. An eight o'clock rendezvous in Aigues Mortes required me to leave my bed before it was even light.

'Salt's always been a precious commodity,' he says, as if to excuse the security arrangements. 'Roman soldiers received part of their pay in salt. Hence the word salary . . . I've been working on a booklet for visitors,' he explains, as if to excuse his erudition. 'When the French kings secured a monopoly, they imposed a tax. The monopoly went with the Revolution but the so-called *gabelle* lasted up until the end of the last war, so customs officials needed strict controls over supplies. Nowadays, it's more to protect the purity of the product that we keep the site closed – except for the guided visits by bus.'

I am beginning to see why no one would visit on foot. We have been driving for a good five minutes and there is still no sign of the sea, where M. Gabanou suggests we should start. We have already passed a number of dune-like salt mountains – *camelles*, he said they are called, although no one seems to know why. Some are a brilliant white, some a duller grey, but all are at least twenty metres high and ten or twenty times as long: surely remarkably plentiful stocks, given the imminence of this season's yield.

'We aim to keep at least a year's production in hand,' he explains. 'Roughly four hundred and fifty thousand tonnes. Just in case bad weather spoils the next harvest. It's thoroughly washed before it's sold,' he adds defensively, as we pass an especially grey *camelle*.

Soon we are surrounded by pools of salt water, extending in every direction and as far as the eye can see, enclosed by low-built dykes. Some are relatively small, perhaps several times the size of a football pitch; others stretch almost out of sight.

'Eighteen kilometres by thirteen,' says M. Gabanou, reading my thoughts and reminding me of Mme Vargas's comparison with Paris. 'Eleven thousand hectares, three hundred and forty kilometres of roads . . . *Mais, c'est beau, non?*' We are passing one of the larger lagoons, which is dotted with pink flamingos, made pinker still by the early light. 'The fact that it's closed to the public makes it a wonderful reserve for wildlife,' he enthuses, pointing out a colony of terns nesting on the other side of the track. 'Don't ask me about the plants, but most of them are quite rare, thriving only in salty conditions.'

'How long has all this been here?' I ask, still patiently waiting for the sea to appear.

'We think it was early Greek settlers who made the first salt here. It's part of the Rhône delta, you see, the word "Rhône" being a corruption of Rhodes, where they came from . . . All in the booklet,' he laughs. 'But it was the Romans who really expanded production, then the monks who kept things going. In the thirteenth century, the Church ceded everything to Louis IX, who made Aigues Mortes his base – both physical and financial – for the crusades. It became a major trading post but the port silted up in the fifteenth century, losing out to Marseille. That left little but the *sauniers*, as the salt producers are called.'

We pass a lorry, the first sign of human life since we left the security post. It appears to be watering the road. 'It's to stop the dust blowing into the pools,' M. Gabanou interrupts the potted history to explain. 'We do it every day. The purity of the product again.'

A lone fisherman looms into view, silhouetted against the low horizon. 'Staff?' I ask, remembering the tight security.

'We issue some permits,' he tells me. 'It's mainly eels that they catch. Not many fish can stand the extremes of temperature.'

'And the Salins du Midi?' I am still scanning the skyline for some sea. 'How long has that been here?'

'Only since 1856,' he laughs. 'At one time, there were seventeen different *sauniers* in the Camargue. That's one of their abandoned houses.' He points to a substantial, shuttered building, one of very few vertical features in this vast, essentially horizontal landscape. 'But in 1842, flooding from the Rhône caused terrible damage to the salt beds. An industrialist, who needed the salt to make soda and chlorine, bought the whole lot very cheaply. The company he founded, the Salins du Midi, now owns all of the French Mediterranean production. *Et voilà, finalement la mer!'*

We have reached a barrier made of neatly cemented boulders, behind which is a narrow beach and the sea.

'You need three things to make salt,' says M. Gabanou. 'Sea-water, sun and wind. Oh, and a fourth thing, as little rain as possible.'

'Is it always sunny?' I ask, looking up at the cloudless blue, so different from the greyer dawn at home.

'Nearly always,' he replies. 'And the dominant winds here are dry ones, the Mistral and the Tramontane. The wet one, the Marin from the sea, is bad news for salt-making. *Ah, mais c'est vraiment beau,'* he enthuses again. 'I used to work as a *saunier* myself. I love it out here.'

He points to some less beautiful machinery, about a hundred metres inland, where a channel runs in from the sea between parallel boulder-barriers. 'Five pumps,' he explains, 'delivering a million cubic metres of water a day. It takes six or seven weeks in the early spring to top the whole system up. Then it's a matter of progressive evaporation, as the water circulates from pool to pool.'

'Using yet more pumps?' I ask, having seen none.

'Just gravity,' says M. Gabanou. 'And a system of sluices. The water starts in the *partènements* – those enormous, lake-like pools that we passed on the way here. A hundred and thirty-six of them, totalling seven thousand, five hundred hectares. The water travels over sixty kilometres, while the salt concentration rises – say, from thirty grams per litre at the outset to two hundred and sixty by the time it's ready for the second phase, the precipitation of the salt in the smaller, shallower *cristallisoirs*. We passed some of those as well. There are fifty-two in all, ranging from five to eleven hectares.'

I feel almost too numbed by the immensity of it all to formulate a question. 'Er . . . What time of year is this? The arrival in the *cristallisoirs*?'

'Late April, early May, often later. It mustn't happen too soon. It's all part of the *maître saunier*'s skill to regulate the water's journey, taking sun and wind and rain into account. He needs to reach the optimum ninety per cent evaporation, in the period with minimum risk of rain.'

'What if it does rain?' I ask, wondering whether the morning clouds might have brought a few welcome drops to those of us outside the salt-making community.

'In the early phases, before the crystallization, we try to evacuate the surface rainwater as quickly as possible, before it mixes too much with the brine and dilutes it and delays the harvest.'

'And after crystallization?'

'You risk the salt dissolving. You'd certainly lose the Fleur de Sel. But fortunately, rain in summer's very rare here.'

'You've started the Fleur de Sel?' I ask and he takes the hint, returning to the car.

'It takes three or four weeks,' he explains, 'starting in mid-July. The regular harvest is later, towards the end of August or the beginning of September. That needs three separate teams working shifts around the clock, seven days out of seven, for the best part of a month.'

'Doesn't that conflict with a certain piece of legislation?'

'We give lots of time off at other times of the year. It's the only way,' he explains, still driving towards our starting-point. 'We have to finish before the autumn rains. But the main harvest is totally mechanized,' he adds, as if to reassure me that I have come at the best time. 'Big diggers, big conveyor belts, big *camelles*, like you saw. Although still very skilled. The salt forms a layer roughly nine centimetres deep and it's a delicate operation to lift it, without digging up the pool at the same time. But the Fleur de Sel's all done by hand . . . Well, except for the loading,' he admits, as we find our side road blocked by a substantial lorry with a crane on the back.

Beside the truck is a scene of curious beauty. 'Curious' because the idea of a dozen young men, dressed in spotless white laboratory coats and white rubber boots, wading about with plastic shovels in shallow water, sounds clinical and prosaic. Perhaps it is merely the effect of the pink-tinted light, contrasting with all that pristine white, but somehow the gathering in of the Fleur de Sel achieves a kind of poetry.

On closer inspection, the water is pinker by far than the early sunshine could explain. 'It's the effect of tiny pink algae that only flourish in very salty water,' says M. Gabanou. 'They provide the food for a tiny pink crustacean, which also likes extra salty water. Look, there are some near the edge there, about a centimetre long. It's what the flamingos feed on.'

'Turning the birds as well as the water pink?'

M. Gabanou laughs in agreement. *'Mais, c'est beau, non?'*

The oldest of the white-coated figures comes towards us and is introduced as Patrick Vergnes, the *maître saunier* in charge of this morning's operation. (He and the other signatories on the boxes in my store cupboard take it in turns.) He explains how the wind blows the surface layer of salt to this side of the pool and how the surface granules are always the finest, the most delicate, almost sweet in their subtlety. The Fleur de Sel should be crumbled on food at the point of serving, he emphasizes, never wasted in the cooking pot. And with that, he returns to his team – mostly sons of older *sauniers*, M. Gabanou explains: the profession is highly dynastic.

Half the younger men are wading three or four metres out into the pool, then gently bulldozing the salt's top layer towards the edge with special high-sided shovels (never treading on the salt to be harvested, M. Gabanou stresses). The other half are using more conventional shovels to pile the salt thus collected on to sheets of nylon sacking, laid out on rafts in the shallowest water. Most of the water is allowed to drain away, before the crane swings into action to hoist the sacking up and away from each raft. The salt is then emptied into a big, square, nylon sack, known technically as *un bigbag*, where it will remain, untouched and unprocessed, in a yard, until customer demand requires it to be packed into cork-lidded tubs, bearing Patrick Vergnes's autograph.

'A marvellous year for Fleur de Sel,' enthuses M. Gabanou, as we drive back towards the entrance. 'Normally we make about three hundred tonnes, but this season we're expecting double that – thanks to the drought and the temperatures. But not so successful for the regular salt. There just hasn't been enough wind.'

'Salt's always been a precious commodity,' he reminds me at the security barrier. 'Men didn't need it when all they ate was raw meat.' He grins apologetically, as he hands me a copy of his booklet. 'It's turning to cooked meat and vegetables that made us so dependent.'

The guard looks sceptically at my surrendered security badge before letting go of my driving licence. You can't be too careful when you're dealing with the stuff of life itself.

*

The Lodève market has never seemed so gloomy. The poetry festival has been cancelled. At the very last minute, a nation-wide technicians' strike has made it impossible.

Garance, of course, is inconsolable, but it is not just the poets who are disappointed. The ordinary residents who were looking forward to a week and a half of music and bustle have been watching the silent dismantling of the unused concert platforms and poetry tents. Moreover, throughout the town and beyond, there are shopkeepers, hoteliers and restaurateurs who have lost important business.

'Catastrophic,' says Laurent, when I meet him at the forbidden *chèvre* stall. (The outlaw still retains my egg business and, apparently, Laurent's cheese order.) 'Never mind the audiences,' he explains. 'I had bookings from a lot of the performers.'

The stallholder serves some other customers, while Laurent, prompted by the strike, expands on some of his favourite themes:

the disaster known as 'the French Economy', the lunacy known as 'the Thirty-Five-Hour Week', the work-shy creature known as 'the Frenchman'.

'Still having fun with the motorway?' I ask him, during a lull.

He pulls a tortured face, then laughs. 'Actually, the good news is, the queues are now so bad, people have started taking the Pégairolles road in desperation. Some are so fed up by the time they reach us, they stop for lunch! Although, as most of them were budgeting for a sandwich at the service station, they're not that keen to spend much. But you've heard about the latest disaster up in the tunnel?'

I knew that the traffic was once again being diverted through Lodève, which seemed decidedly ill-considered, given the late July traffic volumes, but I didn't know it was connected with the tunnel.

'A thirty-eight-tonne lorry caught fire inside it. That was bad enough in itself, but the lorry was full of washing-up liquid and the firemen's hoses washed it all the way down to the Lergue. You wouldn't believe the foam on the river. Several metres high! They say it'll reopen in a day or so, but that won't put the wildlife back. The detergent's destroyed everything for several kilometres.'

There is more bad news at the honey stall.

'We're having to sell the *mièlerie*,' says Claudette. 'That's why I haven't been able to ring you about a transhumance. It's taken all our time making arrangements. It's been such a bad season, the same all over France.'

'Because of the weather?'

'Because of the drought, yes. There just weren't enough flowers. Trust us to pick about the only agricultural activity in France that doesn't get a subsidy!'

'What will you do?'

'We're going to share with a friend, over towards the Cévennes. He's got the space and we've got the equipment.'

'But it's so far away.'

'We haven't a lot of choice.' She smiles stoically.

The only person who seems as cheerful as ever is Pascal Poot, who now has sufficient tomatoes to make it worth his while driving down to the market.

'How's it going?' I ask, hoping for at least a token whinge about the drought.

'Fine.' He shrugs, as if to say he hasn't really thought about it. 'Quantity might be down a bit.' He shrugs again. He hasn't worried much about that either.

I try out the shrug, as I set off home to my sprinklers. I wish I could make it my own; but somehow I can't get the knack.

*

'You can't have bought these eggs from Rens,' said Garance, when I served her what I considered quite a passable tomato (from the Conservatoire) and basil (from the potager) omelette.

'They're organic,' I said defensively. 'From the stall where I used to buy my goat's cheese.'

'*Et voilà, donc,*' said Garance, her worst fears confirmed. 'You can tell they're not from Rens. Her yolks aren't just yellow; they're positively orange.' She toyed with her lunch, as if I'd made it with powdered egg and water; but it wasn't just the omelette: she was also sulking about the cherry orchard.

She should, of course, have been jubilant. The alarming pink posts had merely marked a revised route for our lane, not the motorway. The road was to remain at roughly its existing level, while the new location for the lane would be further from the main traffic than before. But being wrong didn't come easily to Garance. Nor did cycling up the steep temporary surface of the newly bulldozed passage.

'You see what it's done to my back wheel?' She pointed sullenly at the no longer perfect circumference. Then, suddenly more winsome: 'I don't suppose you'd be going that way?'

'To see Rens?'

She knew perfectly well that the cul-de-sac location meant no

one could be 'going that way', unless they were going specifi-
cally to the *bergerie*. Seeing me hesitate, she played the motorway
card again: how she was now the prisoner of her buckled spokes;
how Manu was too busy fussing about his broken exhaust to
repair them; how, as usual, it had all been left to her to do the
complaining . . . until eventually she wore me down. I would go
as soon as the sun got low enough, topping up my own supplies
of Pélardon and eggs while I was there.

There was no sign of goats as I approached along the stream:
a single cow and calf that were not here before, a trailer loaded
with freshly baled hay and more abandoned machinery than I
remember; but no goats.

'They're inside,' says Rens's husband, Bernard Chabrier, when
I find him behind the barn.

'Impatient to be milked?' I ask, extending a hand to shake
his own. His hand being dirty, he proffers an arm instead but
unfortunately it is his left arm and I am already committed to
my right hand, so my attempt at a plausible shake is more than
usually awkward. Too late, I realize that his right arm is badly
withered, almost non-existent in fact, and I wish that I could go
back outside and start again.

'The weather's still too hot,' explains Bernard, giving no sign
of noticing my confusion. 'The goats are spending the afternoons
indoors, which means a lot more hay in the diet. All permitted
by the rules,' he hastens to assure me. 'A lot of people are having
to buy it in but, luckily, we get several crops a year from our
couple of hectares. Normally the rules say you can't buy more
than twenty per cent of the feed; but this year, with the drought,
they've had to make an exception. Otherwise, most people just
couldn't survive. There's no *garrigue* left.'

I can hardly believe that this is the same man who seemed so
taciturn when I first met him.

Still chatting freely, Bernard lets me squeeze in beside
him, in the narrow passage between two waist-high, wooden
platforms, each built to accommodate five goats, with their
milkable ends nearest us. From the ceiling hang five pairs of

automatic milking nozzles which, he explains, can be switched across from one line of udders to the other. On the far side of each platform is a row of personalized feeding troughs filled with the goats' favourite snack: a mixture of corn (off the cob) and vitamin pellets. 'All permitted by the rules,' Bernard emphasizes again.

He opens a tiny door linking the milking platforms to the barn next door. 'It's the same first ten every time,' he laughs, as the keenest members of the herd start stampeding through. 'This is the leader.' He points to the first. 'And that one's her deputy. Always in the same places. They all have distinct personalities, you see. Not like sheep. Take this one for instance, always up to mischief. *"La reine des bêtises,"* I call her. They're also much more sensitive than sheep. If they're unhappy, it affects the milk. Both quantity and quality.'

When the first five are dry, Bernard swings the dangling sets of pipes across to the opposite team and then, when they too are done, he releases both groups by a different gate, leading to another part of the barn, and a second ten are let in.

'The same movements, twice a day, every day,' he says, more contented than complaining. 'It's the same for Rens in the *salle de fabrication.*'

As if on cue, Rens emerges from the holy of holies wearing an incongruous, ankle-length, plastic white apron over her skimpy denim shorts, and a plastic shower cap on her head. Her expression says, 'I know I look ridiculous but this is how I suffer for my product.'

'I couldn't get to the Marché du Terroir on Tuesday,' I tell her, as she assembles both Garance's purchase and my own.

'The "M" word again?' asks Rens intuitively.

'They'd made the bottom end of our lane so steep and rough, you'd have needed a four-wheel-drive to get back up it. I'd seen what it did to my neighbour's van and didn't want to take a chance. By the time I thought about risking the car on the footpath round the back, the market was over.'

'It'll soon be finishing for the year,' sighs Rens, lamenting, I sense, the end of summer more than the narrowing of her sales opportunities.

'You really ought to get them into Le Temps de Vivre,' I tell her. 'I'm sure they'd prefer yours.'

'We still haven't been,' says Rens. 'It's not in our budget.'

'It's less than people think,' I assure her.

'It's 28 Euros for the cheapest menu,' says Rens, more precisely informed than I'd imagined. 'We had lunch on the coast at the weekend for 13 Euros. We took the kids to the beach. Left at eleven, back at four for the milking, and still we had customers complaining. But you've got to let the kids have a bit of a summer, given that we can't go away. You're right, though,' she adds, taking my handful of Euros for the combined purchase. 'The restaurant would be a good shop window.'

*

'Lunch?' I asked incredulously. 'You mean eating? In the middle of the day? In these temperatures?'

Ever since July, when a generous visitor equipped me with an electric juice-maker, my midday sustenance had been almost exclusively ice-cold, home-grown fruit and vegetable cocktails. Perhaps an old favourite, I was thinking when Virgile telephoned: some beetroot from the potager, mixed with early, under-ripe pears from the orchard. Or an experiment: freshly picked carrot and melon, with (yes, the shame of it) ginger from the supermarket. But something served on a plate? Something cooked even? I shuddered at the thought.

'Chez Philippe,' suggested Virgile. 'Down at Marseillan. It's near the port and there's an outside terrace, so there should be some breeze. You could even swim in the Bassin de Thau,' he added, shortly before I gave in.

My normal route via the village was blocked by the roadbuilders' latest efforts to create a plausibly natural-looking link with our relocated lane, so I took the downhill alternative, descending sharply to cross the river at exactly the point where it passes beneath the dual carriageway flyover. As always, a sign at the top carried the warning that the low-slung concrete bridge down below was liable to flooding, but there was little risk of that today. Two-thirds of the river bed had been reduced to shingle beach, and what little water remained was meandering at least a metre below the bridge. And there, in the shadow of the flyover, I found a scene of rare Arcadian charm.

Mindful as ever of seasonal sensibilities, Super U had been running a special picnic-table promotion and here, in the deepest part of the shallow water, stood a gleaming example of their 'top-of-the-range', complete with integrated fold-out benches on either side. The nearer of these was occupied by a familiar figure in blue dungarees, rolled up on this occasion past plump, grey-haired calves to facilitate the freshening of feet in the current. He was too busy reaching out for the nearest of the bottles cooling in the stream to notice my approach.

His wife, on the other side, looked characteristically displeased by my arrival. The plastic-packaged provisions on the table-top were untypically liberally catered and she quickly shuffled them into a single, less abundant-looking mound, as if to emphasize that there was insufficient to share.

'You realize there are people dying in this heat?' said Mme Gros defiantly. She too was frivolously paddling her bare feet but hoped by sheer force of personality to impersonate a woman wearing sensible shoes.

'Mostly old folks,' added Manu cheerfully, as if to exclude present company from risk.

I had read about the death toll in the newspaper: apparently there were thousands of victims, all across the country, unable to cope with the temperatures. I had also read about the processions led by parish priests to pray for rain. Even the tourists, it seemed, were finding the beaches too hot and were heading into the hills for shadier styles of holiday. Almost every day, another coastal restaurateur would be interviewed, bemoaning his worst season ever. But here was I, I explained to my neighbours, off to Marseillan to buck the trend.

'You must be *malade*,' called Manu, stretching dangerously far beyond his bench for a second bottle, as I drove away.

'We've hardly opened a red all summer,' said Magda, when I asked if they'd turn up their noses at rosé.

'It's true,' said Virgile. 'Not even at night. Everyone's the same in this heat.'

'I hope it's cooler for your *vendange*,' I said. 'I've been waiting till nearly sunset to pick my almonds. It's made the job last a week. There are thousands of them but the drought's made them almost uncrackable – they've got incredibly thick shells. There are some in the car for you. Good for your pruning muscles!'

'You're lucky you've got your own water,' said Magda. 'It's rationed in Saint Saturnin. People who want to water their gardens have been given fixed time slots. If they're out and they miss them, tough luck. And nobody's allowed to fill a swimming pool.'

'No wonder my own reds are moving so slowly,' sighed Virgile. 'It seems to be the same in the export market. Ever since the spring, I've had various *palettes* reserved for English and German wine merchants, but now they're back-pedalling.'

'You'd better make some rosé yourself next year,' I teased, but they answered simultaneously with a well-practised '*ce n'est pas la philosophie du domaine*'.

'You'd be amazed,' said Virgile. 'Lots of growers are saying they'll only make rosé in future. If it's cold and wet next year, it'll be a disaster. But everyone's having a hard time.' He looked round at the half-empty terrace of Marseillan's most popular restaurant. 'I bet Laurent's quiet.'

'*Toujours calme*,' I confirmed.

'People are tightening their belts,' continued Virgile. 'It'll be a couple of difficult years for all of us.'

Magda changed the subject back to the happier one of the menu, seeking Virgile's linguistic assistance with some unfamiliar ingredients. She confessed to dropping out of her French course. 'We're always so tired,' she explained. 'Especially Virgile, with so much to organize for his partners. We were planning to go to Poland for a bit of a holiday but it's too much travelling.'

Fifty per cent of Chez Philippe's menu was in fact incomprehensible to all of us. This was because every dish was subtitled in Occitan, the ancient, otherwise vanished language that gave the Languedoc its name. On the page, it looked like some wayward hybrid of French and Italian, but the only vocabulary known to any of us was '*oc*', meaning '*oui*' to Virgile and 'yes' to me. I knew that there were vestiges of the *langue d'oc* everywhere – in surnames and place names, for instance, especially words ending in 'ou' or 'oux', like Salagou and Montpeyroux – but I had always thought it died as an actively spoken language around the sixteenth century, when a centralizing monarchy set out to suppress it. So efforts like this to revive it have always seemed essentially artificial.

Virgile, however, disabused me: it had been a living language for several of his relatives. His paternal grandfather – the one who lives over near Arles and who must be roughly my father's age – had been brought up speaking Occitan. French for him was a foreign tongue but, seeing the way the tide was moving, he encouraged his children to speak it as the language of progress. Indeed, he could manage it himself now. But one of Virgile's aunts had gone to school unable to speak French, yet forbidden by law to speak Occitan, even in the playground. She had a lonely childhood.

Intrigued by all this, I stopped off in the village on my way home. I wanted to consult Monsieur Privat, the retired schoolmaster, but I knew that, at this hour, there was no need to drive as far as his blue-shuttered house at the other end of the main street. He was already seated at one of Babette's plastic tables in the Place de la Fontaine, where the central fountain, like half a dozen others in the side streets, stood dry and silent in response to the water shortages.

He was making a pastis last as long as possible, until it was time to step inside to his habitual corner table for the second of the twice-daily meals which he had been taking *chez*

Babette since the day that Madame Privat died. (No question of defecting to the Restaurant à Vin for him, *coq aux olives* or no *coq aux olives*.)

'They wouldn't have turned the fountains off when I was a boy,' he reminisced, as Babette brought two more Ricards. 'The fountains were the only source of water for the whole village until the 1950s . . . But you were asking about Occitan.'

'Yes, how did it come about, this divide between *oui* and *oc*?'

'Oh, that's quite straightforward. It's all because there was no word for "yes" in Latin.'

'That's ridiculous,' I laughed. 'How did they manage?'

'They said, "this that".'

'They said what?'

' "*Hoc ille*." Don't ask me why but that's how the Romans used to indicate an affirmative.'

'Bit of a mouthful.'

'Exactly. So people shortened it. In northern Gaul, it contracted to "*o il*" – later, the modern "*oui*"; in the south, simply "*oc*". By the Middle Ages, there were lots of different dialects, but in the north there were three in particular, spoken by the Normans, the Picards and the Franks of Paris. When the Franks achieved northern supremacy, the *langue d'o il* became known as *français*. Then in the thirteenth century, when they gained control of the south as well, you find the "*langue d'oc*" used to designate the lands where people didn't say "*oui*".'

' "*Langue d'oc*", not Occitan?' I queried.

'It was only in the nineteenth century that people started calling it Occitan.'

'I see.'

But I didn't really. I should never have agreed to the second Ricard that M. Privat had pressed on me.

I decided to clear my head with a walk home, leaving the car in the square, so it is well after seven when I discover Manu, almost in tears, on my drive.

'I was only out for a couple of hours,' he insists. 'Well, maybe three. Four at the outside. I needed a little snooze by the river,

113

just long enough to forget the wife's picnic. But after that, we came straight back and they were already gone. Not a single one left!'

'I don't understand. What were gone?'

'The greengages!' Manu points dramatically to the pair of well-established trees beyond the swimming pool, now conspicuously empty of the fruit that was bowing their branches this morning. 'I mean, how could she have done it in the time?'

'Who could have done what in the time?'

'Garance. Who else? Denies it, of course. Says she'll never speak to me again. Well, that bit's a blessing but it doesn't bring the greengages back. I tried forcing her door but she's locked it. Pretending she's got one of her migraines, when she's obviously got the greengages in there.'

It is useless to quarrel with Manu's deductive logic; pointless to observe that Garance would have swooned on the first rung of the picking ladder; even more futile to remind him that her *maset* is scarcely large enough to accommodate the crop, without moving the furniture out. He has made up his mind. And anyway, as he rightly said, it won't bring the greengages back.

*

'I see Bové's out,' said Laurent, lingering longer than usual over a midday coffee. Without going so far as to close, he had no very serious expectations of lunchtime customers.

I knew the name. Half the bridges on the motorway have been daubed with exhortations to 'Free José Bové'; but I was still less than certain as to who he was or why he had been deprived of his liberty.

'The militant Larzac sheep-farmer,' added Laurent to help me, but he could see how much the potager had been distracting me from the press. 'About six weeks ago, they gave him a ten-month jail sentence for destroying some genetically modified crops, back in 1999. Now the President's given in to protests and he's out on a closely supervised release programme. But Bové's still complaining. Says the supervision order's just a political manoeuvre to stop him going to Mexico for the summit of the World Trade Organization.'

'Not to punish him for destroying property or anything like that?'

'You obviously don't know many French farmers,' laughed Laurent. 'But you've heard about his finest hour, at McDonald's?' he asked, checking quickly that the car park was still empty.

This was starting to ring bells but I was happy for Laurent to remind me.

'Also in 1999,' he said. 'Around this time of year, I think. The Americans had just slapped a hundred per cent tax on their Roquefort cheese imports and, Monsieur Bové being a Roquefort milk producer . . .'

'You said he was up on the Larzac.'

'I did, but so is the village of Roquefort. About an hour from here.'

'I thought it was much further north,' I answered, feeling foolish. 'I suppose I don't go up that way very often.'

'You should, the caves are interesting . . . You know that Roquefort's matured in caves?'

This was also starting to ring bells.

'Of course,' I bluffed. 'But tell me about Bové. What did he do at McDonald's?'

'Trashed their half-built branch up at Millau. Over 150,000 Euros' worth of what he and his comrades called "symbolic dismantling".' Laurent chuckled at the terminology. 'Ripping off roof tiles, drainpipes, anything detachable; carting the whole lot off to dump it on the steps of the Préfecture, while their wives handed out samples of Roquefort on bits of *baguette*. That earned him another six weeks in prison. Of course, it was a "politically motivated confinement"...'

Laurent's cynical laughter was interrupted by the unaccustomed crunch of wheels on the car park gravel, so I never had a chance to ask more about either Bové or the caves.

I decided to investigate the latter for myself, driving up the motorway, past Pégairolles and through the tunnel that pierces the cliffs to reach the Causses du Larzac. The moorland plateau looked even more austere than usual after several months of scorching heat. The idea of sheep-farming became slightly more plausible as I dropped down to what might, come the autumn, be softer, greener fields closer to Roquefort. Indeed, I saw one thirsty flock gathered round one of the big shallow ponds, which Larzac farmers hollow out from their tough terrain to collect what rainfall they can; but this one was nearly dry.

Roquefort-sur-Soulzon, as it is properly known, sits on a long, narrow shelf between the River Soulzon and the sheer vertical face of Mont Combalou behind it. When water erosion created this dramatic shift of levels in prehistoric times, roughly sixty million years ago, it left a vast network of caves within the debris down below, on top of which the village is built. Vitally for Roquefort cheese production, these caves are ventilated by chimney-like fissures called *fleurines* which connect them to the outside world. Beneath them is a layer of muddy scree which, together with the *fleurines*, preserves a constant temperature of 9° and a consistent humidity of ninety-five per cent.

I wouldn't normally know this kind of thing but the Cave Société has a mechanical scale model (complete with prehistoric storm and landslide effects) to explain it all. It also has a *son et lumière* to relate the legend of Roquefort's origins.

There was this shepherd, we are asked to believe, having his lunchtime bread and fresh cream cheese in the shade of one of the cave mouths, when a passing shepherdess prompted him to abandon the bread and cheese in a crack in the rock and set off in pursuit. Several months later, he stumbled on his forgotten snack and found that the cheese had changed both in texture and in flavour. The bread had acted as an agent in developing the now famous mould which, like all gastronomically curious Frenchmen, he tasted; and the production of blue cheese never looked back.

What the Cave Société doesn't have is any cheese in its caves. I have come at the wrong time of year. Roquefort production is seasonal, beginning when the first lambs are weaned in December – a minimum of twenty days after lambing – and ending when the rams or artificial insemination teams set to work in the second half of June and July. I must content myself with history for today.

The making of Roquefort is believed to date from at least the time of ancient Rome. Caesar himself is recorded as enjoying blue cheese in nearby Saint Affrique. Charlemagne tried it in 778, on his way back from fighting the Saracens in Spain, commissioning a regular supply, but it was Charles VI who made himself the hero of Roquefort protectionists, by granting a monopoly in 1407. The first legislation against fraudulent Roqueforts appeared in 1666 but numerous imitations persisted – some made in faraway parts of the country, others made with goat's or cow's milk, and many going nowhere near a cave – until eventually the cheese was granted an Appellation d'Origine Controllée in 1925, the earliest for anything other than wine. This allowed only unpasteurized ewe's milk from the Lacaune breed, grazed within a delimited area. Then a Millau court case in 1961 ruled that anything bearing the Roquefort name had to be ripened in one of the caves beneath Mont Combalou.

To which I must return, when the lambs have left the udder.

*

'You're crazy!' shouted Manu against the noise of my strimmer.

'I want to make a proper path,' I shouted back. 'In all this time, I've never penetrated this wood. Too many brambles and whatever this thing's called.' I pointed to the greatest enemy of all, an alarmingly vigorous climber, some uncultivated cousin of the clematis perhaps, all but stifling even the strongest and tallest of the trees. I was determined to take advantage of the first cloudy sky in weeks.

'And guess what?' I pointed further into the undergrowth. 'I've discovered a ruin. I need to cut my way in to find out what it is.' I knew that, to Manu, the moss-covered walls were as pointless as a woodland path and this, if I am honest, was part of my motivation. 'It may not be a priority for you,' I began.

'Never mind priorities!' he bellowed, still competing with the machine noise. 'Can't you see the sparks, every time you hit a stone? The whole countryside is tinder dry! Just because the sun goes behind a cloud for ten minutes, it doesn't reduce the fire risk.'

I stopped the engine at once. 'Crazy' was indeed the *mot juste*.

Generously, Manu didn't seek to rub it in. He had his own discovery to show me. 'Can you see it?' he asked, as we stood beside my fig tree.

The windfalls from the early crop had made a thick, sticky paste underfoot which clung like clods of mud to the soles of our shoes. The second crop, however, was already turning from youthful green to soft, ripe yellow. The figs would be delicious in just a few days but the secret of total ecstasy, I had learned, was to wait until they were so bursting with molten juice that they could barely travel the distance from tree to plate. Yet there was always the risk that others, less patient, would get there first. They were Manu's favourite fruit too. It was one of life's great dilemmas.

'Can you see it?' he repeated, pointing to another tangle of the clematis-like menace, growing up a second tree beside the fig. 'Go a bit nearer,' he urged, quite childishly excited; but this, he knew, was impossible. We were standing on the edge of a four-metre precipice. The smothered tree was growing on a different level, far below, and I had no intention of diving into the chasm to identify it. I would have to walk the long way round.

'No, look. Just here!' Manu stretched perilously far into the abyss to pull something soft and pendulous free from the under-growth. Beaming broadly, he offered it for inspection. It was a black fig.

'Try it,' he prompted, but then he reconsidered. He tore the long, teardrop-shaped fruit in half so that we could both have a taste. Then I understood the excitement. This was a fig like no other. It was the quintessence of fig, by which all other figs must now be judged and found wanting. And Manu hadn't even known about this tree! In over twenty years, neither he nor my uncle had found it. A vindication of my strimming policy, if ever there was one.

'Can you see any more?' I asked eagerly.

'They're all a bit out of reach.'

'No, we've got to try,' I insisted. 'Maybe if I sit on the edge here and you hold on to my belt, while I hook that branch with a broom . . .'

'We need your Christmas present,' said Manu, meaning the extra-long-handled fruit-picking device that he gave me at the end of my first year, to ensure that harvests in my absence would not be compromised by his stature. However, even thus equipped, we managed only a dozen fruits.

For once I felt he had earned his share. I couldn't have picked them on my own without scaffolding. But here was Manu, handing me four out of twelve. 'I'd better take some for the wife,' he explained. 'Little peace offering. I promised to be back by noon and it's nearly one now.'

'One o'clock?' I pushed past him. 'I'm meeting someone in Bessan at two!'

'Bessan?' cried Manu, suddenly interested. 'That's the village with the Ricard factory, isn't it? We could call in after your meeting.'

'You need to deliver the figs,' I reminded him and escaped without admitting that my destination *was* the Ricard factory.

'So,' begins Alain Pla, the director, in a way that tells me he will be doing most of the interviewing. 'You do drink pastis, I suppose?'

He has gone straight for the Big Question; and although he is affable enough behind his luxuriant moustache, there is something about the way in which his hands are clenched on the table-top between us that tells me there is only one permissible answer.

'From time to time,' I equivocate. I should never have pursued Monsieur Privat's suggestion of a visit.

'That sounds like a no,' he says gravely, then waits, as if to give me one last chance to change my plea.

'Maybe three or four times a year.'

'That's what I call no.' A guilty verdict therefore. 'So what do you drink as an aperitif?' he asks, sounding genuinely mystified.

'Usually wine.' The thing is, I enjoyed my couple of Ricards with M. Privat and I was genuinely interested in how it was made. I just didn't realize they'd expect me to be an addict.

'Wine's not an aperitif,' M. Pla informs me sternly. 'Muscat, Rancio, Cartagène, they're aperitifs.'

'Each to his own,' I begin in an effort to mitigate my crime.

Monsieur Pla ignores me. 'Wine's for drinking with food. It's got nothing to do with aperitifs.'

'I find Ricard a bit strong,' I explain, as the first plank of my defence.

'It's forty-five per cent,' he concedes. 'But you dilute it with five parts water, which makes seven per cent – half the strength of wine. So you can drink twice as much Ricard without going over the limit.'

The logic seems irrefutable. My modest consumption levels are quite inexcusable, I can see that. I try to make amends by explaining that in so far as I do drink pastis, it is usually Ricard. Practically always, in fact. Whereas Pernod, for instance – I hope this will earn me some remission – hardly ever crosses my lips.

'Pernod's not a pastis,' says my interrogator firmly. 'It's purely aniseed-based. A pastis is a *mélange*.'

He pauses, showing no inclination to expand on the nature of the 'mix', and his glance at his watch discourages enquiry. I attempt a submissive 'couldn't agree more, not a patch on Ricard, can't think why anyone would bother with Pernod' sort of gesture. But M. Pla cuts me short with the news that the Pernod brand belongs to the Ricard group.

'Each to his own,' I nearly say again but remember that this is not a motto to which M. Pla subscribes. My credibility seems to be spiralling rapidly downwards when, mercifully, Francis Vilaro, the *responsable de fabrication*, arrives, offering both a reprieve and a tour of the production process.

'Vilaro's a Spanish name,' he begins gratuitously. 'But I've lived in Bessan all my life – at least, ever since my family left Spain, just over fifty years ago, when I was four.'

The curiously defensive autobiography is delivered as we cross a deserted, sun-baked yard to a warehouse, where he leans his short, stocky frame against a sliding door, revealing the first ingredient of M. Pla's mix: some huge wooden packing cases, filled with dull-looking, dried-up roots.

'Liquorice,' he says. 'Mainly from Syria and Italy. We grind it up and macerate the fibres in water and alcohol, ending up with a liquorice concentrate.'

He scoops some clear, colourless liquid from a nearby vat and pours it on to the palm of my hand. It looks entirely innocuous but, dipping a finger and licking it, I am nearly knocked backwards by the intensity. Then he offers just a sniff of something equally clear and colourless, in a screw-top bottle.

'Thyme?' I suggest, sensing a variety of herbs but assuming that I am meant to pinpoint one.

'*Herbes de Provence*,' he confirms. 'Thyme, rosemary, lavender . . . But now for the most important element of the mix.'

We cross the deserted yard again. I was thinking that everyone must be late back from lunch but, even at three o'clock, the factory is still bizarrely unpopulated. We do find one manifestation of humanity in the distillery but this is only the fourth sign of life, after Messrs. Pla and Vilaro and the receptionist. He is sitting at a large computerized panel, which helps to explain the single-figure headcount.

'Doesn't say much, this one,' says M. Vilaro, in a hoarse stage whisper. 'Came from Marseille. They couldn't put up with him, but we accept anyone in Bessan.' Then he remembers the most important element of the mix: the aniseed. 'We use ninety per cent star anise from China,' he explains, as I admire the impressive metal column of the still. 'Plus ten per cent local fennel, all distilled together.' He gingerly ladles out a glass of the resulting *anéthole* for me to smell. 'You wouldn't want to dip your finger in this one,' he laughs. 'It'd burn it off! But don't worry,' he adds hastily. 'Only two grams per litre.'

The *anéthole* is as clear and colourless as the other ingredients but this, M. Vilaro tells me, is what turns the pastis cloudy when water is added. The thing that makes it yellow is caramel and, remarkably, in the caramel-adding room we find a fifth human presence.

'Another refugee from Marseille,' M. Vilaro teases. 'We're not proud.'

'They were in such a mess,' retorts the exile, his eyes never straying from a second, even larger control panel, 'I had to come and rescue them.'

Not only the caramel input but also the sugar, water and alcohol injections are all, it seems, microchip-controlled. In addition the computer regulates three different filterings. It is never left unmanned. Every litre bearing the Ricard name must be consistent in flavour, strength and appearance and, to reinforce the point, M. Vilaro takes me up to the laboratory, where samples undergo every imaginable test.

'Anything that failed would be sent to the distillery, but it's never happened,' he assures me. 'Not in all the time I've worked here.'

I laugh incredulously. 'This must be the most boring job in the Languedoc. Like a policeman in a town where everyone's honest!'

'Nearly all the lab work's automated.' An expansive gesture encapsulates a battery of unsupervised gadgetry lining the walls. 'We want absolute uniformity. It's an industrial product.'

'Industrialness' is a quality in which M. Vilaro takes unapologetic pride.

'You mentioned water,' I prompt, remembering the widespread shortages, as we return to the heat of the yard.

'Fifty-five per cent of the finished product, yes.'

'Do you have your own *source*?' I ask, as we enter the bottling plant.

'No, the water comes from the town,' he explains above the rattle of glass bottles, juddering down the conveyor belts to be rinsed, filled, labelled and screw-capped.

'And there's always enough?'

'We make sure there's always at least a day's consumption in stock. We filter and pasteurize and chlorinate it; then we de-chlorinate it again, so it's pure but has absolutely no taste.' He greets a younger man, who is checking the good behaviour of the bottling robots. 'Came south, when we closed the Dijon factory,' he whispers to me.

There have to be more than six of them, I am thinking; surely, for sixty million bottles. And then I see a remarkable sight. At the end of the bottling line, beside the last of the automatons, which is filling a succession of cardboard cartons with a dozen bottles each, there are six living beings, each putting two small appliances into every box.

The company is doing a special promotion. One of those quantity-measuring pourers, familiar from French cafés, is being given away with every bottle; but there is no machine to hang them round the bottle necks, so they have drafted in some casual labour, thereby doubling the visible workforce.

'Wouldn't it be cheaper just to give away the bottles?'

M. Vilaro shakes his head with a smile.

'What would you say distinguishes Ricard from other pastis?' I ask more seriously.

'Oh that's easy. When Paul Ricard founded the business in Marseille in 1932, he saw that marketing and distribution were the keys to success. He put six hundred salesmen on the road and set up eight regional factories.'

'No, sorry, I meant what distinguishes it as a drink? Could you pick it out in a blind tasting?'

'I'm not really a great drinker of pastis.'

'Are you allowed to say that?' I laugh, but the laughter soon dies. We are back at the car park and I have forgotten to park in the shade. I am scarcely able to touch the burning handles, as I open both doors to cool the inside. M. Vilaro looks on in puzzlement. He has forgotten that they used to make non-air-conditioned cars.

'I want to drink well and long,' he explains, 'not get plastered on pastis. But I drink enough to know when it's Ricard. Some Montpellier students once tried to catch me out with six different brands, but I got them all. Yet I couldn't tell a basic whisky from a malt. Here, try this.' He hands me a bottle labelled 'Pacifique', as I will myself to enter the driver's seat. 'If you're worried about the strength of Ricard, this is non-alcoholic. Our response to stricter police controls, but still aniseed-based.'

As he waves me off, I realize that he never did tell me what distinguishes Ricard, leaving only one solution: one of which M. Pla would approve and one in which I am sure M. Gros will collaborate. I stop in Lodève to pick up a small selection of bottles, wondering whether to reward him for the fig discovery tonight or tomorrow; but all thoughts of pastis-tasting evaporate as I am leaving the town on the other side.

Some distance up the valley, a dark plume of smoke is rising skywards. The fire is somewhere behind the nearest hill, making it impossible to judge the precise distance. All I can say is that, from where I sit in a traffic jam, the direction looks horribly right for my house. And the smoke is getting denser. The traffic through the roadworks has never seemed slower and I am filled with a sickening, black dread.

A line of four yellow planes flies overhead towards the smoke: no doubt the *canadairs* that I read about at the time of the last forest fires, nearer the coast. Presumably, on this occasion, they will have picked up their water in the Lac de Salagou but they have dipped below the line of the hill, so I can't see where they are dropping it. And the traffic is almost stationary. I half persuade myself that it's too far away but I can't be sure.

At last the traffic speeds up. Then relief as I turn a corner. The smoke and the house no longer line up. The fire must be somewhere on the opposite side of the valley. Then sick apprehension again. The house has been spared but the view must be on fire. It could even be Le Temps de Vivre. We are crawling again and I am too far away. Then more relief. The smoke is coming from *behind* the line of hills that faces the house, well out of sight and well away from Laurent's.

I go straight to the Groses to see what they know and find them both listening silently to Radio Lodève on a crackly old receiver. There are two hundred and fifty firemen, a reporter tells us, drawn from all over the *département*. Later, around eight in the evening, he announces that the fire has been 'circumscribed'. The following morning we learn that 'only' sixty hectares of forest and agricultural land have been destroyed. At least no houses are damaged and no one is injured.

'Do we know what caused it?' I ask Manu.

He hesitates, embarrassed, but Mme Gros, as always, is unafraid to tell me they 'told me so'.

'A strimmer hitting a stone,' she says accusingly.

*

'Something in your eye?' asked Laurent, bumping into me in the Lodève market and seeing me cupping a hand over one of them.

'I can't bear to look at those plum prices,' I explained.

'But they're practically giving them away,' he answered, as if concerned that my circumstances must be more severely straitened than he had thought.

'Precisely. You do all that work, all that planting and pruning and watering and spraying. Then the moment your own are ripe, so are everyone else's and you wonder why you've just spent a whole afternoon picking them, to save how much? No, I'm not going to look! It's the same with most of the potager.'

'I'm sure yours will taste better,' laughed Laurent.

'Not in the case of my melons. Look at that – four cantaloupes for 5 Euros. I spent more than that on the plants alone and I've only managed to ripen two without the ants eating them first. It doesn't even pay for the watering pump. The courgettes, on the other hand, are ripening so fast that, if I turn my back for more than an hour, they've turned into marrows.'

'You'd better hurry home,' he chuckled.

'Not till I've persuaded you to put plums on the menu,' I retorted. 'Even with a house full of guests and two hungry neighbours, I've still got more than I know what to do with. Go on, substitute some *caviar de prunes* for the aubergines – get yourself out of a rut!'

*

'Keep locked away,' read the safety instructions. 'Don't eat, drink or smoke during use. Wear protective clothing, gloves and face mask. Consult a doctor immediately in case of accidental ingestion . . .' The list of health warnings seemed endless.

'Are you really telling me I should put this on my olives?' I asked the Vargases, hardly daring to put the Demethoate bottle on the courtyard table, where my late-rising guests would be breakfasting. 'Isn't there anything more organic?'

'Not to deal with the olive fly,' they assured me in unison. 'And you can't afford to delay. The weather's supposed to break at the weekend. As soon as the temperature falls, the *mouche d'olivier* will be up there, nibbling. Either you spray or you forget about green olives.'

I waited till most of my guests had left for the beach before unscrewing the flagon.

'What are you doing?' asked Sarah, who alone had stayed behind to sunbathe by the pool.

'Deciding which is south-south-west.' I craned my neck to picture the course of the sun in the cloudless sky. 'The Vargases said I should spray from the south-south-west, in a band a metre wide.'

'That's the direction the house faces,' said Sarah with the special certainty of the committed sun-worshipper. I had always thought of this as loosely 'south', but Sarah had spent most of the week rotating a poolside bed to face the ever-shifting sun. 'It's obvious,' she explained. 'If those are east and west, this must be south. Which puts south-west there, then finally . . .' She pointed straight ahead to where the principal trees overhung an inconveniently sharp fall in levels between terraces. 'South-south-west.'

I might have guessed: the one angle from which it was impossible to spray without a crane. A ladder to the west-south-west seemed the best achievable compromise. I tried to interest Sarah in ladder-climbing but the most I could negotiate was a grudging agreement to steady the bottom rungs.

'I thought I remembered these as black olives,' she said, having reluctantly covered her bikini with one of my old coats.

'That's because you were here in November. They turn black as they ripen. All olives do,' I explained, as I warily diluted the Demethoate with water.

'I thought they were different varieties, like grapes.'

'So did I, when I first arrived,' I assured her, adding a second, less toxic chemical, which, according to the Vargases, would attract the flies to the poison. 'I'm planning to make green olives for the table this year.'

'What do you mean "make"?' She reached towards a low-hanging branch. 'Oh, that's disgusting! Why didn't you warn me?' she remonstrated between spits.

'That's another mistake I made myself,' I laughed. 'There's something you have to do to get rid of the bitterness. It's salt, in the case of black ones. You pack them in it for several weeks, stirring and draining them several times a day. I did all that in year one. But apparently it's different for green olives. I haven't had time to look at the Vargases' recipe yet.'

Uncle Milo's half-perished rubber cycling cape and some snorkelling goggles were the best I could find by way of protective clothing and face mask, which meant that Sarah was too busy laughing to be of much assistance in pushing the ladder up through the branches. 'Gently,' I pleaded, as the fruits took a battering. 'I'm not sure whether olives bruise.'

'Wait,' said Sarah, when I finished pumping the spray gun. She went to fetch an umbrella: advisedly, because more of the chemical cocktail landed on her than on the metre-wide strip of tree under treatment; and also because the umbrella served to hide her blushes as she enquired, unconvincingly casual, 'How's Virgile?'

In my first year, Sarah would have known the answer to this question. In those days, when she came to stay, I had almost daily bulletins on Virgile's well-being. Her shortest excursions had a way of detouring through Saint Saturnin, to check that he was blooming. But that was before Magda.

'He's fine,' I mumbled from behind the snorkel mask. 'He's already predicting a good *millésime*. He started the *vendange* a fortnight early, in the last week of August, and finished last Sunday, on 7 September, a day ahead of his start date last year.'

'You didn't want to help?' she asked, as if even she might have given this priority over her bronzing commitments.

'He invited me for the last morning. He was having a barbecue lunch party.'

'But you were too busy looking after us lot,' said Sarah ruefully.

'Too busy avoiding backache,' I laughed the apology aside. 'But I do miss it all,' I confessed, as I started to return to civilian attire. 'Even with so much of my own to look after here. It was a remarkable year. But that reminds me, I haven't looked at my own grapes for nearly a week.'

'I thought your letter said you wouldn't have any – thanks to the rabbits and everything.'

'That's what I was assuming. But look, there must be quite a few kilos,' I enthused, as we walked up to inspect. 'Only on two of the five varieties, admittedly. I had some flowers on a third, but for some reason the fruit on those didn't set. And of course I'm still not sure which varieties they are,' I confessed, handing her a small bunch of black grapes to sample. 'I think these are the Cinsault that Virgile grows. But then again, they do taste a bit like Muscat. The whites definitely look like the Chasselas we saw in the market. It'll be easier when I've got all five, to compare them properly. But whatever they are, it's much more than I was expecting, this early.'

'Pity about the rabbit netting,' said Sarah, puncturing my excitement; and she did have a point. With most of the bunches awkwardly trapped – half inside, half outside the fine metal mesh – my *vendange* would need wire cutters. Perhaps if I trimmed the netting into artistic shapes, I could make the effect in a fruit bowl look deliberate.

'Is this the new fashion?' laughed the Vargases, when I gave them a couple this morning.

I had found them lying face downwards, leaning dangerously far into the gully at the end of their olive terraces. At first I thought they had met with an accident but they were merely struggling with their watering cans, trying to fill them from the nearly dried-up rivulet at the bottom.

'You have been watering yours, haven't you?' they asked as they hauled themselves giddily back to the vertical again.

'My olive trees?' I queried disbelievingly. I had never been anywhere near them with a hosepipe.

'Indispensable,' they opined with their usual unanimity.

So, with olives now to water, along with everything else, I fail to see the funny side of Garance's message left with Sarah: would I please be so good as not to water up near her *maset* this evening? Yesterday's splashing made it quite impossible to write. Surely she could hope that, at weekends, on the two precious days when the roadworks are quiet . . . (Sarah does a respectable, no doubt in different circumstances entertaining, imitation of poetic hysteria – only the top two octaves elude her – but I am in no mood to be amused.) Garance has, it seems, already had one row with Manu, who was strangely disinclined to suspend his *vendange* for the suggested forty-eight-hour curfew, and she expressed herself hopeful that she might avoid another with me.

'We'll see about that,' I mutter darkly, as I switch on the water pump.

Sarah meanwhile resumes the agitated artist impersonation: 'It's all very well for him. He wouldn't be so keen to waste water, if he had a well as low as mine . . .' And so on for a minute or two.

'My *source* has slowed down as well,' I tell her, when the performance pauses. 'It's a matter of priorities.'

'She was also furious that I knew about the ruin,' says Sarah. 'She convinced it's a hermitage.'

'Manu says it's a watchtower. Much more likely, with the view that it must have commanded.'

'I know, but there's no persuading your poetess. She's terrified that, if word gets out, it'll be classified as a national monument, allowing twenty-four-hour access to the public.'

'They could turn her *maset* into a tearoom,' I suggest irritably, more concerned with extension hoses for the olive trees than with the future of local tourism. 'I suppose the next thing will be her asking me to let that part of the wood grow back again!'

'Well, funnily enough . . .'

Her laughter suddenly stops. 'You're not leaving those hoses on all night?' she asks anxiously. This is more, I suspect, out of concern for tomorrow's swimming than for Garance's sleep patterns; but the answer is, in any case, the same.

'I'm making up for lost time,' I announce grimly.

*

'You've heard about Jean-Pierre?' asked Laurent, as I joined him in the Subaru to go bread-buying.

I had heard nothing. With so many visitors – even now, in late September – I had not been near the restaurant for weeks and, when he suggested I come for the busy Sunday lunch today, I told him I was unlikely to finish with breakfast sooner than ten.

'Gone,' he said, before I could ask what news I might have heard. I was too busy clinging to my seat, wishing the Boulangerie Sancho delivered on Sundays, like every other day, while Laurent raced towards Lodève, as if the bread were about to burn. (I should have read the warning written on the wheels: no one with flashy gold hub caps drives sedately.) 'This is my little weekly excursion,' Laurent laughed, accelerating faster round a bend.

'But Jean-Pierre?' I prompted.

'*Il a cassé un câble*,' explained Laurent, leaving me none the wiser. Was cable-breaking a dismissible offence? Or just a figure of speech for resigning? '*C'est ça, la restauration*,' he sighed. 'It's been a difficult year. Ever since his girlfriend threw him out in February, he's behaved like a fourteen-year-old. When he fell in love again in June, I thought things might get better but they didn't. He was forgetting to reorder the wines, going sick without letting me know what was happening, saying stupid things to customers. When I finally tackled him, he went berserk. Well, I tell you, I'd rather have two or three hours' more work in a day than be constantly worrying what he'll do or forget to do next.'

'Will you replace him?'

'We'll probably juggle. Perhaps with me spending more time *en salle*.'

'Can you afford to be away from the kitchen?'

'The summer's nearly over. And Georges is very experienced now.'

'But a day like today, with thirty-two covers?'

'My brother Stéphane's helping. You remember I told you he was managing a London hotel? Well, he's given that up. He wants to work in Indonesia but luckily he hasn't gone yet. I say luckily – this is his first experience as a waiter. Poor Laurence is at her wits' end!' he laughed sympathetically, as we stopped outside Sancho's.

The Grande Rue is, perversely, one of the narrowest streets in Lodève and Laurent's parking effectively blocks it, but he no longer seems to be in any hurry. Entering straight through the door at the side of the shop, he greets every member of the bakery staff with a kiss or a handshake, depending on their sex. Then he introduces me to each of them in turn.

'Don't know why you're bothering with Le Temps de Vivre,' laughs the *patron*. 'This place is much more interesting – been here a hundred years, since 1903.'

'*C'est du folklore*,' whispers Laurent, as I take in the detail of this underlit, overcrowded, flour-dusty room, where little may have changed – neither furnishings nor recipes – in a hundred years. Only the brightly lit rotation of the *baguettes* inside a sophisticated electric oven strikes a false note.

Monsieur Sancho hands us each a box piled high with outsized, pointy-ended rolls – the traditional Paillasses de Lodève – then deposits a similarly outsized, pointy-ended pastry on top of each of our boxes. 'You can't go without the best *pain au chocolat* in the *département*,' he insists,

'Certainly the biggest,' I grant him.

Laurent, driving one-handedly, devours his own at voracious speed, while I – breakfast all too recent – look for a suitable moment to jettison as much as possible through the window.

'Do you see that little château?' asks Laurent, slowing fractionally at the point where the roadworks run parallel with a water meadow. He indicates an attractive, probably early-nineteenth-century building in the trees on the other side. 'That's my dream,' he says. 'It would completely transform my client base, having rooms to offer. Not just for tourists – even places like Le Mimosa, down in Saint Guiraud, say some of their Montpellier customers prefer to stay the night, rather than risk the police on the way back from dinner.'

'Who lives there now?' I ask, as we leave the château behind.

'Nobody.'

'But it's not for sale?'

'Where would I get the money?' laughs Laurent, turning down the drive to his humbler, late-twentieth-century premises.

'We need to start,' says Laurence, urging everyone to their places at the table, on which lunch is already served. 'I must have a shower before twelve. I'm sweating like a lorry driver, after all that furniture-moving.'

I sit down to contemplate my third round of food in little

more than an hour. Everyone else is ravenous, having been hard at work since eight. Georges, Joris and an unfamiliar young face appearing from behind the washing-up counter all take hearty portions of bread and pâté.

Confusingly, the new *plongeur* is, like his predecessor, also called Eric. He worked here before the reign of Eric the Second. He had to leave for some cancer treatment, explains Laurent discreetly; but he's better now. And, well, I've seen for myself, his namesake was very willing but . . .

Another unfamiliar figure joins us from the dining-room. He looks as if he is used to feeling confidently in control: solid, unflappable, authoritative but today with an added veneer of anxiety – an accomplished hotel manager, recast as an inexperienced waiter, perhaps.

'I'd never done this before yesterday,' says Stéphane defensively.

'You'll be okay,' says his brother, with a comradely elbow nudge. 'Only twice as many as last night!'

'Twenty-eight out of thirty-two reserved for twelve-thirty,' sighs Laurence, already halfway through her slice of lamb. 'Not that anyone ever comes at the time they reserve for. Some will be late, others early, but never one of them on time!'

Laurent checks with Georges the quantities of trout and lamb prepared for the main courses on the 28 Euro menu. 'Most will order that,' he assures me.

'What if they all want the *Dégustation*?' I ask him. I have yet to see anyone order Laurent's six-course tasting menu, but you never know. 'Is Métro still open?' I tease him.

'There are plenty of high cliffs round here to jump from,' he answers with barely a smile, as he rises to make everyone coffee. 'But Jeanjean – the wine *négoçiant* at one-thirty – he'll order the *Dégustation*, I'm sure. Either that or à la carte.'

My money is on the à la carte. Moon's First Law of Catering, formulated in earlier services, says that the later a person's booking, the less likely he is to order a menu. It seems to be part of the same independence of spirit. But there is no more time for speculation. Laurent hands me an apron, asking Georges to keep me busy.

'*Ça va chauffer,*' he promises, alluding, I think, to the metaphorical heat that I'm about to feel in the kitchen. However, he could equally have meant the weather. The sun has unexpectedly broken through the morning clouds and it is now the most perfect afternoon for the lazy poolside lunch that my friends will be enjoying.

Georges puts me to work on a vase of flat-leaf parsley, plucking thirty perfect leaves for some later decorative purpose. He shows me how to keep them moist beneath dampened kitchen paper; then he sets me combing the vase again for thirty perfect *tiny* leaves to decorate the new *amuse-bouche* of marinated salmon. He says he'll appoint me the '*chef des amuses*' today but first there are copious quantities of rocket from which to eliminate the stems. This undoubtedly beats all previous records for tedium and fiddliness and, as the first customers arrive, there is hardly sufficient for two of the four *goujonettes de lisette* that they might be about to order. Humiliatingly, Eric the First is drafted in to help, while Georges spoons finely diced salmon into the miniature dishes that were supposed to be my domain.

Joris works away as silently as ever, preparing a supply of potato *galettes,* infused with hazelnut oil and topped with matching roasted nuts. The *gratin de blettes*, which once taught me how to loathe a bunch of Swiss chard, has been superseded as the new accompaniment to the lamb – sabotaged by popular mutiny, I shouldn't wonder.

Suddenly Joris's silence is broken by a yelp of pain. He has burned his hand and is heading for the sink to cool it but Laurent calls him back. He needs Joris's help. With customers expected any minute, there is no time for sympathy; and anyway, apprentices must learn from their mistakes. But for most of the rest of the service, whenever there is a second's respite, Joris furtively nurses his hand.

Laurent goes to the dining-room to greet each party personally. He goes again to take their orders, returning briefly to the kitchen to rattle off the details. One of the tables for four is down to two (but no one thought to telephone). Another of the fours goes up to seven (and still no one thought to telephone, even though this means Laurence and Stéphane having to set up a much larger table). But am I the only one to notice that this leaves the numbers one up overall?

I stare at the *amuse* dishes anxiously. Is there any more salmon for an extra serving? Or should I simply steal a tiny spoonful from each of my thirty-two, while the going's good? Suddenly everyone is too busy for me to ask.

I have often wondered how a hectic restaurant kitchen keeps track of its progress in fulfilling all the various orders. Well, here the answer lies in a double row of hooks on the wall near the fridges. There is a hook in each row for each table and Eric the First – the only person not currently frantic – explains how the system works.

As Laurent announces each new order, he tears the corresponding sheet from his notepad and impales it on the upper row. When the command is given to activate the starters, the appropriate entries on the paper are ringed; when the dishes are served, they are crossed out. If the menu includes a middle course, the process is repeated; then the same for the main courses, except that now the note descends to the bottom row. Dessert selections are usually made after the main course, even if cheese is served in between, and at this point, the table's choices are scribbled on the back of the travelling sheet of paper and it moves to a separate row of hooks above the narrow worktop by the window, where the puddings are assembled. Thus, everyone can see at a glance how many tables have reached a particular stage. With a slightly more detailed scan along the rows, they can tot up where they are in terms of demand for specific dishes.

Later than he might have wished, it dawns on Georges that they have underestimated today's demand for the trout. It must be the sunshine, he says, but extra fish will have to be boned. More importantly, in terms of preparation time, extra *tians provençaux* will have to be produced to accompany them.

I have no idea what a *tian provençal* will turn out to be but that doesn't stop me fantasizing that this might be my lucky break, the moment when the inexperienced *ingénu* steps forward from the chorus line to save the show. I hear the clamour from the dining-room, demanding who could have made such incomparable *tians*; I feel the rush of blood to my cheeks as the doors swing open to applause; but it is Eric, flushed with his recent triumph on the rocket, who is already slicing the requisite aubergines, courgettes and tomatoes. This is, however, just as well because Laurence is calling for the first four *amuses*, which are going to need all my attention.

The little dishes of *tartare de saumon* are perched on top of the sorbets in the ice-cream fridge. A tub of whipped cream mixed with chives and lemon juice sits waiting in the main refrigerator. All I have to do is fashion four perfect egg-shaped quenelles of cream with the aid of a teaspoon and balance them on four servings of salmon, not forgetting four of my parsley leaves planted firmly on top.

When Georges gave a demonstration, the spoon needed only the gentlest of scrapes across the surface for the cream to curl itself up into the requisite ball, without even waiting to be asked. The secret, he explained, was cold cream and a hot spoon. 'Couldn't I just quietly get them ready in advance?' I asked but no, Georges insisted, they had to be done at the last minute. Otherwise, the quenelles would collapse. The trouble is, in my hands, the scooping takes so long that my first has nearly melted before I can manage even a second. And Laurence is waiting for four of them.

The idea was to heat the spoon in a saucepan full of boiling water but this meant moving the pan from the stove to my working area and the handle, I painfully discovered, was blisteringly hot. I had started the session, like everyone else, equipped with a tea towel for such eventualities but, somewhere along the line, I lost it. Remembering the lack of sympathy for Joris, I tried to manage with the hem of my apron but this made for such an awkward, stooping scurrying across the kitchen that I was behind the anticipated finishing time before I even started. Laurence takes another spoon and deftly flicks up the third and fourth, while I anxiously nudge the second into some sort of shape that will not be greeted with outright derision.

'I want a word with you later about your brother,' says Laurence to Laurent, sounding fraught. Then, *'Deux amuses,'* she calls to me, before I can even recover from the first four, and I realize that I have forgotten to put my cream in the fridge or my hot water back on the stove.

'Hey, Georges, that's three of your father's wines I've sold today.' Laurent sprints upstairs with a bottle, grabs a decanter from the middle room and dashes through the swing doors. There is no longer the manpower for Jean-Pierre's more elaborate tasting rituals, but all but the very humblest reds are still decanted.

Georges explains that his father has vines in Corbières, the wine district south of Narbonne. He will be leaving at the end of the year to set up a restaurant of his own on the family estate. 'Simpler than here.' He smiles modestly. 'At least to begin with.'

He passes me the bowl of vegetable salad, which he has already dressed with walnut oil to accompany a serving of *lisette*. It is my relatively undemanding role to pile this up inside a circular metal mould in the centre of the plate, while Joris places the hot pieces of fish around it. Georges then removes the mould and tops the circle of vegetables with a neat mound of rocket, just as Laurent passes by to taste the remaining salad in the bowl.

'Too little salt,' he judges, making Joris scrape the salad back into the bowl to start again. No one mentions the fact that it was Georges who dressed the first attempt. Joris takes the blame without demur.

'Is the hotel your brother managed still in business?' whispers Laurence to Laurent, sounding increasingly harassed. He grins supportively, then issues the command for the first of the main courses: *'Ça marche: deux truites, trois souris.'*

Surely I must have misheard. Two trout, yes, I know about

those. I have observed my colleague Georges in the act of boning them. But *trois souris*? The order quite puts me off my quenelle production. I mean, snails and frogs' legs, certainly; obscure bits of offal, by all means. But surely the French don't eat mice now?

I consult the menu on the wall. *'Souris d'agneau,'* it says. So Laurent's new lamb dish is 'lamb's mouse'. No wonder nobody ordered it last time. But then I see Georges putting three already slow-cooked pieces of lamb on to the hob for a final simmer. *'Souris'*, it seems, is the culinary term for 'knuckle', or even more accurately, a small but highly esteemed muscle on the knuckle end of a leg of lamb.

'What can we do for a child who doesn't like the starters?' asks Laurence, looking ever more strained.

'I don't know,' says Laurent, preoccupied with the arrival of Jeanjean. 'What do they expect in a restaurant like this? A fried egg?'

Laurence goes to consult the infant again, returning to report that she has persuaded him to have a little vegetable salad on a big bed of rocket. *'Et sept amuses,'* she adds to me: a serious challenge now to finish a seventh before the first has liquefied.

'Et quatre Dégustations, la table Jeanjean,' announces Laurent, obliging me to modify my First Law. I suppose the real point about late arrivals is that they never order anything simple. The six courses on the tasting menu will occupy the kitchen until at least five o'clock, by which time the preparations for the evening service will need to start.

Laurent takes personal charge of the VIP order, leaving most of the more routine courses to Georges and Joris, which unfortunately results in a routine manifestation of the vegetable salad when Laurence comes to collect it: a small mound of rocket on top of a generous, circular pile of vegetables; not the small vegetable salad on the more substantial bed of rocket requested.

Laurent, preoccupied with Jeanjean's lobsters, looks baffled by the distinction.

'I relay the customers' wishes,' says Laurence tartly. 'All you have to do is listen.' It takes the chef only a second to decide that it would be better for his marriage if he reconfigured the infant's salad. '*Et dix amuses*,' Laurence adds, all too audibly not in the mood for melted cream.

It is approaching three o'clock when Laurent realizes that there is no aïoli in the fridge. A generous dishful of this garlic-flavoured mayonnaise is urgently needed for the Jeanjeans' monkfish but Laurent is already busy with advance work on their pigeons and Georges and Joris are fully stretched, producing a dozen assorted desserts.

'You've made mayonnaise before?' says Laurent, more as a statement than a question, having passed me the garlic, mustard, eggs and oil. He is then called away to say goodbye to the first departing table, before he can hear my nervous 'Not really.'

Georges takes sufficient pity on me to fine-chop the garlic and beat it rapidly into the eggs and mustard, with the requisite pinches of salt and pepper. I am then on my own for the crucial addition of the oil. I need to confess to someone that this has always been the moment when my own attempts have curdled, but no one is listening.

I start to drip the oil in, whisking anxiously as I go: so far so creamy. But the fish will soon be ready. I have to speed up. The drips become a drizzle and still the sauce remains homogeneous. Now Laurence is calling to Laurent, 'How long?' I have to risk a steadier stream, so with aching wrist and pounding heart, I pour faster.

'*Ça arrive?*' presses Laurent, already arranging the fish in the four waiting dishes. I go for broke, holding my breath as I drain the last of the oil. '*Impeccable!*' is the improbable judgement, as he pounces on the bowl. A momentary tasting, a rapid ladling on to the steaming *baudroie* and already, before I can savour my triumph, the heat of the fish has turned the once miraculously stiff emulsion to a liquid sauce. '*C'est normal*,' he assures me, sensing my disappointment.

There must be at least another two hours' work still to do but my reward for successful mayonnaise is a dispensation to return to my guests.

'You've missed some unbelievable weather,' cries one of them from the poolside, as I stumble from the car, too exhausted to think or speak. 'The last of the summer sunshine, to judge from those clouds.'

'Too hot really, for us,' says another, patting the last of her Factor 30 on to a pale white forehead. 'We were almost envious at one point, thinking of you over there in the shade. But anyway, raring to go now, if you feel like a gardening session.'

Autumn

'*Annulé*,' said the airport departure screen the next evening. It should hardly have come as a surprise. The daytime storms around the house had been nothing particularly unusual for the time of year; the longed-for rain nothing truly out of the ordinary to warn me that my guests would be extending their stay; but as we drove into Montpellier, it soon became apparent that the weather there had been the stuff of headline news. A wall had collapsed across the main road into the centre. Abandoned cars were everywhere, with banks of debris washed against their wheels. Scarcely any of the traffic lights were working. The city looked like a battle zone.

My friends were treating me to an early supper before their homeward flight. They had booked a table at the Pourcel twins' La Compagnie des Comptoirs on the edge of the city centre. ('We'll take you over the road to Le Jardin des Sens, when we've stayed a month,' they promised.) Sarah was worrying that she might be underdressed in her travelling clothes, but the manager greeted us in jeans and T-shirt. He was mopping pools of water inside the front door.

'*Une table à l'intérieur?*' he quipped, as we sprinted across the threshold. The friends had booked an outside table by the fish pond but tonight the patio was almost a pond in itself. We settled by the floor-to-ceiling windows of a spacious veranda, the better to watch the other diners splashing through the courtyard in their smart shoes. We then thought better of our choice, when the water seeping beneath the windows threatened to cut us off from the kitchens.

'It hasn't stopped all day,' said the maître d'hôtel, now more dignified in expensively casual black. 'And worse to come tonight,' he added, above the drumming of the rain on the low flat roof above us.

Every new arrival had some tale of devastation to tell, some never-before-in-Montpellier extremity to recount; but still we none of us thought to telephone the airport. Even as we drove out of town on the fast, slightly raised urban motorway – now a dramatically isolated causeway between deeply flooded side streets – nothing dented our mood of blithe invincibility. Perhaps a momentary ripple of anxiety washed through the car when we found the usual access route to the terminal submerged; but I was confident that we could find another and we did: only to find the flight cancelled.

Unwilling to invoke the procedures for a landing on water, the relevant plane was still in London and intending to remain there.

'Good thing we didn't have time to strip the beds!' said Sarah, determined to look on the bright side.

'We'd better hurry back,' I fretted, remembering the promise of worse to come; but my friends could only focus on their diaries, on the meetings that needed to be cancelled, the responsibilities that had to be delegated.

'We can't leave without rebooking,' they all agreed; but a similar notion had already occurred to several hundred other travellers, who had not lingered over second espressos in restaurants. Indeed, the queue at the airline's single computer screen was surely longer than the capacity of the cancelled flight.

This, it transpired, was because the Germans, in the best traditions of European holiday-making, had got there first. The airline's earlier flight to Frankfurt had also been cancelled and, not unreasonably perhaps, the over-stressed youth at the solitary computer considered it his duty to resolve the itineraries of those passengers first. The problem was, the Germans had diaries and meetings and responsibilities as well; and so determined were they to return to them that they preferred to put their towels on the next available flight to London and then change there for

Frankfurt, rather than wait an extra day or more for something direct.

'You'll be at least an hour,' said a lugubrious security guard. 'Not that it matters. You won't get away from here tonight in any case. Have you seen how heavy the rain is? I've just phoned the wife to say I'll be sleeping here,' he added more gloomily than ever.

It was in fact two and a half hours before my friends learned their fate: the Teutonic competition had snapped up everything for the next three days. They had also, of course, occupied all the airport seating.

'Which do you think would be worse?' I asked despondently. 'Sleeping on the floor or in the car?'

'I think we can sleep in our beds,' called Sarah brightly, from one of the exit doors. 'The rain's stopped.'

We decided to risk it, finding that our hours in the queue had given the local fire brigade time to pump an escape route through to the higher, somewhat drier land, away from the coast.

This morning, however, some alarming newspaper photographs of the vineyards near Montpellier prompt a visit to see how Virgile has fared.

The gravel in Saint Saturnin's village square, where the senior residents play afternoon boules, appears to be half washed away. At Le Pressoir, the restaurant immediately opposite Virgile's cave, Pius and Marie-Anne are surveying the damage to their terrace awning.

'Hardly worth repairing at this time of year,' says Marie-Anne glumly.

'We were planning a winter refit anyway,' says Pius, more philosophically.

But Virgile seems unperturbed. 'The rain's done the vines good,' he says, looking thoroughly relaxed in the doorway to his *cave*. 'A different story though, for anyone with two or three days to go. *Très problématique* . . . How did your neighbour get on?'

'He finished picking the day before the rain.'

'Is that good news or bad?' laughs Virgile.

'Good for his temper. Bad for my liver. But he's complaining about the quantity. Only two thousand litres to get him through the year.'

'Quantity's down here,' calls Magda from the back of the *cave*, although it doesn't look like it. Never, not even in the whole of the year that we worked together, have I seen the diminutive space look so crowded. Everything remotely portable has been carried out to the square to make room for the morning's labours but, even so, there is hardly space for an extra grape, let alone an additional body.

'I bought all these extra fibreglass fermentation tanks,' says Virgile, squeezing in between two of the smaller examples to help Magda's sister, Martha (who is showing no signs of forsaking the Languedoc for Poland) pump some Carignan off its lees. 'I wanted to vinify everything separately – each of the different parcels of land and grape varieties. It's amazing what you can cram in, if you fit the little ones into the curves between the big ones.'

'Pity there's no room for the hosepipes,' complains an invisible Magda, aerating some Syrah at the rear.

'It's the same all over France,' says the invisible Virgile. 'Small quantities, I mean. The lowest for ten years. But how about you? Everything alright at your place, after the storm? None of your terrace walls down, I hope.'

'No, they're fine. Some animal or other has been digging up the potager, but that'll be the shepherd's dogs. Nothing to do with the storm. It's amazing though – in just twenty-four hours, the land already looks greener. Fresh wild flowers appearing overnight . . . Is that your phone?' I can hear ringing from Virgile's office upstairs.

'They'll try the mobile if they really want me. The number's on the answerphone message. But there's something I haven't told you, he says, as he inches back out through one of the gaps. 'I've broken off the partnership. I did their *vendange* but that'll be it. It just wasn't working. I even consulted a lawyer but, in the end, I decided it simply couldn't be viable.'

'That's your mobile.'

Virgile scowls as he answers it, then passes it to me. 'It's for you.'

It was Garance.

But how could it be Garance? She didn't have a telephone. And she didn't even know I was with Virgile. She must have tried everywhere.

'You've bought a what? . . . Oh, bought a mobile,' Virgile hears me say. Then a long pause. 'Oh, I understand. Yes, I'm sure the mobile makes you feel more secure up there on your own . . .' Another long pause. 'Yes, well, clever of you to track me down. I can see that you wanted to test it, yes . . .' Equally long pause. 'Was there anything special you wanted?' Brief pause, while Virgile chuckles. 'The roof? . . . Oh, after the storm . . . Yes, I agree it's disappointing. A centimetre of water everywhere, you say? . . . No, but be reasonable, we've not had any rain to test it till now . . .' Virgile finds this hilarious. 'Garance, it's rather late to start repairing it now.' Exceptionally long pause.

'I'll come straight back.'

*

'It's well outside the village but you'll see a sign eventually,' said the only resident of Combaillaux who seemed to have heard of her neighbourhood award winning olive oil mill, Le Moulin de l'Oulivie. (Regional gold medals cut limited ice, it seems, among the immediately local population.) 'Take the track by the sign,' she advised, as she neared the end of her complicated directions. 'It's a bit rough but just keep going up and up.'

My informant had not allowed for the storm. Mere roughness had been rendered positively crater-like and, for every three wheels that went 'up and up', the fourth seemed to be going down again. I was half-expecting the Vialla brothers' olive grove to be washed away, but the trees shading three small children, playing quietly beside the new-looking building at the top of the hill, were apparently undamaged.

'Monsieur Vialla,' seemed to mean little to the children but 'Papa' rang more of a bell. The eldest obligingly ran inside, disappearing through the back of what appeared to be a shop. A few minutes later, he produced the next best thing: their uncle.

'The storm didn't harm the trees,' says Rock Vialla, escorting me straight into the heart of the grove. 'In fact, the water did them good. But you saw what it did to the track?'

I confirm that I more than *saw*; both I and the Renault are still in a deep state of shock. However, I am not too traumatized to miss the implications of a small group of pickers – many shirtless in the late September sunshine – filling plastic collecting crates slung round their necks like cinema usherettes' ice-cream trays.

'You've started.' I state the obvious in my dismay that the weekend Demethoate prevents me doing likewise for another seventeen days.

'They're ready now for table olives,' he says, confirming my fears. 'Green ones, that is. Another seven or eight weeks for black. It's the Lucques we're picking today.'

'How do you tell when they're ready?' I ask, hoping that mine, at their higher altitude, might be lagging behind.

'Partly size,' he says. (Could mine be considered smaller?) 'Partly colour . . .' (Were mine any less intensely green?) 'We're only picking the biggest for now. We'll pass round again in a week or so . . .' (Perhaps there's some latitude, after all.)

'You can't just shake the trees?' I ask, appalled at the labour-intensive activity, which I shall soon have to replicate.

'They're much too firmly attached when they're green,' Rock explains. 'And you have to be very gentle with Lucques at this stage.' I have already noticed how carefully each individual olive is being plucked. The trees are sufficiently laden to pull the fruit off by the handful but apparently the Lucque shows every tiny blemish and the pickers are even instructed to trim their fingernails. (If only I'd been more delicate with the ladder at the weekend.)

'What do you do for water?' I ask, thinking my all-night

drenching session might give me *some* advantage, even if I fail on so many other counts.

'We drilled a well,' he answers. 'An olive tree drinks two hundred litres a day. Mostly from the soil but, in a hot summer like this year, we give each about forty litres a day.' He kicks aside some twigs to reveal a network of irrigation pipes beneath our feet. 'Drop by drop,' he emphasizes, making me wonder whether my single belated deluge will have been remotely beneficial.

'How much land do you have?' I ask, as we return to what I assume to be the mill building.

'Seventeen hectares,' he says matter-of-factly. 'Planted by my grandfather, just after the 1956 frosts destroyed nearly all the *département*'s olive trees. But they'd been abandoned for years when Pierre and I decided to make a go of things in 1990.

'Is your brother here today?'

'He mostly concentrates on the indoor work. It reflects our different training.' And true to the norm, we find a less sunburnt Pierre inside with a machine that is cleverly calibrating the olives into six different sizes.

'Are the bigger ones more expensive?' I ask, shaking his hand.

'Not here.' He relinquishes the machinery to Rock and moves away from the rattle. 'It's to make sure the olives get the right amount of soda treatment.'

'Soda?' I query, having yet to study the Vargases' instructions.

'Caustic soda,' he confirms, and he sees me looking shocked. 'No, really. They have to be soaked in it to get rid of the bitterness – normally for four to eight hours. You rescue them when the soda penetration reaches a millimetre from the stone. We start them off when we're going to bed, in the hope of getting up only once in the night to check.'

'What would happen if, say, you left them too long?' (I know I shall not be good at these inspections in the small hours.)

'They'd go soft and shrivel.'

'Ah . . . And too little, for instance?' (An abbreviated session, squeezed between picking and bedtime suggests itself.)

'They'd stay too bitter.'

'But if you follow the rules,' (I've resigned myself to the precision timing) 'they'd be ready to eat?'

'What, steeped in caustic soda?' he laughs. 'No, you have to rinse them twice a day for three or four days, every morning and evening.'

'And then they're ready to eat?' (Do I sound impatient, I wonder?)

'You have to salt them in brine, both for flavour and preservation.' (That sounds easy enough.) 'But it's important to get them acclimatized slowly, increasing the salt concentration gradually over several days.' (Maybe not so easy.)

'What if you simply plunged them straight into maximum strength?' (I know myself too well.)

'The exchange between the water in the olives and the brine would be too rapid. They'd go soft and shrivel again.'

'Or if you left them in the weak solution too long?' (Something is bound to distract me.)

'Then you run the risk of harmful micro-organisms.'

There seems to be no room for compromise; but as we pass back through the shop towards the sunshine, a brighter prospect catches my eye: some bottles of truffle oil, displayed on the counter.

'Are there truffles on your land as well?' I ask excitedly.

Manu must, I believe, have cracked the identity of the little truffle oaks behind my own olive grove. I often see him hovering there, as if willing them into production in his lifetime. I am also convinced that he (and he alone) knows the whereabouts of some already mature sources of truffles on my land. He always insists that the secret died with his brother, Ignace, who sold the land to Uncle Milo; but Manu's cousin Babette thinks otherwise, and Babette is seldom wrong. So, all in all, I could usefully learn about truffle-hunting.

'You must come along with us in the winter,' offers Pierre

with surprising openness. I always thought these things were secret, but perhaps he intends to take me blindfolded to some never-again-identifiable part of their estate. Or maybe I'll have to swear some terrible oath of silence. For the moment, he is more concerned with his children, who are settling into a simple picnic, brought down by their mother from the flat above the mill building.

'Not far to commute,' I congratulate him.

'I'm lucky,' he laughs, as his son tries to drag him over to the sun-dappled tablecloth beneath the trees. 'Rock lives in Aniane. But the important thing about living on the estate is, it's easier to monitor the health of the olives.'

'Do you spray?' I ask, now certain that I have got this wrong as well.

'As little as possible. There's been no risk for most of the summer, because the olive fly can't survive above thirty degrees. Most people have been spraying systematically, every two weeks, but we've done it only twice all year. We use pheramone traps, you see.' He shows me a triangular 'tunnel' made of cardboard, hanging from a branch. 'It's only when and if they appear in the traps that we resort to Demethoate.'

'It didn't exactly sound nutritious,' I grant him.

'It's not so much the health of the consumer I'm concerned about,' Pierre explains. 'The poison stands very little chance against all the soda and so on. It's more the air that my family breathes here. Look after them and the customer's got nothing to worry about.'

As if to prove his point, the youngest member of the Vialla family comes tentatively across to offer me what I confidently assume to be a Demethoate-free biscuit.

*

'Someone's building a wall between your pool and the potager,' said Manu, as if I might not have noticed. He had been down amongst the vegetables, trying to scrape together sufficient *haricots verts* for our respective suppers. 'You might need to fill up on potatoes,' he advised, as he parted with my personal portion. 'A wall won't keep the dogs out,' he continued. 'They'll still come in from the other end.'

'I just thought it would look nice,' I explained. 'I'm going to put some terracotta urns on top,' I added, to make my frivolousness unambiguous.

Manu shook his head despairingly. First my crazy wood-clearing, now this; and all the time there were winter greens to be paid for and planted.

It hadn't really been my idea. It was Arnaud, the young electrician whom I met on Virgile's *vendange* two years ago, who suggested it, when he was fixing up an outside light near the pool – I was tired of stumbling back through the lettuces, after midnight swims in the summer. He had told me it would only take a week or so.

'Something modest,' I had emphasized, with an eye on the budget. 'Nothing too high or wide. And of course rustic – as much as possible like the existing walls supporting the terraces.'

'It needs to be *quite* high,' said Arnaud. 'The ground slopes away and, if it doesn't start high at this end, there'll be nothing at all up there.'

'Okay, but not too wide.'

'It needs to be *quite* wide,' he said. 'Otherwise, it might not be stable.'

'All right, but definitely rustic. Nothing too smooth and refined.'

'It needs to be *quite* smooth,' he said. 'Certainly on the top. Otherwise, the rain will get in and freeze and crack it.'

'Very well, but rustic-sided,' I insisted. 'Try to think of something that will last for thirty years. I'm not so worried about the rest of the century.'

'Of course,' he said, putting the finishing touches to some silky-smooth grouting on the side.

I suppose I shouldn't have been surprised. Arnaud had been trying to grow a beard and moustache since his *vendangeur* days, but he was otherwise the same unswervingly meticulous perfectionist. Hence his modest achievements in the first fortnight.

The idea was to gather up the rocks impeding the tractor's passage round the terraces and then use them as building materials. A quick and economical solution, I thought; but it must have taken him all of a weekend to select and sort surely less than half the quantity needed. He then started cleaning each piece before using it. I even caught him sanding some of them to produce a smoother surface. Indeed, whole hours have been devoted to chiselling the faultless right-angles for the top edges.

'Don't run your hands along those,' I warned Manu. 'You might cut them.'

*

'*C'est très simple,*' says Laurent.

Foie gras served *mi-cuit* (literally half-cooked) has for long both intrigued and delighted me in equal measure. 'Like savoury ice-cream,' was Sarah's judgement, when she sampled Laurent's version last month. But simple? Surely not, or everyone would be making their own.

'No, really,' he insists, taking a pile of specially fattened duck livers from the fridge, as a white van draws up beside the glazed door.

It is Monsieur Jouvigné, of trout-farm fame. There is no *truite de Labeil* on the autumn menu but instead he is delivering the crayfish that Laurent needs for a new dish of duck carpaccio.

'You farm *écrevisses* as well?' I ask.

'They come from Turkey,' he says regretfully, depositing a lightweight wooden box containing the live crustaceans beside the livers. 'They died out locally thirty or forty years ago, even though they're one of the region's most traditional foods.'

'There was a sort of "black plague",' says Laurent.

'Coupled with over-fishing,' says his supplier. 'The result of too many people with cars.'

'Do you keep them in the fish tanks?' I saw none when I visited in May.

'Too much risk of illness,' says M. Jouvigné, preparing to leave. 'Much safer in the fridge, where they live quite happily for a fortnight.'

Laurent finds a space in his own fridge and returns to the duck livers. 'We start by removing the veins,' he begins, but then he lays down his knife at the sound of another van.

Enter Sancho's delivery girl, asking how many *paillasses* are needed today. *'Toujours calme,'* she commiserates, when Laurent tells her. Then she finishes her customary coffee and goes on her way with a cheery *'À demain!'*, leaving Laurent once again to the livers.

'You break the bigger ones up a bit,' he explains, taking a long, narrow cast-iron dish from beneath the worktop. 'Then you simply put them in here with some salt and pepper – some people add brandy or even truffles – and pop them in a low oven . . .'

A third rumble of engine noise interrupts his flow. This time it is Rens, chauffeured by Bernard and bearing one of her brown paper carrier bags. The mixture of pride and excitement beaming from behind her spectacles shows that Le Temps de Vivre has finally switched its allegiance.

'I put in one for you and Laurence,' she says, with a characteristically bashful shrug.

'No comparison,' says Laurent, when she has regained the van. 'I should have done it months ago . . . But where was I?'

'You were putting the livers in the oven.'

'Yes, for thirty-five minutes,' he resumes. 'Just to heat the middle to 70°: 63° is enough to kill bacteria. Then you press them.' He shows me how one of the heavy terrines fits conveniently on top of another. 'And then . . .' He pauses, almost as if he expects a fourth vehicle to cut him short. 'They'll be ready for slicing.'

'That's all?'

'I told you, *très simple.*'

'I suppose, with this much traffic, it has to be,' I laugh, as van number four does indeed cast a shadow through the glazed door. My laughter quickly subsides, however, when I notice that this van is red.

'Garance said I'd find you here,' says Manu, bursting theatrically into the kitchen like a cuckolded husband. 'She's told me your little secret! And there was I, thinking the reason we couldn't go wine tasting any more . . .' His voice trails off, as he notices Laurent; then he gives a stiff, embarrassed cough and introduces himself. 'Sorry about all that,' he adds, more to Laurent than to me, and he shuffles awkwardly from one short leg to the other. 'It came as a bit of a shock.'

'We'd finished really,' says Laurent, still baffled.

'I'll call you,' I promise apologetically.

'It's a question of trust,' mumbles Manu resentfully, as I open a conciliatory bottle back at home.

'I didn't think you'd understand.'

'Well, I don't. And if it weren't for that woman's mobile, you'd still be up there.'

'Garance rang you to say that I was up at the restaurant?'

'She rang me to ask if she could come round to charge the phone. I told her I didn't mind, but really she'd be better asking you – the wife being more of the "should have thought of that before she bought it" school of thought – and she said she'd already tried you. Well, that's when she spilled the beans – said you were always up at Le Temps de Whatsisname these days – and before I could ask her what she meant, the phone went dead. Battery used up.' He smiles more amiably, as a third glass slips down. 'It can only be a matter of time before she's round here,' he chuckles, sinking back into his favourite armchair.

We listen out for footsteps and, before many minutes, are rewarded. Except that the tread sounds altogether heavier and fiercer than that of Garance.

'How could you?' cries Mme Gros, as she flings open the front door like a jealous wife.

'It was only a quick one,' bleats Manu, putting his glass down.

'I don't mean the wine, I mean the mobile – telling her you didn't mind! Now we're stuck with it. And you mark my words, it'll be the thin end of the wedge!'

*

It was supposed to be a treat: a birthday supper for Mme Vargas.

Knowing that oysters were one of their favourite foods, I had driven down to Bouzigues to be sure of the freshest possible, bred only metres away, in the Bassin de Thau. I had even invested in a special short-bladed oyster-opening knife. (I hadn't a clue how to use it; but in this, as in so many things, I was willing to learn from the Vargases.) Then I followed the oysterman's advice, storing the box in the cool of the garage, with a stone on the lid to stop the shells opening.

'You're really spoiling us!' exclaimed the Vargases, when they saw the distinctive box. 'We never have oysters at home. We've no idea how to open them.'

I thought they were joking but no; this was something they had always shied away from.

'It can't be that difficult,' they insisted gamely, as Monsieur took up the knife.

The most promising entry point for the blade seemed to be a little indentation at the pointed end of the oyster but no amount of wiggling produced any movement. The shell remained obstinately closed. We all took turns, attempting different methods and angles of attack. Our hands were soon bleeding, either gored by the jagged outer surface of the shells or stabbed by the knife, as it slipped from the point of incision.

From time to time, an exhausted specimen would give up the struggle and surrender. Indeed, after a couple of hours of poking and prising, there were six available to each of us and we all agreed that this was as many as we could manage, so late in the evening. They were tepid rather than chilled, and many of the shells had splintered at the edges; but they were undeniably open.

'Mmm,' murmured the Vargases bravely, as they picked a few shards of shell from their lips.

*

'Not from a teabag?' Garance winced at my proffered selection of post-lunch *infusions*. I thought I had done well, adding Verveine and Camomile to the garden mint and lemon balm; but apparently not. 'It's not difficult to get proper herbs,' she continued. 'In fact, I've heard there's a specialist grower on the Larzac, not far from La Cavalerie.'

'The Templar village?' I enthused. Perhaps if we were quick, there would be time for the medieval Knights as well.

'An hour's round trip,' Garance estimated but, as usual, her grasp of distances beyond the range of her bicycle proved unreliable. It takes us all of an hour just to reach what might be the herb farm's signboard, standing bleakly isolated in a barren tract of moorland.

'Homs! That's the name,' she says, but I am unconvinced as I take the track leading down to an unpromising cluster of buildings, huddled away from the wind in a hollow at the bottom. There is, however, a flowerbed beside the car park, filled with neatly labelled thyme, lavender, sage, oregano, hyssop, marjoram, tarragon, savory, even absinthe – which, I have to concede, goes some way to substantiate the presence of a herb gardener.

'But the sign said Pastis de Homs,' I quibble.

'I'm sure this is the place,' she insists, adding, 'Homs means elm in Occitan,' as if that put the point beyond doubt; but just as there are no signs of elms in the landscape, there are no signs of *infusions* in the nearby 'boutique'.

A proprietor-like man is on the telephone in a back room, so we examine the assembled produce. We sniff our way through nine varieties of vinegar, mostly herb-infused with tarragon and thyme but extending to the more intriguing 'rose'. We note some similarly herb-influenced honeys and various bottled drinks, including a pastis, corroborating the signboard, but no *infusions*.

'We used to do them,' says Pierre-Yves Boissieu, introducing himself. 'But it's a very marginal business. People would buy a few sachets for the winter and most of them would still be in the cupboard in the spring.'

Garance looks scandalized. 'This can't be the easiest climate,' I interpose, before she can voice her feelings.

'It wasn't what we set out to do. Thirty years ago, we bought this as a *bergerie*, starting with goats and switching to sheep ten years later. We were building up the herd,' he continues, looking anything but herdsman-like today, in all-black shirt, waistcoat and corduroys. 'Everything progressing nicely, until two dry summers in '85 and '86.'

'Worse than this year?' I ask.

'The same. But then we had two in succession. I had to buy so much feed to keep the animals alive, I was forced to sell off half the herd just to settle my bank debts. That's why I went into herbs – they need little money and little water. But I soon found you couldn't make much of a living from *infusions*.' Garance looks ready to explain how little it would take to rescue the world from this benighted state but he continues too quickly: 'I looked for other uses, starting with the vinegars.'

'Yes, we saw those. You make the vinegar here?'

'In this climate?' he laughs. 'No, I buy it from an organic winemaker. Most people think vinegar's just a wine gone wrong, but in fact it's a wine that's finished. It's completed the natural cycle, which the *vigneron* normally arrests. Anyway . . .' He reaches for one of the bottled drinks. 'In the early '90s, a customer brought me an old family recipe for "Eglantine".'

'Dog rose?' queries Garance, sensing new infusing opportunities, as the owner of a *maset* half-surrounded by wild roses.

'Exactly. You must have seen lots on the way here. The hips

picked a couple of days ago are fermenting downstairs. When they reach about 12°, we'll add pure, neutral alcohol to bring it up to 16°.' He reaches for some tasting glasses but Garance shivers a refusal, saving herself for her own unfermented macerations. 'Very popular with ladies,' he tries in vain to encourage her.

The addition of the alcohol halts the fermentation, he explains, maximizing the natural fruit flavours; and refreshingly fruity the Eglantine aperitif proves to be: appley, yet pleasantly nutty at the same time.

'My pastis is also very popular with women who never normally drink it,' M. Boissieu tries again, but Garance knows how many dark days the resulting migraine could cost her.

'I try to emphasize the herbs,' he says, pouring me a single measure, 'all the ones you saw by the car park. I also use more fennel and less star anise than most people. And the fennel's home-grown. I'm about to try growing liquorice root as well. After all, they have it in Provence, so why not here?'

'And caramel?' I ask, remembering the Ricard recipe.

'I don't use it. Do you see?' He tops my glass up with water. 'It stays pure white.' Then, as I taste it, he talks me through what I ought to be experiencing. 'The aniseed should dominate at first, then fade a bit, revealing a nice long liquorice flavour underneath, and finally you get the herbs.'

The back-room telephone spares me any comparable commentary of my own. Suffice it to say that I need no encouragement to finish my glass while I wait.

'VAT,' he says, returning ten minutes later. 'The time on administration must have doubled in the last few years. Come, I'll show you an example.'

He takes us down past the field, no more than a hundred metres square, where the main supply of herbs is grown in orderly rows. At the bottom of the slope, the doors of the original *bergerie* are open and inside is an assortment of rusty metal cylinders, with convoluted pipes protruding in all directions. It could be a collection of hot water tanks, awaiting a bid from a passing scrap merchant.

'My new stills,' he explains. 'Well, new to me. I found them in the Lozère. Very few left these days. Next year, when I've reconditioned them, I'll be doing all my own distilling.'

'For better quality control?'

'Partly,' he says, 'and partly to be able to distil at any time of year. Most distillers' ateliers are only open for a few months between now and the end of the year, which is fine for fruits but very restrictive for pastis. Anyway, I was telling you about the admin. You need a customs authority to transport anything to do with alcohol in France. Not just the alcohol itself, but everything involved in making it. Each bit of those stills has a number and, if it isn't on your permit, you can't put it in your van. You wouldn't believe how complicated it was moving this lot.'

'Is your other drink ... Chantelune, was it? ... Is that something you distil?' asks Garance unexpectedly, perhaps in the hope that it might even be non-alcoholic, or perhaps because she now wants to wrap things up quickly to pursue the Templar alternative.

'You'll find this quite different,' warns M. Boissieu, back in the boutique, as he pours a single glass of amber-coloured liquid. He does not even try to tempt Garance with this one.

'I wanted to complete the *apéro* selection with a bitter,' he explains. 'It uses gentian roots from the Cévennes, macerated first in neutral alcohol, then blended with white wine. The same principle as the big brand, Suze, but drier.'

Being unfamiliar with Suze, I have no idea what to expect and, in the circumstances, a more cautious sip might have been prudent.

'An acquired taste,' is M. Boissieu's understatement, when I have finished spluttering.

He has certainly succeeded on the bitterness front. I always regarded aperitifs as something to stimulate the taste buds but the Chantelune leaves them quivering. Garance can never know what she has been spared.

*

For once it is green olives, not Garance, that have made me late.

Yesterday's picking proved less than straightforward. I had equipped myself with a dozen new grape-picking buckets, reduced to half-price in the farmers' co-operative at the end of the *vendange*, but I failed to fill half of them. The trees just wouldn't stay still in the wind. I needed at least three hands: one to steady the branch, one to pick and one to cling for dear life to the ladder. As the day wore on, my assessment of a year's supply underwent several downward revisions, until eventually I convinced myself that five bucketfuls were ample. However, by now it was nearly nightfall and no time to be reading caustic soda health warnings.

'Keep locked away. Wear protective clothing, gloves and face mask . . .' Thus far, all remarkably familiar from my *mouche d'olivier* days; but the soda bottle listed an additional horror, unknown to Demethoate users. 'Causes severe burns,' it cautioned, above a picture of a bathroom sink, the unblocking of which seemed to be the product's primary role in life.

I checked the Vargases' instructions. I checked my memories of the meeting with the Viallas. It didn't seem possible, but both were adamant. No green olive could be contemplated that had not been soaked in the stuff.

I had felt insufficiently robust for the encounter last night, but I knew I had to leave for Bouzigues by nine this morning. I'd tried to calculate how early I would have to rise to complete the operation before I left. The Vargases prescribed a four- to six-hour soak; the Viallas up to eight. It all depended on the time it took the soda to reach the crucial millimetre from the stone. I'd compromised on seven and went to bed early, setting my alarm for two o'clock.

Only when it went off did I realize the stupidity of the strategy. I was no more robust, just considerably more sleepy. I succeeded in measuring out the soda solution and plunging the olives into it, but then dared not go back to sleep. Instead, I checked the soda's progress at half-hourly intervals. It seemed slow at first but suddenly, at six o'clock, the deep brown stain hit the limit.

It was time for urgent action, but just as I was picking up the first of the buckets, the telephone rang. It was Garance, on her mobile.

'There's a man in my garden,' she almost screeched.

'It's probably Manu,' I suggested, anxious to get away. 'He's always in my garden at night.'

'No, he's in bed,' she continued at the same piercing pitch. 'I tried him first but he refused to get up.'

'I can't come now, Garance. I'm rinsing my olives.'

Then a click.

'Garance?'

No answer. Understandably not believing me, she had rung off and I worried for a moment who she might be trying next. Did she know the poor Vargases' number, for instance? Then, still in my dressing-gown and barely able to keep my eyes open, I rushed outside to the space near the umbrella pine, where the hazardous fluids would escape down the drive. It was difficult to see by the light of the moon but I rinsed for half an hour with a hosepipe, as if my life depended on it. I then fell asleep in a chair, waking up again at precisely the time that I was supposed to present myself at the oyster-farm in Bouzigues.

The blinds of the shop at Les Jardins de la Mer are ominously down. A message chalked on a blackboard between the blinds and the windowpane confirms the impression of inactivity: 'Due to the closure of the lagoon the shop will be closed until . . .' Then a blank: they don't even know when it will open again. I might as well go home.

But wait. Sounds of table-laying can be heard from the adjoining restaurant, so there may still be hope.

'My husband's at the market,' says Madame Balcou, bringing me a much-needed espresso. 'Buying oysters. The lagoon was closed a week ago.'

'An outbreak of algae,' her husband explains, having returned with a boot full of oyster boxes, labelled in Spanish. 'Alexandrium, it's called. I'm sorry, I didn't have your number to ring you.'

'Are they dangerous?'

'What, the algae? Only if you consume them by the bucket-load; but you know the authorities. And this is on top of all our problems in the summer.'

'I remember something in the paper. Was that algae too?'

'No, that was something called La Malaigue. Mainly lack of oxygen, caused by the heat and lack of wind. But some otherwise harmless algae made it worse by monopolizing what little oxygen there was. Normally – under water – oysters stay open all the time; but they close up if there's a problem, like lack of oxygen. They can live autonomously like that for a while, but not indefinitely. Some people lost every single oyster. Our own survived but we lost eighty per cent of our mussels.'

'Is there no way of preventing it?'

'There are things that would help, but this was the first occurrence since the 1980s. Most people don't think it's worth the investment.'

'Should I come again, when it reopens?'

'It's up to you. There are some things you'll only really understand if you touch them.'

'How many weeks will it be closed?'

'I wish I knew. Another week or two probably. Anything more would be disastrous. I mean really disastrous, for all of us. There's a protest rally in Montpellier this afternoon, outside the Préfecture. We're all being asked to go. It's crazy really. There are parts of the lagoon that aren't even affected, including our own. But as I said, you know the authorities. It's administratively simpler to close all seven thousand hectares.'

'Early November?' I suggest. 'To be on the safe side?'

'Early November,' confirms M. Balcou. 'If it isn't open then, there'll be war.'

*

One of the principal methods of keeping out the cold in the mountainous region behind us is the copious consumption of *aligot*. Made exclusively from potatoes, cheese and cream, it sounds like the perfect dish for anyone observing an intensive carbohydrate and cholesterol diet. Yet, staunchly traditional as it is, it makes an ideal foil for the resolutely modern main courses at Montpellier's Restaurant Cellier-Morel (located appropriately in the Maison de la Lozère – the Lozère being the most mountainous, not to mention *aligot*-loving, of the Languedoc's four *départements*).

At Cellier-Morel, it is often the serving as much as the eating of the *aligot* that people remember. The cheese on which the dish depends must be exceptionally elastic. The waiters stretch the finished product to spectacular, gravity-defying lengths, juggling a portion high in the air with a fast-rotating spoon and fork, teasing it out until the spoon and the fork are almost a metre apart. Then, as the table holds its breath in disbelief, the centre starts to sag. The spoon and fork come swiftly together, sending the *aligot* spiralling rapidly round itself, as it drops dramatically towards the table. Of course, it never falls *on* the table, but rather just in the centre of a challengingly tiny side plate.

What really draws the crowds, however, is the creative energy of thirty-five-year-old Eric Cellier's cooking: where else can you enjoy a dessert of caramelized aubergine slices, served with potato ice-cream? Hence the amount of creative energy devoted on my part to contriving Montpellier-focused missions around lunchtime.

It must have been my sixth or seventh performance of the *aligot* routine when I asked Pierre Morel – the other half of the partnership and in charge of the dining-room – whether it took a lifetime to learn. It was only a casual question. Learning that they both knew Laurent, I had mentioned my adventures at Le Temps de Vivre; but not with any intention of extending my culinary research. On the other hand, the signature potato dish was interesting . . .

'*Consommé de sassafras*,' said Eric Cellier, the following Thursday morning, when I asked what he was preparing.

I knew a bit about consommés but nothing about *sassafras*.

(Subsequent dictionary research revealed that the English for *sassafras* was 'sassafras', taking me little further.) 'It comes from the herbalist across the road,' the chef explained, straining a sieveful of woody-looking residue from a dark orange-brown stock. 'I use quite a few of her things: *ronces*, *genêts* . . .'

I knew a lot about *ronces* and *genêts*. These were the brambles and broom, of which I had super-abundant quantities. I could supply the restaurant direct with all it needed and cut out the middle man; but I had never knowingly cultivated sassafras.

'It's for a new *foie gras* recipe, entering the à la carte tomorrow,' he said. Experience told me that his cheapest menu featured three new dishes every week – a starter, a main course and a dessert – but this was extra: the creative urge would out. 'Sometimes I change the presentation of a dish in the middle of a service,' he admitted. 'It drives the staff mad. They get two tables side by side, making the same selection but receiving something different.'

'Has anyone ever complained?'

'Not yet,' he chuckled; then he showed me round his crowded kitchen.

There were eight or nine assistant cooks, plus two *plongeurs* at separate sinks for kitchen and dining-room utensils. Theoretically, there were separate, in some cases partitioned, areas for cold dishes, fish dishes, meat dishes and desserts, along with storage and refrigeration sections; but I would soon see how swiftly territory was surrendered under the pressure of a busy service. Similarly, everyone had his primary role. Misashi, for instance, a diminutive *sous-chef* from Japan, was Eric's number two on meat, while Thomas, an altogether sturdier type, had equivalent responsibility for fish. Yet all such demarcation had to bend, not only to the peaks and troughs of customer demand, but also to the comings and goings of each person's rest days.

Today, it was Thomas, the fish specialist, who was putting the huge pan of potatoes, still in their skins, on to boil for the *aligot*.

'Did the Maison de la Lozère put a clause in your rent agreement?' I asked, only half in jest.

'The *aligot*?' Eric laughed. 'No, it's not an obligation. But it's part of the restaurant's folklore. We've served it ever since we opened in 1991. I come from the Lozère, you see. My parents had a hotel-restaurant in a village up there. I was already washing up at twelve and receiving customers at fifteen. It's sold now, closed down in fact. I tried to help my mother when my father died, but it was too far away.'

'Was your father the chef?'

'No, my father raised cows and grew vegetables. My mother was the cook. There's always a difference, I think, between women's cooking and men's.'

'Are you allowed to say that?' I laughed, with a glance at the kitchen's only woman, responsible for the *amuse-bouches* in the cold section, as well as one of Eric's most popular starters, a carpaccio of beef, served with shavings of parmesan, artichokes, broad beans, fennel and figs.

'With women, there's always an accent on the family, on children,' he insisted. 'But then again, my own cooking's changed since I had daughters.'

Thomas's potatoes were now boiled and peeled and he was busy forcing them through what looked like a large garden soil sieve, using a broad plastic spatula. I asked whether this was a crucial part of the tradition.

'No,' he laughed. 'We normally use a machine, but it's broken.'

It was nearly time for lunch. The *amuse* chef was hosing the floor with a mixture of detergent and disinfectant, piped directly from a plastic jerrycan on the wall. Aprons were being untied and simmering stocks turned down. Only Thomas was still preparing food, cutting a large slab of cheese into small, thin slices which he would leave to melt on top of the hot mashed potato. It was a special, three-day-old cow's cheese, Eric explained, from Laguiole, more famous for older, Cheddar-like *tomes* and expensive steak knives. The town itself was up in the Aubrac mountains, north of Millau, but the catchment area for the milk included parts of the Lozère, he was quick to emphasize.

Eric then suggested a visit to the herbalist's, while everyone broke for lunch, after which I could watch Thomas finish the *aligot*, see a little of the service and finally – if I cared to – eat some lunch. So, convinced by three-quarters of the programme, I went warily over to the source of the sassafras: I hadn't spent six months resisting most of Garance's dietary dogma, only to succumb to some joyless régime of broom and brambles.

I hid myself behind a display of soaps and lotions, drawn from the wilder reaches of the hedgerow and scanned the shelves stacked with beautifully labelled, apothecary-style porcelain jars. *Genêts*, yes; *ronces*, I could also see; but the formidable-looking *herboriste* behind the counter was determined to be helpful.

'Can I assist?' she asked for a second time, peering suspiciously round the weirdly constituted cosmetics.

'I'm interested in sassafras,' I said, prompting an enquiry as to how much of it I wanted. 'No, I mean I'm interested in it,' I explained. 'I wondered who buys it, apart from chefs making consommés. And . . . well . . . what it is, really.'

'It's the bark from a tree root. In a tisane, it's used to purify the blood.' She eyed me expectantly, still wondering how much she should be weighing out.

'What about brambles?'

'Good for the throat.' She stroked her throat expressively, as if my knowledge of anatomy might be as poor as my understanding of herbalism. Then she resumed her ready-to-receive-an-order manner.

A customer, seeking relatively mainstream camphor and comfrey, provided a breathing space, in which I speed-read the entry for 'sassafras' in a handy herb encyclopaedia: 'Grown down the eastern side of the United States . . . Astringent taste . . . Fragrant odour . . . Scenting cheap grades of soap . . . Cure for rheumatism, skin diseases and syphilis.' Then, more disconcertingly: 'A teaspoon of sassafras oil produces vomiting, dilated pupils, stupor and collapse.' I made a discreet exit, repeating to myself, 'It's only the bark, not the oil that Eric uses.'

I thought I had only been gone a few minutes but already

the team are back on duty, with Misashi now taking charge of the *aligot*. A small, intense whirlwind of activity, he is visibly happiest when most thinly spread: the cheese having melted into the potato, he is stirring the resulting purée with a vigour that makes me fear for his wrist, yet all the while supervising countless bubbling pans on the meat section. Thomas, in contrast, is equally happy leaning nonchalantly against the pass to chat with Sébastien, the head waiter.

'I've been thinking,' says Eric, returning to the kitchen from his office where he and Pierre Morel take their meals. 'A dinner service would be much more interesting for you. Not tonight. We've got a party of fifty, taking the whole restaurant. That'll simply be a factory. But with only sixteen for lunch today, and most of them likely to order the first menu, it's too easy. Why not just enjoy some lunch and come back one evening next week? I could serve you the new *foie gras* dish.'

'Only the bark, not the oil,' I tell myself, as the plate is set before me.

*

'You drove a hundred kilometres for a cup of fizzy water?'

It is hard enough for Manu to accept how little time I have for cellar crawls these days, but this latest excursion suggests dangerously disordered priorities. 'If only the wife had kept her mouth shut,' he recriminates, recalling the late summer lunch that set me on the trail.

Exceptionally, I had invited all three of my neighbours for a barbecue in the courtyard. I remember that Manu was in a particularly bad mood, having (unusually for him) been woken early by the road-builders' stone-breaking machine, and I was working hard to keep him off the subject, for fear of another Garance tirade.

The heat was such that even Manu had grumpily forsaken manly red for rosé.

'But none of your water.' He waived the proffered jug aside.

'And there's no need to tell me how much good it would do me,' he told Garance irritably. My aim had been to broker some kind of reconciliation, after the greengage episode, but the peace process had foundered before the end of the first course. 'You know your uncle had it analysed?' He turned more amicably to me. 'Part of his crazy idea of bottling it for sale,' he chuckled nostalgically.

'Second most important *source* in the Languedoc after Perrier, it was going to be,' laughed Mme Gros, little knowing where her unaccustomed jest would lead.

'In the Languedoc?' I queried. 'I thought the Perrier spring was up in the mountains, over near Switzerland somewhere.'

While Manu and his wife pulled their 'does the man know nothing?' faces, Garance seized the initiative: it was down near the coast, between Montpellier and Nîmes, near Vergèze, to be precise. (Another chapter from the children's treatise, I could only assume.) A great favourite with the Romans, though more of a bubbling swamp in those days – did I know it was naturally sparkling? ... Well anyway, it frothed away, more or less forgotten, till the great days of hydrotherapy under Napoleon the Third, who granted the 'mineral water' classification in the 1860s. However, nothing much came of this until a certain Dr Perrier bought the *source* at the turn of the century.

The lunch must have been all of two months ago. It took most of the first month to get an appointment. My request bounced from Vergèze up to Paris and back again, convincing me that the main board of Nestlé, the parent company, must be meeting to sanction my security pass. In the end, a rendez-vous with Monsieur Traup, the Communications Director, was promised but, when I telephoned the day before for directions, his secretary said he had been 'just about to call' to explain to me his unavoidable detention at another Nestlé-owned *source*. Then, when an early October substitute date arrived, it was only at the reception desk, a hundred kilometres from home, that I learned that the Communications Director had, this time, forgotten to

communicate an urgent, six-in-the-morning departure for Paris.
So yesterday I phoned ahead to confirm again.

'*Mais, bien sûr que c'est confirmé,*' said M. Traup, in the manner
of a man who had never missed a meeting in his life.

This morning, however, the Perrier car park was almost
empty. I parked beside the only other car, in front of a pair of
imposing, château-like gates, beyond which were well-tended,
formal gardens. Behind me stretched the rough, arid, even
today in mid-October, sun-drenched landscape of Vergèze
– about as far from my preconceived sylvan mountainside
as anything could be. I was beginning to resign myself to
a wasted morning when, at one minute to eleven, a breath-
less Thierry Traup appeared on the other side of the gates.
Unlocking them, he ushered me through the deserted gardens
to the modern, all-glass visitor centre, which we also had
entirely to ourselves.

The absence of other human life was oddly underlined by the
presence of several hundred bottles of the famous fizz chilling
expectantly in a gigantic circular vat in the centre of the reception
hall. Not even Ricard had trimmed its workforce to this level, I
marvelled, as my host poured us each a paper-cupful of water.
This, he explained, was a new, only-gently-sparkling house
water named 'Eau de Perrier', to distinguish it (inadequately, I
couldn't help thinking) from another, more familiar *eau minérale*
called 'Perrier'.

'I'm sorry, I forgot when we made our appointment for a
Friday ... The thirty-five-hour week ... The factory functions
only four days a week, outside the summer, so we no longer
do the visits on Fridays. But this should tell you all about the
history.' He presented me with a large and beautifully illustrated
book entitled *Perrier*, as if that almost concluded our meeting,
but then he sensed the disappointment behind my thank-you. 'I
thought it was the history you were interested in,' he apologized
again.

'Oh, it interests me a lot.' I tried to leaf more appreciatively
through what appeared to be principally a compendium of

Perrier's publicity campaigns from the 1860s onwards. 'It's just that I was hoping to see a bit of how it's done. How the water's extracted, for instance. The idea of naturally sparkling water, straight from the ground, has always seemed incredible.'

'Oh, well, that I can show you.' I was expecting to descend to some subterranean pumping room, but we stopped in front of an incomprehensible cross-section drawing on the wall. 'First, we extract the gas, at a depth of five hundred metres. Then we extract the water, at a depth of one hundred. And finally we put the gas back at the bottling stage.'

'Why do you take it out and put it back?' I asked, wondering whether the process was really so natural.

'To ensure consistency. Very important when you're selling eight hundred million bottles a year. Come, this should give you a more concrete idea.'

Hopes rose anew but we stopped beside a model of the whole huge complex – the glass works alone (Perrier produce all their own bottles) occupying twenty times the area that I had so far seen for myself. 'We're here.' He pointed to a tiny building in the foreground. 'And here's the underground room, where we used to capture the gas. Normally I'd take you down there, but it was flooded in the storms the other day.'

'But it's no longer functioning?'

'No, purely historical. Right up your street, if it hadn't been for the rain.'

I ignored the continuing misapprehension and asked him where – in terms of the model – the actual *source* was located now.

'That I can't tell you,' he said, as if this were only to be expected. 'It's a secret.' Then inspiration struck him. 'I could show you a video.'

While he organized a private screening in his office, I asked whether Perrier production was seasonal, explaining how my own spring was conspicuously feebler at the end of the long, dry summer and was only now speeding up.

'Oh, definitely seasonal. We sell very much more in summer.'

'No, I meant production. Is the *source* less abundant after a drought?'

'We have big reserves underground.'

'But in a year like this,' I persisted, 'do you find you're dipping into them?'

'We just take what nature gives us,' he said, as if determined to avoid the issue. Another secret, it seemed.

'It was an Englishman who bought the *source* from Dr Perrier . . .' M. Traup steered the conversation safely back to history. *'Monsieur 'Armsworth.'* He wrestled simultaneously with the difficult English name and a roller-blind to reduce the glare on the television. 'When a motoring accident left him paralysed below the waist, he took up Indian clubs to keep fit. Hence the famous Perrier bottle-shape . . . *Et voilà!'*

The film show was ready. The mysteries of Perrier extraction were about to be revealed on screen.

We began, however, with some low-budget special effects to dramatize the all-important planetary convulsions of one hundred and twenty million years ago: the geological phenomena that created the *source* and made this improbable underground fusion of water and carbon dioxide possible. Then we cut to the present (or rather the 1980s, when the film was made – everything was much more state-of-the-art today, my host assured me). But we were nowhere near the *source*. We were in the Perrier glassworks. And we lingered either there or in the bottling plant for roughly fifteen times as long as the geology demonstration. Then the film was over. The secret remained intact.

'I could show you the château,' suggested M. Traup, in the hope of keeping me amused. Or rather, he would have been able to show it, if he had known how to open the electric glass doors that were Nestlé's contribution to the period façade.

The builder, St John Harmsworth, was the younger brother of Lords Northcliff and Rothermere, proprietors of the *Daily Mail* and *Daily Telegraph*. In 1902, they sent him to France to learn French but instead he bought an obscure sparkling spring, promising the vendor to keep the name. His early marketing was targeted on England and its Empire, especially the troops in India, who welcomed Perrier as a safe accompaniment to their whisky, and by 1905 it was being served at Buckingham Palace.

I knew all this because I had time to look at my book while M. Traup, having entered by a side door, searched everywhere behind the glazed entrance for a switch. I learned how, in 1947, Harmsworth's heirs sold the business to Gustave Leven, a shrewd French stockbroker who noted how the water sold for three times the price of wine or milk, without even needing raw materials. 'This has to be a bargain,' he told himself. It was Leven who insisted on total integration, right down to in-house label-printing. He also invested heavily in advertising, the image always one of style, elegance and fun. By 1990, his heirs were producing 1.2 billion bottles. And then came the US benzene affair that I only half-remembered.

'You'll have to use the side door,' mimed M. Traup from behind the glass.

Most of the château interior had been engulfed by the creative outpouring of a hyperactive merchandising department: you've drunk the water, now wear the T-shirt, baseball cap and full matching wardrobe. Feigning interest in a co-ordinating umbrella, I asked as casually as possible, 'So what exactly happened with the benzene?'

'Oh, that was thirteen years ago,' said M. Traup evasively, doing his best to distract me with more recent measures to safeguard the seventy-hectare site, not to mention the nine hundred hectares that Perrier owned around it, plus the incentives to 'go organic' offered to farmers working the adjoining land.

'Is that what happened with the benzene?' I persisted. 'Was the *source* contaminated?'

'Not at all. Benzene's a perfectly natural element in the soil. It's considered slightly carcinogenic, but I mean slightly. A lifetime drinking Perrier equates to about an hour sitting next to a smoker! But even so, the levels permitted in mineral water are regulated and what happened in 1990 . . .' He found himself reluctantly answering my question and started steering me discreetly back to the garden. 'Two or three bottles in the United States were found to be above the American limit, even though still below the European one. It sparked an amazing press campaign, mostly orchestrated by our rivals. You see, we had eighty per cent of the US imported water market.'

'How could you tell how many other bottles might fail the test?'

'We couldn't. We could only destroy our stocks. Logically, this could have been confined to the US, but we decided we had to go further. We destroyed our entire world supply – a total of two hundred and eighty million bottles around the globe.'

'And that saved the Perrier name?' I asked, as we walked back to the gates.

'We survived. I mean, we could have been wiped out! But sales suffered. Production fell to seven hundred and fifty million bottles. Nestlé bought us in 1992 and we're slowly climbing back. You know what 'Armsworth used to say?' (I didn't but Harmsworth's ornamental ironwork had prompted a return to the comfortable security of history.) 'What was it now? Rather clever . . .' He remembered as we were shaking hands: 'Every man has two countries,' he said approvingly, 'his own and France.'

I waved goodbye, happy to let St John have the last word.

*

'Quick!' called Manu. 'I think your electrician's about to lay a stone.'

'Not another?' I joined in the joke. 'That must make six today.'

However, I didn't find it quite as funny as Manu. The joke was uncomfortably close to the truth. It was nearly dusk and the progress since yesterday was almost imperceptible.

Arnaud had changed his mind about the beard and moustache, shaving them off since his last visit, and sadly he was proving equally indecisive when it came to stone selection, trying many different pieces for size, shape and, of course, stability before proceeding.

'I hope you're not paying him by the hour,' laughed Manu, as he went down to pick the leeks that were the object of his visit.

This I didn't find funny at all because Arnaud was indeed on an hourly tariff. The only consolation was that I paid him weekly and the job had gone on for so long (with so many days, even weeks lost to inactivity, when the climatic conditions were sub-optimal for stability) that I had lost all track of the total.

I had joked with Laurent that, if the first half were finished by the end of the year, the project might still cost less than the value of the house; but secretly, as Manu counted out my leek ration, I wondered how far this might be from the reality.

*

'At least the physical work's eased off for a while,' sighed Virgile.

He and Magda had driven up for lunch and we were taking a late, drizzly walk in the last of the daylight, enjoying the longed-for renewal of green in the lately parched landscape, the revival of thyme and heather on the once scorched terraces.

'The trouble is, there's so much paperwork to catch up on,' complained Magda.

'Plus all the challenge of the sales effort,' added Virgile. 'We're about to start opening the *cave* for tastings on two afternoons a week. And we've only just got back from a marketing trip to Belgium and Luxembourg. Thank goodness we've got Martha now, as an extra pair of hands. But isn't this a wonderful time of year?' He gestured through the drizzle towards the golds and ochres and reds of the neighbouring vineyards, the dying leaves almost glowing as the dusk descended.

'You're pleased with this year's wines?'

'Apart from the quantity. But what should help us a bit is that all of the red wine can now be classed as Appellation d'Origine

Controllée. I've bought some small *parcelles* of Grenache Noir and Syrah, so I no longer have an excess of Carignan, forcing me to downgrade a percentage of the red as Vin de Pays . . . Hey, did you see that?'

An extraordinary creature has just scuttled passed us in the almost dark, disappearing under a boulder near the footbridge. It looked a little like an overweight lizard, except that its skin was jet black, with improbable brilliant yellow spots.

'That was a salamander,' says Virgile. 'Only the second time I've seen one. But this is just the right time of day and season. You really are close to nature here. But of course, winemaking's a bit of a sideline these days,' he chuckles, as we return to the house past the compost-maker. 'The *tri sélectif* takes up most of our week.'

'It's reached Saint Saturnin?'

'Since the beginning of the month. But it's worse than for you. We have to keep our two enormous bins in the flat! We start the week with the biodegradables, wheeling them out and leaving them in front of Le Pressoir.

'Pius and Marie-Anne must be happy!'

'They're furious,' he laughs. 'But that's where the Mayor says we've all got to put them. Then on Tuesdays we wash the biodegradable bins. Wednesdays we have free for sorting out the glass and paper and packaging, and on Thursdays we wheel out the residual stuff.'

'Also outside the restaurant?'

'Correct. I mean, it's one thing in October, when it's cold and there's no one eating on the terrace, but imagine it next summer!'

'What about Fridays?'

'Washing the residual bins, of course.'

*

It is 8 p.m. at the Maison de la Lozère. The first customers could arrive at any moment. Eric is finishing his dinner in his office, while the others prepare for the onslaught in their different ways.

Thomas (Mr Fish) leans nonchalantly against the pass, discussing with a junior his plans for his day off. Misashi (Mr Meat) runs to and fro fetching ingredients, climbing up on a low metal rail to peer inside the biggest cooking pot in the kitchen and jumping high in the air to toss a pan of mushrooms (lending fresh meaning to the French verb, *sauter*). It was the same at the end of the lunchtime service last week: Thomas perched unflappably on a worktop, compiling the shopping list for the following morning, Misashi frenetically scrubbing and hosing everything in sight. They will both go far, but for different reasons, I feel.

They have a party of fifteen booked tonight, from something they call the *laboratoire*, meeting first in a room belonging to the Lozère tourist office, then eating later; they also have an impressive number of twos and fours; but they cannot quite be full because Sébastien suddenly announces *'quatre qui passent'*.

The *amuse* section switches into immediate action: some snails are battered and plunged into bubbling oil; some crayfish tails are set on a purée of carrot and coriander in tiny glasses. Then, only minutes later, Sébastien returns to say that the *'quatre qui passent'* have passed into the street again. 'Too expensive.' He shakes his head disbelievingly. 'There's a menu outside. Can't they read?'

The first table of two orders the familiar *foie gras* in the sassafras consommé, except that already the dish has evolved. The balancing of the liver on the *pain d'épices* and fried *courge* was judged too unstable. Eric has also added the contrasting sweetness of a chestnut madeleine on a side plate. He gives me one to taste and I can imagine its inspired contribution to the whole.

The bringing together of these separate elements for the early dishes is a remarkably leisurely affair. Almost too many hands are available for the final draping of the single, obscure oriental salad leaf on top of the whole meticulous assembly. However, when early main courses begin to overlap with later starters, I watch bedazzled as three people slide the dozen or so individually prepared ingredients into their carefully allotted places within seconds, whilst all the time supervising something completely different, with half an eye and half a hand elsewhere.

Nothing leaves the kitchen without the chef first making sure of its perfection, administering a final wipe to the edge of a plate or a tweak to the angle of a spear of chive. There are no tantrums, no aggression, simply total authority.

As Thomas pours the extraordinary chestnut cream that I remember from my lunch over a fillet of red mullet, and Masashi positions the contrasting filo pastry parcel of olives, anchovies and tomatoes, I hesitantly ask Eric, 'Do you sometimes . . . as it were . . . give them a chance to express themselves?'

'Definitely,' he assures me. 'It's very important for the young, if they're going to develop.' Then he makes it clear that such youthful self-expression is strictly confined to the occasional small suggestion in the *amuse-bouche* department. He retains total control of everything else. '*Il le faut!*' he adds, putting the point beyond debate.

Pierre Morel brings news of the laboratory party. They are ready to go to their table but their numbers have risen from fifteen to twenty. 'It's going to be cosy,' he laughs, hugging his elbows to his chest to demonstrate, and I wish I could be in the dining-room to see twenty elastic portions of *aligot* descending from a great height, over each diner's head.

The full complement of waiters is dispatched to re-lay the table, while everyone else, except the *plongeurs*, helps with the required twenty carpaccios. The frosted glass plates are so big that five of them alone fill the pass, requiring every other horizontal space not ruinously close to a heat source to be requisitioned, until the command is given for '*Service!*'

In a moment of relative calm, Eric tells me he is planning a week in Vietnam in the spring, cooking in Hanoi's best hotel, and is curious to see how it influences his cooking. So, I assure him, are his customers.

The more we talk, the more I am aware that there is seldom

more than seventy per cent eye-contact. The other thirty darts ceaselessly from station to station, monitoring every micro-detail; meanwhile, behind those penetrating eyes, I sense he is constantly thinking ahead – not merely to the dishes still to be served tonight, but to future creations, as yet unattempted.

A dessert making its debut tonight says much about his cooking: *La pomme Reinette du Vigan de Monsieur François Valette rotie au four au vinaigre de Banyuls, glace confiture de lait, sel de Camargue.* Not just any old apple but the relatively rare Reinette du Vigan; and not just any Reinette du Vigan but one from the orchard of M. François Valette (whoever he may be – Eric is suddenly too busy for me to ask); roasted (daringly) in vinegar but not just any old vinegar, one made from sweet Banyuls wine; served with 'milk jam' (whatever that might be – the entire kitchen is too frantic for me to ask); and then the crowning originality: Camargue salt. I must return while it is still on the menu.

As I am saying goodnight, I notice a name-tab discreetly stitched to the seam of the chef's smartly pressed black trousers. I know it is only the gimmick of some kitchen fashion designer, whose thoughts were far from the Maison de la Lozère when sewing it there; but nothing could more aptly supplement the 'Eric Cellier' embroidered on his starched white jacket.

'Star Chef,' is the verdict of the trouser-epithet.

*

'Does your electrician always work in the dark?' asks Manu, returning from the twilit potager, bearing most of the contents of the spinach bed.

'Only when he's had a difficult day. He's had a lot of problems since the rain and he likes to feel he's made some progress before he goes home.'

'You mean, at least one stone laid,' chuckles Manu, sharing the spinach between us in the usual proportions and casting an eye around the dining-room in search of a suitable aperitif.

'Have I told you about your uncle building this place with stone from the roadworks?' He sees that he hasn't and, finding a nearly full bottle of Picpoul in the fridge, settles in his preferred armchair to do so. 'When they built the dual carriageway, this is. Milo used to be down there every evening, shovelling whatever they'd excavated into his wheelbarrow. You couldn't do that today, of course. Not with that stone-breaking machine crunching everything into hardcore. But yes . . .' He looks at the rough stone barrel-vaulting above us and the matching stone walls to either side. 'Your uncle used to sit here, like we are tonight, looking at that ceiling, and he'd say to me . . . Don't mind if I open a second bottle, do you? . . . He'd say, "*Chaque pierre*, Manu. I remember every stone." Those were the days,' he sighs, untypically sentimental.

'And the whole thing finished in less than twenty years,' I laugh, wondering what on earth Arnaud can be doing out there in total darkness.

*

'Oysters are successive hermaphrodites,' shouts Guy Balcou, above the clank of the oyster-cleaning machine. 'First male, then female. Each lays a million eggs in the course of the summer, only ten of which reach adulthood. They swim around, looking for a bit of old shell to fix themselves on to. The *captage*, they call this bit, but the Bassin de Thau doesn't suit it. There's no tide and the water's too warm. So from October onwards, we buy our shells from Arcachon, with the larvae already attached.'

He fishes a handful from a long concrete tank to show me the barely visible 'pimples' and then demonstrates how the shells are slotted into loops on lengths of rope and hung for twelve months in the lagoon, using wooden frames known as 'tables'. A pile of one-year-old ropes has just been brought ashore, but there is no longer any sign of the original shells. Each is now hidden by a dense cluster of baby oysters, clinging on at every conceivable angle.

A youth in wellington boots and waterproof dungarees is breaking these off by hand and placing them in twos down one of a dozen grooves running the length of a five-metre table. He lays a rope along the line, between the pairs; then ladles a blob of cement from a small mixing machine on to each of the points where the rope touches the oyster pairs, before glueing a third on top of each dollop.

'A hundred and fifty to a rope.' M. Balcou spares me counting. 'They'll go back on the tables in the morning for another year.'

'How did they manage before cement?' I ask.

'They didn't,' he laughs. 'Oyster farming only started here in 1925, with a man called Louis Tudesq. He already had a mussel business but his main activity was masonry. That's what gave him the cement idea. At first he fixed the oysters to pyramid-shaped frames on the seabed, near the shore; but they were eaten by sea urchins, so he switched to tables and ropes.'

'We've got six tables,' he continues, 'with a thousand ropes on each. It used to be anarchy out there, until the end of the '50s; but as you've seen, it's very well ordered now. Everyone has a twenty-five-year lease, with standard-sized tables and a regular layout – all very important for a good circulation of water, and therefore of oxygen.'

'I meant to ask – how did you get on with the algae?'

'It never affected our part of the *bassin*,' he says, sounding bitter rather than relieved. 'We didn't lose any stock,' he explains. 'Just masses of sales in the month it was closed. Like I told you: "administrative simplicity".'

'And the process?' I indicate the youth and the cement mixer. 'Is it seasonal?'

'It's all year round, except for July and August, the peak egg-laying period, when we only disturb what's needed for immediate sale. Oh, and except for Christmas, the peak selling period, when everyone's flat out, getting extra stock ready for sale. You saw the boats, did you?'

I had, although they looked more like rectangular floating jetties, complete with machinery to rip the two-year-old oysters free of their cement, as the ropes are winched aboard. (All this apparently happens at daybreak and I shiver at the thought: it was 5° when I left home at nine o'clock, so I hate to think what it might have been at dawn.) The oysters drop directly into plastic bins, which are loaded on to miniature railway tracks and wheeled the couple of hundred metres up to the atelier, where we are standing.

The shells are barely visible beneath a year's encrustation of algae, mussels and other assorted lagoon life. M. Balcou is about to explain how they are cleaned when the youth in the water-proof dungarees empties a tub on to a small, upward-sloping conveyor belt that leads to a violently noisy machine, rendering explanations both impossible and unnecessary. First a vigorous buffeting knocks away most of the alien life forms, then the shells roll out on the other side for a brisk manual scrub.

'Then straight to the restaurant?' I ask, thinking the oysters must now be past caring.

'Not at all,' says M. Balcou. 'They go back in the water for a week in nets, to recover. They need to heal any fractures in their shells after the cleaning, so that they can retain a supply of water in between leaving the sea and being opened. Otherwise they'd die. We build up our Christmas stocks in nets in the same way. Then whatever we bring in for the restaurant, we keep in oxygenated, temperature-controlled water until the last minute. We really pamper them!'

'So are you responsible for both the oyster farming and the restaurant?'

'Oh no. Nicolas, my son, took over the production side six or seven years ago.' He indicates a younger man of about thirty, packing oysters into wooden boxes for the takeaway market. 'That's the fourth generation you're looking at!'

'So just the restaurant?'

'Not too much of that even,' he admits with a grin. 'I'm taking a back seat.'

'There's just one more thing . . .' The most important question remains unasked.

'Anything,' says M. Balcou generously.

'Oyster opening,' I explain. 'Can you show me?'

'Ah, for that you need to see the expert,' he laughs, taking me into the kitchen.

'Lesson one,' says the grey-haired Master Opener. 'Never open an oyster without these.' He holds up his thumbs, sheathed in what look like the thumb pieces cut from extra-thick gloves.

'What should I do at home, without thumb protectors?' I ask.

'Buy some supermarket gloves and cut the thumbs off,' the MO suggests, before getting more technical. 'Hold the oyster flat side up, with the narrowest end towards you. Push the point of your knife in between the two halves of the shell, about a third of the way down on the right hand side. It's best, if the blade's just a couple of centimetres long. What you're looking for is the ligament that joins the flesh to the top shell. Once you've cut through that, it's easy enough to prise the top shell away, keeping the bottom level, so as not to spill the juices.' He passes it to me to taste. 'Presumably, the fact that you've come to ask all these questions means you like oysters?' he asks, passing me a second and a third in rapid succession.

Yes, but ideally not at 11.30 a.m., I would like to reply, as another two pile up. And preferably with a squeeze of lemon (two more); even a slice of rye bread and butter (a further two, and I have eaten only one); in a perfect world, a chilled glass of Picpoul (now three: he is determined to ensure that I master the methodology).

'*Voilà, une belle douzaine.*' He pauses, urging me not to hesitate if I want any more.

'No, no,' I protest. What I really want is to try the technique for myself but that would only add to my digestive difficulties.

Eleven oysters later, I escape to the nearest sea-front brasserie, where the first mountainous *fruits de mer* platters are already appearing at neighbouring tables. Immediately beside me, two curvaceous middle-aged ladies are devouring them at speed, as if they were ice-cream about to melt in the unexpected lunchtime sunshine. They have even stripped to their bras, in the hope that these will pass for bikini tops, while in England, it occurs to me, they are lighting Guy Fawkes bonfires. 'We normally have the bigger platter,' says the hungrier-looking of the two, as she starts to dismember a crab. 'But not in this heat.'

'Just a coffee,' I tell the waiter, feeling suddenly nauseous, as I notice a plaque on the wall above us, naming the waterfront, 'Avenue Louis Tudesq'.

That man has a lot to answer for.

*

'Zero,' said Laurent last night, when I asked him 'How many reservations?'

'But it's Saturday,' I pointed out superfluously.

'Don't rub it in,' he answered. 'It's also mid-November. *C'est ça, la restauration. On ne sait jamais.* You'd have been better coming yesterday. Fridays are often busier now. It's this thirty-five-hour week. More people are taking long weekends.'

My idea had been to work a busy Saturday night and follow it with an even busier Sunday morning, to see how it felt, sweating well into the small hours, then reporting back early the next day for a second round. It had meant saying 'no' to the Viallas, who were picking their black Lucques for oil production, and now I wished I had gone there instead.

'Not much point in your staying,' said Laurent, as embarrassment mixed with glumness behind a brave face.

I could in fact see plenty of point in staying. I was curious to know how he and Georges would spend the evening, watching the silent telephone, listening out for an unexpected car in the car park; but my coming had already done more than enough to compound his woes.

'How was lunchtime?' I hardly dared ask.

'Nearly as bad. Just two covers. The cheapest menu, the cheapest bottle of wine from the Co-op and no aperitifs or coffee. It hardly paid for the electricity!'

'So did you get an early night?' I ask him this morning, as I put on my apron.

'In the end we had six,' he says. 'A couple of late reservations. But not very interesting for you.'

Nor for you, I think to myself, although perhaps it paid for both the gas and the electricity.

'I've made all the staff redundant,' he explains, when Georges has disappeared downstairs. 'From now on, I'll pay them according to the services that they work, which is all the more important now that I'm closing on Mondays, Tuesdays, Wednesdays and Sunday evenings.'

'You're not afraid of losing them?'

He shrugs to indicate his lack of choice. 'Georges was finishing at the end of the year anyway. And Joris can only do weekends and holidays, while he's studying.'

This morning, Joris has added hoover-training to the curriculum, his time apparently more usefully employed preparing the dining-room than preparing food, which causes me agonies of status-anxiety as to the relative rankings of my potato peeler and his vacuum cleaner. It would be sad if my absence for much of the autumn had cost me my place in the hierarchy. However, Laurence explains that the apprentice will be working as a waiter today, the anticipated twenty-two covers being too many for her alone, even with Laurent doing the order-taking. When I ask Joris which he prefers, he shrugs, as if to say 'they both pay the same', and sets about cleaning the windows.

Meanwhile, Georges gives a lesson in the subtle art of chive-chopping. He takes the sharpest knife he can find and then sharpens it some more. Taking a fat bunch of herbs, he trims the straggly ends to make them all the same length. Then a few rapid flashes of the knife generate several hundred immaculate chive-specks, not one of which is more than a millimetre long.

'The secret's a sawing movement,' says Georges, as he hands me the knife. 'Never press down or you'll crush the juice out. And remember, as tiny as possible.'

Yes, Georges. The trouble is, the lighter, the more saw-like my strokes, the longer the pieces cut. Equally, the more I concern myself with size, the more conspicuous the pool of green on my chopping board. I don't know which to do first: mop up the chlorophyll or shovel the more embarrassingly twig-like portions into the bin before my instructor notices.

'Here's the new *carte*,' says Laurent, producing a couple of sauce-stained computer print-outs. 'I've simplified things to allow me to spend more time *en salle*.'

He has done away with the first two set menus in favour of a single, so-called *menu-carte*, giving a selection of four savoury dishes. Customers can pick any two of them for one price and any three for another, with cheese and dessert included in either case. The six-course *Dégustation* formula has survived, but with the dishes now unspecified. Instead, they will be 'according to the market place', to avoid carrying major quantities of every ingredient, just in case. Or there is always the full à la carte.

My subterfuges with the chives must have succeeded because Georges is now bearing down on me with a tub of cooked lobsters to accompany the sweetbreads in what Laurent tells me has become another 'fetish dish', like the *foie gras* and smoked salmon. 'The customers won't let me take it off,' he says.

All I have to do, says Georges, is remove the meat intact from the shell. Not forgetting the pincers, of course. It's especially important that the claw meat emerges undamaged. I look at him closely to judge whether he might be joking. I've only ever once tackled a whole lobster and that was in England, when a lazier chef had left me to my own devices. Then, it hardly mattered that my results looked more like dressed crab. I could cover them with mayonnaise and hope no one noticed.

But Georges is not joking and, after a quick demonstration, I am on my own. My hands feel paralysed by the thought of those devotees of the famous *fricassée de homard*, some maybe driving all the way from Montpellier, braving even the roadworks, only to find their lobster shredded.

'Relax,' says Laurent mischievously. 'It's only my most expensive ingredient.'

The service starts slowly and, for a quarter of an hour, everyone, even Georges, looks as if they are searching for things to make themselves look busy, to justify their existence in this brave new post-redundancy world. Eric the First, in particular, seems to be competing with me for the handful of tasks in my repertoire. Soon, however, the pace becomes frantic – especially when an additional six *de passage* arrive late and (true to my Law) order à la carte.

Just welcoming the customers and taking the orders keeps Laurent away from the kitchen for a surprising proportion of the time, in addition to which Laurence frequently needs to call him back for advice on wine.

'Tell them La Grange des Pères '96 will be perfect,' he jokes, when the pressure in the kitchen is particularly fierce.

The current *amuse-bouche* is Laurent's most ambitious to date: a rich, warm pumpkin purée, topped with a light, frothy mushroom velouté, served in tall glass dishes which emphasize the contrast in colour between the two separate layers.

Always assuming that they have indeed remained separate – because unfortunately for me (once again the *chef des amuses*) the glass dishes also show any hint of intermingling, as well as every imperfect drip and splash. Ladling the purée is one thing: by my fifth or sixth attempt the thicker, heavier pumpkin preparation is satisfactorily subjected to my will; but the foaming velouté still has a mind of its own. If I spend any more time dabbing away at my smears, it will all be as tepid as my supposedly chilled salmon *tartare* in the summer.

For every batch of *amuses*, the saucepan of velouté has to be restored to a peak of perfect bubbliness with a single-blade electric whisk. To achieve the required degree of frothiness, I am supposed to point the whisk into the bowl of my ladle, holding both below the surface of the mushroom mixture as I whip. The ladle, of course, requires the hand not already claimed by the whisk, which is fine, so long as there is plenty of whiskable velouté in the pan. The trouble starts as the level falls.

'Tilt the pan,' advises Laurent.

But that needs a third hand.

Laurent shows me how to tilt the saucepan on the edge of the worktop, using only his stomach to balance it there.

'Did I tell you about the wine dinners?' he asks, as I perform a kind of belly dance to achieve the required angle. I need to hurry. Joris wants the *amuses* and Laurent will soon want the whisk for the similar-looking but in his case fish-and-wine-based sauce served with the perch-pike.

'I'm organizing a series of monthly events,' he explains, putting the fish on to fry. 'Each of them hosted by a leading local wine-maker – featuring his wines and including, I hope, some that customers couldn't ordinarily get hold of, with the grower there to talk about them. Most of the dates are already fixed. I've got Olivier from Mas Jullien, Laurent Vaillé from La Grange des Pères.' He takes over the whisk as Joris collects the *amuses*. 'Pass me the fish sauce, will you? No, that's the mushroom, the other . . . Hang on! What did you put on the pumpkin? *Oh, mon dieu* . . . JORIS!'

Halfway into the dining-room, the apprentice stops in his tracks. The swing doors swing closed again. With only seconds to spare, the late-coming table of six has been saved from my pumpkin purée with novelty fish topping.

'Serves them right for ordering à la carte,' I mutter mutinously, as Laurent calmly tells me to start again.

One of the six has ordered, all for himself, a dish that is intended to be shared between two, comprising a whole mallard, accompanied by a tart filled with *cèpe* and *girolle* mushrooms and rocket salad. Laurent decides that the only way to make sense of it for one is to present it in two successive servings: the first as normal, with the tart and salad; the second with just a handful of mushrooms for decoration but extra salad.

Note, in passing, this advanced example of Moon's Law – the glutton's double service ensures an even later end to our labours. Indeed, it seems an age before he is even ready for the second helping.

'He wants to know why there isn't a second *tarte aux cèpes et girolles*,' reports Laurence.

'I thought it would be too much,' says Laurent.

'He says he's paid for it,' says Laurence.

'Very well,' says Laurent, starting a new tart from scratch, as the end slips further out of sight.

*

At the end of my first year, the Vargases gave me a mushrooming knife. To a novice in these matters, it looked much like a penknife but to the Vargases it was uniquely *pour aller aux champignons*; ever since Easter, they have been promising to take me to an abundant source of supply, allegedly half a kilometre from my postbox.

'Can't think why you never found them yourself,' they have chorused throughout the year. 'As soon as the rain stops, we'll show you,' they added all last week. 'The sunshine ought to bring up hundreds,' they told me, quite childishly animated, this morning. 'Especially with a full moon last night.'

'Where's Manu?' they ask conspiratorially, at the bottom of my drive. It seems he knows nothing of these marvellous mushrooms and, given Mme Gros's famously bottomless freezer, the Vargases prefer to keep it that way.

'He's sorting out his well. The water level's been rising all week, but this morning it started overflowing.'

'Into the stream?'

'Into the house. Apparently, it's never happened before, but of course that hasn't stopped Manu being blamed for not having the sandbags ready.'

The Vargases laugh sympathetically, hobbling ahead of me down the edge of someone's cherry orchard, towards a line of poplars.

'It's the poplar roots they seem to like,' they chorus excitedly, already unfolding their own special mushrooming knives. 'Got your basket ready?' they call, positively keyed up to fever-pitch. Then suddenly they teeter to a stop, bewildered.

'Surely this is the spot,' mumbles Mme Vargas perplexedly.

189

'I was half afraid of this,' says Monsieur. 'It happened once before, after a long, dry summer.'

'Even after all this rain?' I ask, still unwilling to face disappointment.

'It came too late.' They shake their heads sadly.

'You don't think someone got here first?' I ask, with a glance towards my neighbours, but they shake their heads again.

'You know something else?' says Monsieur even more dejectedly. 'There'll be no truffles for Christmas.'

'Not even for Manu,' they add in unison, making two brave attempts at a smile.

'I'd better go and see how the flood barrier's going.' I try to sound positive.

'Just the man I wanted to see,' calls Manu, as I cross the bridge towards his cottage. I assume this means that I am about to be conscripted to help with the rescue operation but, drawing nearer, I find that his inundation seems to be forgotten. Instead, he is busy hacking at the base of a vine with a pickaxe, while Mme Gros watches sternly, close by.

The optimistic thought occurs that Manu has at last accepted a subsidy to rip up the low-grade, high-yielding Aramon with which he makes his *rouge*, in favour of some nobler variety; but surely not on a morning when there is water lapping round his kitchen table. Or could this be Mme Gros, exacting terrible retribution for his lack of anticipation in the dyke department: the destruction of his means of production?

'We've got to make a channel,' grunts Manu, apparently embracing me in the 'we'. 'Diverting the overflow into the river.'

'Sacrificing some vines,' adds Mme Gros, finding the silver lining in the cloud.

'I thought maybe the tractor to pull up the roots,' explains Manu.

'It's down at the garage, remember.'

'Of course. Sorry, can't think what happened that day. Skidding on the wet grass, I suppose.'

Manu then outlines the potential virtues of a second, spare tractor for emergencies. His cousin has left Monsieur Bricolage but there's a hunting companion, who has owed him a favour since last year's truffle season . . .

'I'm going to check the *source*,' I cut him short, taking the quick route over his fence.

The water supply has certainly recovered from its late summer slow-down – I have never heard such a torrential delivery inside the collecting chamber – but the system appears to be coping. On the other hand, about twenty metres away, there is water pouring from the terrace walls in two separate places where there has never been water before.

'Never in my lifetime,' confirms Manu, who has followed me up. 'You need to channel that lot down to the river before it brings the walls down. I'd fetch a pickaxe, if I were you,' he suggests. 'Then perhaps you'd help me with that vine on your way back. But you know what you really want for these jobs,' he calls after me. 'One of those mechanical excavator things. Like for the roadworks, but smaller. Not to buy,' he emphasizes, ever careful with my savings. 'But that hunting pal, I mentioned . . . He does a very reasonable rental.'

Winter

I have been reading Claudette's bee book on the subject of stings.

'Without the sting to protect the honey,' it said, 'a hive would lose everything to predators and starve during the winter.' This sounded reasonable enough, but hardly reassuring on a day when Claudette was taking me to visit some of her colonies. Another paragraph offered a crumb of reassurance: 'Bees do not lightly use their stings on human honey-thieves, because they cannot withdraw them from human flesh. In their efforts to do so, they tear the whole mechanism from their bodies and die shortly afterwards.'

Claudette said we were unlikely to collect any honey, so surely our benign intrusion would never warrant a suicide sting; but reading on, I grew nervous again. 'When the sting enters the body, two natural antibodies are produced to neutralize the venom: Immunoglobulin E and Immuno-globulin G. If your body produces more of the G than the E, you should have no problems. Indeed, over time, as your antibody level builds up, very little reaction to bee stings is noticed.' So far so good but there was more. 'It is when you generate more E than G that problems arise. The histamine produced by this antibody limits the effect of the venom but causes swelling in the area of the sting.' Then the crunch: 'In a small number of people, it can cause more frightening effects, from giddiness to difficulty in breathing and unconsciousness.'

On a scale from nought to ten, the speed of inflammation after my poolside wasp attack scored around nine and a half. Does that mean I'm awash with E? Would I survive a multiple bee attack? I wondered, as I drove up to Soumont.

'I'm not sure my overalls will fit him,' says Dominique, eyeing me doubtfully, as he fills his pipe.

'Too small,' says Claudette, cheerily pouring us each a coffee. 'But never mind, the bees shouldn't be too excitable at this time of year. Maybe he could just wear Martin's top.'

With her own 'I used to be afraid' still ringing in my ears, the merest flutter of excitement seems to me to merit total coverage and, much to my relief, Dominique agrees.

'He ought to have a complete suit,' he says sombrely, from behind a cloud of pipe smoke. 'Especially with the Marin blowing. For some reason, bees really hate this wind from the sea.' My stomach is already sinking with the weight of Immunoglobulin E, when Dominique glances down at my feet. 'Boots would have been better,' he advises with a frown. 'The legs of the suit will be a bit short and boots would have helped protect your ankles.'

'Bees always go for the articulating body parts,' Claudette explains breezily. 'They're warmest, you see. But you're wearing long socks, I assume? . . . Oh well, never mind.'

I ask myself whether there is time to drive home for my boots, but there is not. The van is already being loaded and it is time to face the enemy.

As we drive the few kilometres to the first of the *emplacements*, Claudette's elderly Pyrenean sheepdog cowers under the dashboard beside my feet.

'She's terrified of bees,' laughs Claudette affectionately. 'Always hides in the van.'

An option, disappointingly, not open to me, I reflect, as we come to a halt in a clearing, where an alarming quantity of hives – perhaps fifty of them – stand in four formidable rows, like the tents of a medieval army. The air is filled with noisy (surely angry) buzzing. Claudette seems in no particular hurry to don her protective suit, so it seems cowardly to hurl myself into mine. I try to look nonchalantly interested in the pine needles that she is stuffing into a curious metal canister with a sort of bellows attachment at the side.

'It calms them down,' she says, setting light to the needles and closing the chimney-like lid. (From someone who assured me that they wouldn't be excitable, this is less than comforting.) 'They smell the smoke and think the hive's on fire,' she explains, with a squeeze or two on the bellows to get it going. 'They think it's their last chance for a honey binge, so they gorge themselves until they're too fat and drowsy to want to sting you too much.'

But how much is too much? I wonder, as we clamber at last into our suits.

'Do you recognize those trees?' Claudette indicates the dominant surrounding species. 'They're arbutus, easy to identify because they produce flowers and fruits at the same time.' I had been too busy trying to make my socks reach the bottom of the suit to notice the simultaneous whitish blossoms and reddish berries. 'Makes horrible honey,' she says, showing me how to improve the hermetic seal round my head. 'Not sweet at all. But very expensive.'

'Who buys it?' I try to sound interested, caring only at this moment about the vulnerability of my ankles.

'Italians,' comes the answer, as if to say 'what do you expect?' But already she is puffing the smoker close to the bottom of a hive and opening it up at the top. 'I was hoping to give you a taste, but look.' She beckons me closer and, reluctantly, I advance a few centimetres. 'There's scarcely enough to last them the winter.'

I am wondering how we can make it unequivocally clear that we have no designs on their rations, when Claudette issues a public statement.

'*Ne vous inquietez pas, mes pauvres, mes belles,*' she addresses the hive's population. '*On va juste vous fermer les portes.*'

The 'doors' which we are about to close are the narrow openings, about two centimetres high, at the bottom of each hive. Into each of these holes we are to wedge a strip of wood which has been chiselled away to leave just the slimmest possible entrance for winter. In a few cases, Claudette needs a tool like a small machete, to chip away the inhabitants' own efforts to seal themselves in, using a home-produced, honey-based concrete-substitute called 'propolis'. In nearly every case, we need to rip away brambles impeding our access.

'Sometimes they really go mad when you do that,' laughs Claudette, as I wrestle with a particularly stubborn clump, and I stretch my socks even higher.

'Those were the top priority,' she explains, when the last hive is shuttered and the equipment back in the van. 'They get the least sun here. But now for the windiest location.'

The windiest location of all, it seems to me, is the van itself, because the continuing fumes from the smoke appliance require us to drive with the windows down. The smouldering canister has been wedged in the back, inside a crate of the stick-like wooden 'doors' that are worryingly reminiscent of kindling wood. A sudden emergency stop makes me fear that the fire has spread; but no, it is only because Claudette has spotted some mushrooms.

'Hardly enough for a single portion,' she sighs as she accelerates onwards. 'The worst year I can remember, even after all the recent rain. But did I tell you about the house – that we're having to sell it?'

'As well as the *mièlerie*?'

'It's been such a bad season, with the summer drought – about a third of our normal yield. Like the mushrooms, the rain was too late to help us.'

'What will you do?'

'We own the building next door. It's uninhabitable but luckily some neighbours who spend only the summer here are lending us their place, while we work on it. Business-wise, we're scaling back on our hives – two hundred instead of three hundred and twenty. And Dominique's diversifying into sheep.'

'A bit of a change!'

'His family used to breed them. He feels he's returning to his roots.'

At this point the sheepdog at my feet starts yelping and

fidgeting and retreating as far as possible beneath the dashboard. Claudette is quick to spot the cause. A bee has travelled with us from the last *emplacement* and is crawling up my left arm. I am still in my suit but have unzipped the head section, letting it dangle down my back. It can only be a minute before the bee will reach my neck.

'I know it's silly,' I begin, tensing rigidly in my seat. 'But I'm worried about this bee.'

'Oh, no need to worry,' Claudette says brightly. 'At this time of year, it'll still be accepted in one of these hives.' We have arrived at the second *emplacement* and the bee leaves my arm to review the accommodation prospects.

The hives here have been arranged in a single row, their backs to the prevailing westerly wind. The dominant flora is heather, 'Bruyère Collunes' to be precise, as the resulting honey's label will eventually say.

'What kind of vegetation do you have on your land?' asks Claudette, sharpening her machete on a stone.

For a moment, the tempting prospect of the Napoleonic kilogram per five hives rises before me; then I remember the Immunoglobulin. 'Brambles mainly,' I prevaricate.

'Here you *can* taste some honey,' she declares, opening the nearest of the hives and passing me a sample on the blade of the machete.

I am not sure which seems more dangerous: licking the newly whetted knife or licking the honey that a swarm of bees may be about to defend to the death. 'Delicious,' I pronounce, hardly aware of what I am tasting, as Claudette begins the door-closing.

'*Ah, mes pauvres!*' she exclaims, spotting some bees in a puddle. 'I know it's not worth the time,' she admits, as she crouches to fish them out. 'I just don't like to think of them drowning.'

'Time for one more colony?' she asks, when the round is completed. 'It's right by the village.'

She gives the smoke machine an extra blast to make sure the fire is alive and puts it back in the van with the kindling wood.

'And here we are, worrying about bee stings,' I whisper to the dog, as I resume my place in the passenger seat.

We return to the village by a different road, passing some oddly sinister-looking agricultural terraces just below the ramparts. It takes me a moment to realize that the reason they look sinister is that many of the trees are black and bare; and the reason they are black and bare is that they are burnt. A summer fire, I assume, as Claudette turns the van into the heart of the charred landscape.

'It happened last September,' she says. 'Dominique let the smoke machine fall over. The fire brigade were here within minutes – he had his mobile telephone. But you can see how far it spread. We lost a lot of hives, including six in which we were raising new queens for next year.'

'Is it your land?' I ask, looking round at the damage.

'We rent it,' she says.

'What does the landlord think about it?'

'Fortunately, he understands that these things happen. It was covered by our insurance but you can't put the landscape back in a day. Could have been much worse though, especially so near the village.'

I smile sympathetically but make a mental note to decline the *emplacement* at home.

*

'Can we just put these in your tumble dryer?' said four nearly naked English friends, holding armfuls of dripping wet clothing. They had volunteered for a 'working weekend' to help me open up the wood, but they had forgotten to look at the weather map. Two cherished such romantic notions of the southern climate that they had travelled without even jackets.

I explained that I didn't have a tumble dryer. It wasn't usually necessary. I did my washing when the sun shone or at least when a dry wind was blowing. So I rigged up a washing-line near the hot-water tank and the friends formed a bedraggled huddle by the fire.

'You didn't make them work in this?' laughed Laurent, when they trooped into Le Temps de Vivre on Saturday evening, wearing motley combinations of whatever they possessed that was water-free and some ill-fitting borrowings from me.

'We insisted,' they said. 'It was either work or his uncle's jigsaws. Easy choice really.'

In the end, we had worked on the stream, not the wood. It was suddenly too exciting not to. They had all visited before in the summer and, where once there had been a trickle, now they saw a powerful torrent. The waterfall at the top, normally ten to twenty centimetres across, gushed two metres wide, round either side of a massive, apparently unperturbed oak tree. I possessed a water feature that landscape gardeners would kill for but most of it was invisible behind a dense wall of scrub and brambles.

The project had meant working in the stream as much as beside it, clearing fallen branches and other debris that were hiding most of the beautiful, smooth boulders over which the water should have been cascading. 'If everything else is wet, why not the feet?' laughed the friends, when they found that most of my uncle's wellie collection leaked. It was all I could do to rein them in to leave a little screening at the point where the brook divides my land from Manu's: his wife's surveillance activities were intensive enough as it was, without opening now lines of scrutiny.

'You're crazy!' said Manu, when he stepped across to 'borrow' some kindling wood for their afternoon fire. 'You'll never get any more fish that way. And the crayfish are gone for good.' Our lack of utilitarian purpose bewildered him even more than our determination to defy the elements.

Laurent, laughing at our account, promised more rain for Sunday. He hoped it would encourage saner folk to go out to lunch. He now needed busy weekends more than ever, having decided to close on Thursdays, as well as Mondays, Tuesdays and Wednesdays, at least until the early spring. 'More time for *la chasse*!' His grin made a virtue of necessity but did not entirely hide the underlying strain. With only five services remaining, the books would not be easily balanced.

Unfortunately Sunday's rain is heavier still – not so much a rain to invite restaurant expeditions as one to make the contents of even the dullest deep-freeze seem unexpectedly appealing. I picture the scene in half a dozen different households: 'Do you think it's too early to ring to cancel?' Yet the fearless four are undeterred. Left to myself, I might have tidied out the tool-store, found a forgotten spare room to redecorate, even unpacked a jigsaw; but if my workers are determined to get wet, how can I remain dry?

Later in the morning, there comes a point when the current is simply too strong to stand in the stream. 'Let's go and see what this is doing to the river,' proposes William, and I suggest a walk to the scene of Manu's river picnic, back in August. I am curious to see how the road-builders are progressing with the widening of the flyover at that point.

As always, a sign reminds us that the bridge at the bottom of the steep descent is potentially floodable. 'Who cares?' says William. 'Our feet are wet already . . .' but his voice trails off in shock. The concrete crossing is completely impassable. What normally flows at least a metre below is, this morning, pounding half a metre above it. The water is hurtling towards Lodève with terrifying force. Manu's neck at his picnic table would be worse than submerged; it would be broken.

If only the prayers of those priests for rain had been a little less fervent.

*

'Couldn't your friends have done this?' asks Manu, holding a corner of my newly purchased olive-picking net as high as his restricted stature allows.

'I thought it was bad for the olives to pick them in the rain,' I answer, climbing a little way up the ladder to shake a branch.

'You're thinking of grapes,' says Manu, switching from one weary arm to another, as the first black Lucques start to fall.

'And now half your crop has been battered to the ground by the rain,' grumbles Mme Gros.

Of course, when she says 'your crop' she means 'our crop', which is why she is reluctantly holding another corner of the net. Mme Gros is very fond of olives. They, more than anything, might tempt her into one of her special-occasion Noilly Prats; but she will happily eat them by the fistful without. Indeed, she has never quite forgiven me for taking most of the harvest in my first year to be turned into oil, at the Clermont l'Hérault co-operative. When I asked her what became of last year's crop she laughed at me scornfully: 'You don't think I've got time for all that soda and salt palaver, do you?' So this year's efforts need to compensate for long months of scarcity.

'And it's so cold,' whines Garance, her efforts to hold a third corner being severely impeded by a double layer of gloves (the first worn indoors, with the second, larger pair deployed as a supplement for outdoor activity). 'It's all very well for you, but I start off frozen before I even leave the *maset*.'

She was even more reluctant to help than the others but she has at last picked up on the force of Mme Gros's resentment over the mobile telephone and now wants to switch the recharging contract over to me. So I did a deal. But she is right: it is numbingly cold.

The fall in temperature has already called a halt to wall-building. Arnaud was three-quarters finished but said it was no longer safe to use cement until nearer the spring. 'Otherwise it might not be stable,' he stressed, as he shrouded his pride and joy in lurid blue plastic sheeting.

'You realize that tarpaulin's the first thing I see, when I pull back the bedroom curtains,' carps Mme Gros, as a forceful shake of the tree sends a barrage of olives in her direction.

'Surely that's enough,' whines the man with the aching arms.

'It's getting colder,' snivels Garance. 'It's all right for you . . .'

'Just be grateful he's helping at all,' snaps Mme Gros. 'It's not every day he takes time off from catering school.'

My leadership skills seem to be failing me. 'Let's try to finish this row before lunch,' I suggest diffidently.

'Lunch!' laughs Mme Gros, in the same scornful vein. 'No use inviting him to lunch any more. Honest home cooking is no longer good enough. Time was, of course, when he used to invite us. Moves in different circles now. But yes, I enjoyed a pleasantly quiet *anniversaire*, thank you for asking.'

Two years ago, in October, I treated her to a birthday dinner, with the partner of her choice, at Saint Guiraud's matchless Le Mimosa. I still lie awake at night, reliving Manu's more embarrassing contributions to the evening, but I have slowly started to come to terms with the experience. I have even been back there for several meals this summer, with friends from England. However, as far as the Groses are concerned, I always thought of our soirée as an insurance premium for my time away, not the start of a long tradition.

Unfortunately, to judge from her tone, Mme Gros views things differently. 'He'll be on his own for the salt treatment,' she informs the community.

*

It seemed such a good idea on Armistice Day.

I was accompanying Virgile on a barrel-buying expedition to the Charente and it was one of the sunniest mornings that could ever have favoured 11 November, warm enough indeed for a picnic, but Virgile had something more substantial in mind. About half an hour before Toulouse and more than half an hour before noon, he left the motorway for Castelnaudary.

'It's the birthplace of cassoulet, one of my favourite dishes,' he explained, as we killed the remaining time before the restaurants opened. 'The town was under siege in the Hundred Years' War against the English,' he whispered at the back of the Saint Michel church, where the Remembrance service was drawing to its close. 'The people of the town were running desperately short of food. On the eve of the last great battle, they put every bit of meat they could find into one final dish – duck, pork, sausages – all cooked up together with beans . . .'

'Who won?'I whispered back.

'You wouldn't ask, if you'd tasted the dish,' he assured me with a grin. 'But we'd better make haste,' he added, as a rousing organ voluntary began. 'This congregation looks hungry.'

We were lucky to get a table. It was a public holiday and within half an hour of our taking the only unreserved places, the restaurant Le Tirou was full with, needless to say, nearly everyone ordering cassoulet. At first, all I could see in the steaming earthenware bowl served between us was a bubbling stew made of white haricot beans; but buried within it, we discovered hunks of sausage, pork and duck leg.

'No one in their right mind would cook this at home,' laughed Virgile. 'It takes forever to make.'

'Come back and see for yourself,' the chef's wife encouraged me, when Virgile mentioned this habit that I seemed to be forming of invading unfamiliar kitchens.

At the time, a return to sunny cassoulet country needed little encouragement, but that was three weeks ago. This morning at six o'clock, it had been raining for forty-eight hours and the rain seemed to be getting heavier. It was barely light when I left home (it would prove in fact one of those days that was barely light at any time) but I could see that the footbridge between me and the Groses was, for the first time ever, under water. As for the bridge over the river beneath the dual carriageway, I don't know why I even considered going that way. The water had surely risen another metre since the last storm. Even a heavy truck would have been swept away. Then, nearer Pézenas, I found the whole of the raised-level road now a causeway between flooded vineyards – in many cases, so deeply submerged that the water was lapping at the door lintels of the agricultural buildings.

So, all in all, not a perfect occasion for the two-hundred-kilometre drive to Le Tirou.

'I'm afraid we've made a start,' says an ebullient-looking Jean-Claude Visentin, indicating a saucepan the size of a small dustbin on the hob. 'We weren't sure you'd make it.'

I sympathize. I wasn't sure myself. Arriving half an hour behind schedule, at 9.30, I was almost too dazed to locate the door in the kitchen's wall-to-wall, floor-to-ceiling windows. Blinking in the glare of the strip lights, I realize too late that the chef is already detailing the contents of his pot.

' . . . and finally, herbs and spices,' he concludes what may have been a long list. '*Très simple*,' he adds, so presumably not. There must have been onions and garlic in the *jus*, but I can't ask him to start again. 'Oh, and just a hint of tomato paste,' he says, stirring in a spoonful so tiny in relation to the cauldron that it is difficult to believe it can be detectable.

'Have you always wanted to cook?' I ask, feeling the question rather superfluous. One look at M. Visentin's figure tells you there were never more than two career possibilities: the chef and the operatic tenor.

'My parents were Italian,' he begins. (So I was right about the opera.) 'They weren't cooks, although my mother made good cassoulet. They did factory and farming work. That's why they came to France. But I couldn't do either of those.'

He heaves a second giant saucepan on to the hob. This one is filled with dried haricot beans ('from Castelnaudary – the best,' he stresses) which he leaves heating gently in water. 'Never salt them till the end of the first cooking,' he advises. 'Otherwise the skins go hard. There . . .' He leans heavily against the worktop for a moment. 'Should be done by 12.15.'

'Isn't that cutting it a bit fine?' I imagined that his earliest customers might be here at noon.

'Oh, these are not for today. They're for the ones we'll be making up tomorrow. Enough for fifty.'

'Are you expecting many today?'

'Not in this weather,' he says, signalling the resumption of activity with the tossing of some pig's trotters into the simmering *jus*. 'We had a party driving up from Montpellier but they cancelled.'

'More sense than me,' I laugh, already dreading the return journey.

'This is Sébastien.' M. Visentin introduces me to the contrasting figure of the *sous-chef* – as angular as his employer is rounded, as sombre as the other is jovial – who has appeared with four or five large expanses of pork rind, each a metre long and maybe fifteen centimetres wide. These he rolls up like a pile of rugs and ties in a bundle ('not too tight, to let the *jus* in,' the chef emphasizes). Then the parcel follows the trotters into the pot.

'What would you say distinguishes your cassoulet from everyone else's?' I ask.

'It's better,' says Sébastien unhesitatingly.

'That and the fact that not everyone puts the rind and trotters in,' laughs his employer, already busy with two large hunks of pork. 'This is what's called *échine*,' he explains, pointing to his upper back. 'Plenty of fat to keep it moist.' Then quickly, casually and apparently without counting, he trims what must be twenty-five pieces from each on to a tray, which he slides into a low oven, leaving a pile of spare-rib-like bones, which he consigns to the *jus*.

Sébastien is meanwhile cutting twenty-five duck legs in half. 'These are *confits de canard*, of course, from a Castelnaudary farm, but we do the *confiserie* ourselves,' explains M. Visentin 'This lot we cooked yesterday and salted two days ago That's how long the process takes. To eat cassoulet on Sunday, you need to start on Thursday.'

A white van draws into the car park. The driver unloads a large box and struggles with it through the rain towards the panoramic windows.

'Do you mind being so exposed to your customers?' I ask.

'It means we get to see some daylight,' says the chef. 'Well, not today, of course,' he laughs.

The van driver, shaking himself like a dog on the doormat, is delivering coffee. Products unrelated to cassoulet are permitted to come from as far away as Narbonne, and he has tales to tell of ships thrown up on to the foreshore, near the motorway by which I must shortly drive home.

All this while, a third cook has been preparing vegetables in a dark corner. Now summoned into the glare of the strip lights, to lay out the dishes for today's fifty cassoulets, he looks barely fourteen and I start to wonder about child labour laws in Castelnaudary.

'Julien's on work experience from school,' explains the chef. 'There's normally an apprentice, but it's his day off. The wonderful thirty-five-hour week.' Julien smiles shyly and returns to his corner, leaving ten small dishes and twenty larger ones on the pass. 'Ten for one and twenty for two,' says M. Visentin. 'Don't ask me why, but it always seems to work.'

He takes yesterday's batch of pork chunks from a fridge and passes them to Sébastien for sharing out, along with the *confit*, while himself distributing chunks of raw sausage. 'The first time we've made our own,' he says proudly.

'You really are gluttons for punishment!'

'Our supplier changed his recipe and I couldn't find another that I liked. Now for the beans.' Yesterday's beans have already been mixed with yesterday's *jus*, but today the *jus* has set solid. 'I've never known it so hard,' he grunts, as he packs the jellified beans round the meat in each dish.

'Don't try this at home,' I remind myself, as the beefy M. Visentin groans with the physical effort of stirring and scooping.

'Only remains to add a bit of water,' he says, when the bean allocation is finished. Improbably, every dish is perfectly filled to the brim, with not a single bean left over. He has certainly done this before.

'So you'll cook these to order at lunchtime?' I ask, oddly relieved to have reached the end of the three-day process.

'No, these are for tonight. We'll cook them around three o'clock, at the end of the service.'

A waiter, introduced as 'Anthony, the best cassoulet salesman in the world', whisks the new production away to an air-conditioned storeroom.

'There's enough left from yesterday for lunch,' says M. Visentin, transferring some ready-cooked examples from the fridge to the low oven, from which they will pass to the hotter one if Anthony achieves his sales targets.

Another van draws into the car park and an almost unrecognizably drenched Mme Visentin dashes in with the bread. 'People are abandoning cars out there,' she reports.

'You'll stay for lunch?' her husband asks me.

'I ought to be getting back.'

'Anthony will feel he's failed.'

But I insist.

'So, how do like working in a kitchen?' I ask Julien, as I prepare to leave.

'*C'est différent*,' the boy answers shyly.

'You won't think that when you've made cassoulet every day for ten years,' I think to myself, as I sprint through a squall to the Renault.

*

I didn't in fact make it home that day.

As soon as I left Le Tirou, I realized that I should have stayed for dinner as well as lunch. The signs at the Castelnaudary motorway junction were barely visible through the battering rain but one, I knew, said Montpellier, while the other said Toulouse, and suddenly the latter – perhaps only half an hour away – seemed irresistibly nearer than home. All I needed to do was turn right instead of left. Toulouse must have a cheap hotel and a toothbrush shop, I told myself; not to mention warm, dry cinemas. And it also had Betty's cheese stall in the covered Victor Hugo market.

You would not think so to look at her, but Betty was born on the day that France was liberated at the end of the Second World War. She is French through and through but, in thanks for freedom, her parents named her (more or less) after Britain's young Princess Elizabeth. She told me all this two years ago, when she also introduced me to her incomparable truffle-flavoured cheese ravioli.

'We can't afford to make them,' she laughed, when I explained my return. 'Have you seen the price of truffles this year? There are none to be found.' So I contented myself with more conventional pasta, filled with cheese and herbs: delicious but not incomparable.

And, of course, some cheeses. Lodève's market stall is all very well but Betty's reminded me of de Gaulle's remark about the impossibility of governing a country having two hundred and sixty-five cheeses. She seemed to stock all of them.

I mostly bought what was least familiar but I also asked for some Roquefort, because Betty's was a variety that I had never seen at home. It even had her name on the silver-foil wrapping.

'Do you make it yourself?' I asked naïvely.

'The Carles family make it for us,' she said, pointing to the 'Carles' beneath the 'Betty'. 'They're one of the smallest. Not farmhouse. There hasn't been any *production fermier* – using home-produced milk – since the '30s. But Jacques Carles is one of the last two "artisanal" producers. In fact, such are the big industrial monopolies like Société, that he's one of the last seven altogether.'

I decided to go to see Monsieur Carles, while there was still time.

The voice on the telephone this morning sounds elderly and tired, the sort of voice that could suddenly sell up and retire: there may not be a moment to lose.

However, the season has barely started, he tells me patiently. January production levels will be three times what they are now, rising to a peak in April. It would be better to come after Christmas.

*

A neatly serried rank of toddler-sized tractors and trucks dramatizes the absence of the Moulin d'Oulivie's younger generation.

They are at school and their place has been taken by a minibus-load of mentally handicapped adolescents, enjoying their first experience of an olive oil tasting on the veranda. Pierre Vialla's unflappable wife is showing them how to dunk a slice of *baguette* in a bowl of *extra vierge*, preferably without too much spattering of fellow participants.

I am here for a tasting myself, and apparently a professional oil taster who advises on blending is also coming. I never knew that there were such people so I have no idea what to expect. Certainly not the formidable, expensively dressed lady who is striding up the drive, having presumably (and wisely, given the latest storm damage) abandoned her car at the bottom.

'*Je m'appelle Françoise.*' The single declaration introduces her to everyone, from the minibus driver to me, but most especially to the handicapped contingent, with whom she establishes an immediate, easy rapport – the finer points of power-dressing being, I suppose, beyond their experience. Pierre waves from his office window, with a 'trying to wind up this telephone call' gesture, while the tasting grows more messily animated under Françoise's enlivening influence.

'We're harvesting the Picholines,' Pierre explains, when finally free to escort us into the olive grove. 'The Lucques and Verdales are already in,' is what I think he says next, but his words are drowned by the noise of the picking operation. The Picholines are falling fast on to large, plastic tarpaulins (no fancy nets for the Viallas). The rapidity, like the accompanying racket, is primarily attributable to a pair of motorized branch-shaking machines, each with a fierce-gripping claw at the end of a long pulsating arm, wielded by two of the workforce. A third is tickling any last tenacious fruits from the branches with a gentler but only marginally less noisy appliance, resembling a vibrating rubber-pronged pitchfork. The fourth and final harvester has the tedious but silent task of gathering in the percentage of the crop that bounces clear of the tarpaulins.

'How many can they pick in a day?' mouths Françoise slowly

and deliberately. To help Pierre she performs a mime of someone lifting two heavy buckets.

'Two tonnes,' he appears to be replying. At least, he holds up two fingers and he can't be saying kilos.

'I'm surprised you don't use nets,' is the contribution I should have liked to make. 'Less bouncy than tarpaulins.' But I'd never be heard. And anyway, the Viallas no doubt have their reasons. So, as we turn back towards the mill and the decibels diminish, I confine myself to surprise that the bulk of the harvest should still be green.

'Yes, people think they have to be black,' says Pierre with a smile, 'but perfect maturity for oil production has nothing to do with colour.'

'How else do you tell?'

'Laboratory analysis. We send samples to Provence.' In the shop, he produces a bundle of faxes, charting the Picholines' progress towards the optimum picking point. 'This measures flavour.' He points to one graph. 'And this measures oiliness.'

Smiling sheepishly, Pierre dons a huge pair of ear muffs. Françoise and I exchange looks of renewed dismay and follow him into the heart of the building, where we learn that picking was tranquillity itself, compared to oil extraction. Ninety per cent of Pierre's detailed commentary is inaudible, so we must deduce what we can by observation.

The first device is plainly a conveyor belt, transferring the olives from their collecting crate to a vigorously churning vat of water, washing away leaves and twigs, as well as general dirt (evidenced by Pierre plucking a sprig from the waves). The next piece of equipment, after another conveyor belt, must be grinding up the olives (even without Pierre's grinding gestures, I can infer this from the fact that the following appliance is kneading the resulting paste). This kneading will apparently continue until the paste is smooth and homogeneous (only a mime artist of distinction could manage 'smooth and homogeneous' but Pierre is such a one). Then the biggest challenge of all: how to explain the horizontal cylindrical drum which is connected to the kneader by a pipe.

The drum is completely sealed, giving little clue to its interior activities. Some spectacularly green oil is emerging from a smallish pipe at one end, while water is expelled from another; and a glance outside, through the window, shows the solid leftovers exiting down a third, more substantial pipe. But what goes on inside the machine to achieve this?

'Is it a press?' I act out a pressing motion.

Pierre shakes his head. He thinks for a moment, then his arm starts spinning furiously along the line of the drum. Next his hands make as if to part an invisible wave and his fingers mime the trickling down of liquid.

'No, don't tell me, It's coming . . .' Then enlightenment dawns: 'CEN . . . TRI . . . FUGE?' I shout and Pierre nods applaudingly; but now it is time for Françoise to take centre stage.

In the quiet of Pierre's office, she explains how I should swill a little oil in my mouth, really 'chew' it, sucking plenty of air across it. Very inelegant, she promises, looking impeccably elegant as she demonstrates. The back of my tongue should taste the bitterness (a good quality in oil, she emphasizes); and my throat should feel the fieriness (another good quality). A really fine example should make me cough. I mustn't feel embarrassed. She coughs gracefully herself, to show me how easy it is. But first, as with wine, I must appreciate the colour and smell of the oil in my glass.

Pierre distributes small plastic beakers, pouring some deep, straw-coloured Verdale into each of them.

I must warm it first, Françoise instructs, cupping the bottom of her beaker in one hand and rotating the flat of the other over the top. It tastes best at 22°, she says; then recognizing the improbability of achieving such a temperature before the spring, she takes a swig.

I follow suit but, in my nervousness to get things right, swallow my sample straight away. I continue chewing air and sucking across an empty palate, hoping that no one will notice, while Françoise and Pierre compare notes. A little sweeter than last year? Not quite so herby? But definitely quite fiery, yes. I join in the general appreciative coughing but, even with my second, unswallowed sample of Lucques, I am not much better at finding these subtleties. Perhaps a little 'thicker' than the Verdale? 'More unctuous,' Françoise and Pierre agree.

'You know the trouble with Lucques?' asks Pierre. ('Trouble' is hardly a word that I want to hear in the context of the dominant variety on my own land.) 'There's a very narrow picking window. Miss it and you've missed all the Lucques-like quality. And as I told you before, they're the most delicate, the most easily diseased and damaged. The oil doesn't keep as long either. Six to twelve months at the most, before it starts to decline, whereas Picholine . . .' He pours a sample of the newest and greenest of his three oils. 'Picholine actually improves with a bit of ageing and then keeps for three or four years without the slightest deterioration.'

'So Françoise, what kind of blend are you going to recommend?' I change the subject to less sensitive terrain.

'That depends on Pierre's objectives,' she answers non-committally. 'The style of the *assemblage* that he wants. Also the amount of single variety oil that he needs.'

'I hope to blend everything eventually,' Pierre tells me.

'I thought the single varieties were supposed to be the best.'

'Not in my opinion. Blends are much more interesting. But most of our customers are still at the stage of getting interested in the single varieties. It's the same as with wine – people need time to familiarize themselves with the individual flavours before they can appreciate the harmonies and contrasts in a blend.'

'So, what happens at the moment if, for instance, Françoise wants all of the Lucques for a blend and you want half of it for single variety customers?'

'He'll tell me to get lost,' laughs Françoise, before Pierre can put the point more delicately.

*

, as he showed us to a table in the deserted veranda. It
seemed that Sarah's early Christmas treat for me was going to
be a mixed blessing for him. 'I suppose it's only to be expected,'
he added, bringing the glasses of champagne ordered by Sarah
before we even sat down (she had just driven from the airport).
'A Thursday night and only a week before the twenty-fifth.'

'Will you be busy on Christmas Eve?' I asked, assuming this
to be one of his most hectic nights of the year.

'We'll be closed,' he answered simply. 'It's a Wednesday. I'm
going to give the family priority for once. But we'll be doing New
Year's Eve, serving an eight-course gala menu. I must be *malade*!'
he chuckled. 'At least, I'll still have Georges. I've given him a
night off this evening, but the Réveillon will be his last service.'

'Well, Patrick's cooking for us that evening!' Sarah decided to
make one thing clear.

'I'll tell you my biggest headache,' said Laurent, when he had
taken our order. 'I've stuffed the menu full of truffles but I don't
know where I'm going to find any this year. *Mais, c'est ça, la
restauration!*' he laughed, as the swing doors closed behind him.

Feeling restless from an afternoon of sedentary travel, Sarah
got up to explore, taking her champagne with her. 'You didn't
tell me about this,' she chastised me, returning from the main
room behind us with an album of news-cuttings

'You didn't tell me about this,' I in turn chastise Laurent, when
he appears with miniature versions of the famous *foie gras* and
smoked salmon dish as our *amuse-bouche*.

'I thought I'd shown you the press-book,' he says, looking
suddenly self-conscious.

'Not these articles.' There are several devoted to his nomina-
tion by the trade magazine, *Le Chef*, as 'Tremplin de l'Année'
(the French culinary equivalent of 'Most Promising Newcomer')
for the year that he opened. He shrugs the reports aside, as
something that happened long ago. 'But it's a fantastic achievement,' I insist, as he heads off to attend to our first courses.
Having given everyone, except Eric the First, the night off, he is

215

managing all aspects of our meal on his own. 'Wait till the new guides come out in the spring . . .' I call after him, but he has gone.

'It says here, he doesn't want a Michelin star,' says Sarah, always one of my more achieving friends and unable to relate to such lack of ambition.

'I don't think he'd turn it down,' I reassure her, as we browse through the remaining cuttings.

We find several recurring messages, some of them familiar: how rooted he is in this valley where his grandfather culti-vated vines and olives; how close to the soil and to nature; how passionate about the region's products (witness the *petit gris* snails with our salt-cod starter). But some are newer to me: I never knew that at twenty-nine, when he left Le Jardin des Sens, he was already the *chef de partie* responsible for fish, with five assistant cooks in his section and only the Pourcels themselves and the *second de cuisine* above him in the hierarchy.

'I don't think we should remind him of that bit,' whispers Sarah, when Laurent comes to clear our empty plates.

National, local and professional presses are also united in something close to awe that the Pourcel twins not only attended his opening ceremony but also spoke so warmly and support-ively about him.

'I never stopped learning from them,' says Laurent, when he returns to serve our roasted pigeon with its *mille-feuilles* of aubergine caviar, in which wafer-thin, oven-crisp aubergine slices usurp the place of pastry. 'Not just lessons in perfection and precision,' he elaborates, 'but lessons in humanity, simplic-ity and listening.'

'There's something else I haven't told you,' he later confides, above the rumble of the approaching cheese trolley. 'Something much more important than that old stuff. I've bought a house.'

Sarah and I exchange glances that both say, 'On these profits?'

'The next house along this lane. You might have noticed the postbox on the verge.'

'Is there much work to do?' I ask, wondering how soon they can enjoy the extra space.

'It's a total ruin,' he laughs, cutting our selections of Pélardon and Roquefort. 'I couldn't have bought it if it wasn't. We won't be moving in for at least two years. And that's if I can afford all the work that needs to be done.' He indicates the otherwise empty veranda and then laughs philosophically: '*C'est ça, la restauration!*'

*

'I did warn you,' said Rens, with a sympathetic chuckle.

She was right. She had warned me and, intellectually, I knew there would be none of her goat's cheeses produced between the middle of December and the middle of February. I simply hadn't accepted it as a practical reality. Two months now seemed an impossibly long time and I should have built up my stocks, like Laurent.

The forbidden stall in the market is still there, piled just as high as at any other time of year with little *chèvres*.

'He must be using frozen curd,' says Garance disgustedly, darting rapidly round, as if to hurl herself between me and temptation.

But she needn't worry. I'm not going back. It's Betty's Roquefort for Christmas.

*

The Groses' grandchildren, who are visiting for the festive season, have decided that the persimmon tree beside my swimming pool produces quite the funniest fruit in the world. This is because the French for persimmon is *kaki* and this, of course, is quite side-splittingly close to *caca*, which in turn is French for 'poo'.

Yet even those deaf to such *jeux de mots* must surely grant that there is something wittily surreal about a fully laden *kaki*. Perhaps, in my first December here, I was too busy packing up

217

to leave; or perhaps the tree simply didn't bear fruit that winter. I could hardly have failed to notice this profusion of vivid orange globes, suspended gaudily on the bare wood, like so many Christmas tree baubles, the weight dragging many of the branches down to the ground.

I sampled my first several weeks ago, as soon as the leaves started dropping. They all looked magnificently ripe and I imagined the fruits ending up, like the leaves, on the paving stones, if I didn't harvest soon. I took an enthusiastic bite, expecting some kind of cross between a tomato and a citrus fruit.

'I was about to warn you,' chuckled Manu, as I spat out the bitter, indigestibly fibrous mouthful.

'Don't tell me these need caustic soda too,' I spluttered through lips almost glued to my teeth by the dryness of the flesh.

'You have to leave them on the tree till the first frosts,' explained Manu. 'They should be ready by Christmas.' But now that the frosts and Christmas Eve have come in that order, the *kakis* look much less inviting. The skins have turned a deeper, less appetizing red, almost black and bruised-looking in places. The insides feel almost too squashy to pick, like balloons filled with water. The birds have gorged themselves on several but what sort of recommendation is that?

'Trust me,' says Manu, arriving with a wicker basket (as though I could break the habit of our whole acquaintance). 'No, wait,' he stops me, as I psyche myself up for a taste. 'You'd be better indoors with a plate and a spoon.'

His advice proves sound. Merely pulling at the stalk bursts the bubble, and the molten interior pours out across the dish. The bitter fibres of November have liquefied to a sweet creamy purée: the colour a vibrant swirl of yellow and orange, the flavour deliciously reminiscent of *crème caramel*.

'*Il va manger du caca*,' chorus three gleeful grandchildren, as I go back down to the poolside for my remaining share.

*

Manu swears that not even he saw so much as a sliver of truffle for Christmas.

Pierre Vialla tells the same story. 'You'll have to come "hunting" another year,' he says.

'Does that mean no more truffle oil?' I ask, having almost finished the bottle that I bought when we first met.

'You'll have to ask my cousin. It's him who makes the truffle oil, up at Saint Guilhem-le-Désert. But if you'll excuse me . . .'

Pierre has even more important matters on his mind because – not content with their ultra-modern operation at Combaillaux – he and his brother are today inaugurating an ultra-traditional mill on the outskirts of Aniane. He dashes over to a huge granite wheel, nearly two metres in diameter, grinding merciless circles inside an equally huge stone trough filled with olives. They found the wheel in Italy, Pierre explains when I catch him up. Eight hundred years old, he believes; unlike the formidable wooden press, erected nearby, which is also from Italy but is no more than four hundred years old. Even younger is the mighty waterwheel outside, driving the rotation of the mill: mere nineteenth-century, he confesses, but Italian again. The single twenty-first-century solecism is an electric pump, powering an artificial millstream for the waterwheel.

The press, in contrast, is entirely manual, as Rock is about to demonstrate. Gathering olive pulp from the trough, he packs this into circular, basket-like containers and piles five or six of them on top of each other, beneath the corkscrew shaft of the press. Then he and a friend slot a pair of wooden poles into opposite sides of the screw and start the circular, oxen-like pushing process that brings the weight of the press spiralling downwards, while the oil oozes out through the mesh of the baskets and into a waiting tub.

'Why?' is the question that springs to mind. 'Isn't Combaillaux enough work?'

'It was a challenge,' says Pierre, coming over to monitor the results. 'And a homage to tradition.' Coupled with a bit of marketing, I reflect, surveying the striking, architect-designed glass pavilion, packed with oil enthusiasts who might otherwise never have found their way to the family estate.

'We'll mainly do this on Sundays,' says Pierre. 'Maybe more often in summer.'

'What will you do for olives? Surely this must be near the end of the season?'

'We'll use frozen ones. It's what the Romans did,' he adds, offering a taste of the latest pressing.

I suck and chew it as Françoise taught me, buying time while I grope for the forgotten vocabulary.

'Fiery?' I suggest, waiting for acclamation; but Pierre has returned to the mill, too busy throwing olives in the path of the wheel to comment.

*

'You've chosen a good day,' says the young Lionel Giraud. 'We're introducing the winter menu.'

Like his father Claude, whom he succeeded last April, Lionel changes the menus at Narbonne's La Table de Saint Crescent every three months, taking advantage of seasonal produce. I tell him it's depressing – after the weather conditions of the last few weeks – to be told that the middle of January is the start of winter; but Lionel is too preoccupied to see the joke.

'Keep it moving,' he shouts at the assembled company. 'It'll be twelve o'clock and half your ingredients won't be ready.'

You have only to notice Lionel's intense, dark eyes and his fastidiously trimmed moustache and goatee beard to recognize an unrelenting perfectionist. Claude Giraud, by contrast, making periodic appearances in blazer and tie, seems the very personi-fication of relaxed bonhomie. Perhaps he was different when he was in charge but in retirement the father's eyes twinkle warmly with ironic amusement, where the son's tend to pierce with authority; and the older man's flamboyantly upward-twirling moustache is something of which Salvador Dali would not have been wholly ashamed – the artist more than the autocrat.

Claude is, however, keen to stress that he hasn't put his feet up. He now runs a printing business.

'Do you miss this?' I ask him.

'You have to make way for the young,' he answers and disappears to his office.

The staff in Lionel's kitchen are exclusively young and male; in at least one case, barely out of school. The frenetic activity seems to keep all of them exceptionally trim, which is just as well because the space between the worktops and cooking hobs is by no means exceptionally wide – especially when you are running.

Lionel explains that they are understaffed today. The *sous-chef* in charge of fish is having a knee operation and someone else left on Sunday, so he will be manning the fish station himself. Lean and hungry Mike ('he's French but Mike sounds more American') is on meat, helped by marginally better nourished Christophe. An anxious-looking, rake-thin Japanese boy is making the starters, while Sébastien ('Bas'), the most skeletal of all, the very antithesis of a pastry chef, is running the dessert department. That leaves the hapless little school-leaver, Philippe, peeling tomatoes.

Philippe is working immediately next to Lionel. This may be deliberate, for supervision; or it may just be Philippe's bad luck. Either way, it exposes him to constant criticism: 'Philou, that's a knife you're using, not a pickaxe. It's a chef you're trying to be, not a farm labourer. And get a move on! You can't spend all morning on a dozen tomatoes.'

Lionel, always dangerously close, is spreading something greasy on to dainty slices of sea bream fillet. 'It's duck fat,' he explains. 'A Chinese technique. You wrap them up and steam them. They'd use a banana leaf or something in China but here we use cling film.'

'Have you worked in China?'

'I learned it from Michel Guérard, at Eugénie-les-Bains. Now, who was that English chef I met there? Marco Pierre-White.'

'How did you find him?'

'Excitable. And the chef from Claridges – what's his name?'

'Gordon Ramsay?'

'Also excitable. *Très vio.*'

Another of Lionel's own persuasively violent rounds of censure suggests that Messrs Ramsay and Pierre-White may be not so much acquaintances as role models. This time, it is the Japanese *commis chef* who bears the brunt.

'Naioki, what are you doing? Were you in here yesterday? Were you watching when I showed you?' Lionel barks from a distance of two or three centimetres. Naioki nods nervously. This is not a moment to say the wrong thing. 'Did I cut the herring into pieces that size? Come on, you're not a baby. You're twenty-seven. You're a *commis de cuisine.*'

The look in Naioki's eyes betrays a fear that only two out of three of those propositions may be true by the end of the service.

Then, as if nothing had happened, Lionel returns to personal biography. He has worked at many top restaurants, including L'Oustau de la Baumanière in Les Baux de Provence. He has also run his own French restaurant in Bucharest. And he is still only twenty-five.

'Come on!' He switches to his principal mission, that of spurring the troops on to victory. 'We've been talking about this menu for a week.' Then a revealing variation a few minutes later: 'We've been talking about this menu since Sunday.' (That was two working days ago.)

Philippe has finished tomato number twelve and now faces twice that quantity of yellow peppers. He is, however, finding it difficult to work the peeling knife round the contours, and the skin remains stubbornly, provocatively in evidence in every indentation. It can only be a matter of time before Lionel notices. He hunches defensively over his work. Maybe, if he can make himself very inconspicuous . . . But it is useless.

'Philou, what are you doing?' Lionel practically screams, as he grabs both the pepper and the knife. He shows the boy how to cut the vegetable into quarters, down the lines of the indentations. He scrapes away the seeds and the pith and only then, much more easily, does he shave away the skin. 'This isn't cooking with grandma, Philou. This is gastronomy!' he shouts at point-blank range. Then suddenly, quite chattily, to me: 'Is there anything particular that interests you?'

I explain that I have eaten here twice – once under Claude's regime, during my first year, and once a few months ago, without in fact realizing that there had been a handover – and while nothing had failed to impress, the most remarkable things had been the desserts made with olives. Claude served a collection of four small desserts, conceived as the olive's 'Odyssey' around the Mediterranean, or the Oléade as he punningly called it: an olive oil sorbet, an olive *crême brulée,* a compote of red fruits with olives, and an olive-filled *patisserie.* Then last time, under Lionel, sweet-toothed olive lovers could choose between summery strawberry and olive tartlets and a richer, more autumnal olive 'cake' – the only English word on his menu.

'You're in luck,' says Lionel cheerfully. 'I'm doing various things with flavoured oils in the new menu.' He produces an armful of jars from a storeroom: vanilla, ginger, grilled cashew nut and smoked oils, according to the marker-pen inscriptions. 'And you remember Naioki's herring? That's for a variation on the classic salad with potato. We're giving each customer two little bottles of different oils to experiment with – one young and fruity from Narbonne, the other more robust from Provence . . . Hey, Naioki!' he calls to the starter chef. 'You've finished the herring?'

'*Oui, chef.*'

'And the oil bottles?'

'*Oui, chef.*' He is sounding, for the first time, more confident, more pleased with himself.

'So that leaves you just the onions, the salad, the carrots, the chives . . .' Undaunted, indeed almost smiling now, Naioki produces the onions, already diced and neatly wrapped in cling film. 'I don't believe it!' Lionel throws down the uncooked prawn that he was peeling and charges across the kitchen. 'Were you in here yesterday?' he thunders, as he wrenches the parcel from the assistant's hand. 'Did you see me do that yesterday? Did I put the onions in cling film? Could you really not find a dish? They'll be sweating.' He opens the package triumphantly. 'See! What did I tell you?'

Naioki watches as his onions land in the dustbin and silently adds them back to his 'to do' list.

Claude, meanwhile, passing through to see how things are going and incongruously still in his blazer and tie, has quietly picked up the peeling of the prawns where Lionel left off. This is not an activity that is easily combined with the smoking of a large cigar but somehow Claude manages.

'It's always tense on the first service of a new menu,' he confides in my ear. 'But wait till after the service. You'll never have seen such close friends.'

Philippe's progress in the pepper-peeling division is proving disappointing. To be fair, which on this occasion Lionel isn't, Philippe, as the youngest member of the team, does have to spend a lot of time racing off to the storeroom for whatever ingredient Lionel needs next – the last request being a hundred grams of peeled ginger.

'Philou, what are you doing?' demands Lionel. The boy is weighing two small pieces of ginger root, fetched at the double from the cold room. 'You can see that you haven't got enough.'

'That's all there is, chef. I used the rest yesterday.'

'What do you mean, you used the rest yesterday? You're supposed to be in charge of *checking* the cold room!'

For a moment Philippe hovers nervously between the ginger and the peppers. Then, recognizing the former as a situation that he cannot win, he reverts to the latter where at least he has a chance. But Lionel remains disappointed. 'Hey, Bas!' he calls to Sébastien. 'Can you spare a couple of minutes?'

The pastry chef finds himself drafted in to peel, while Philippe makes a more focused effort on the quartering and seed- and pith-removal. However, even with Sébastien's greater experience (he is, after all, senior enough to have his name on his jacket

– an honour that Philippe, in his present emotional turmoil, can hardly dream of), it is more like thirty minutes before they are finished.

Or think they are finished.

'I don't believe it!' cries Lionel, before Sébastien has been back with his desserts for more than a moment. 'I told you to remove the skin!' he shouts, at the point-blank range to which Philippe is becoming accustomed. 'So what's this? Is that skin? Is that skin? Is that skin?'

'*Oui,*' mumbles Philippe eventually.

'*Oui, chef!*'

'*Oui, chef.*'

'You'd better go through the whole pile again.'

No one, certainly not Sébastien, likes to mention that it was Sébastien who was on skin-elimination duties. Sébastien instead creates a diversion. A big brass bell on one of the walls has been intriguing me since I arrived but Sébastien's spirited ringing now reveals its function as a warning signal: it is already half past eleven.

'Naioki!' Lionel's long-distance scrutiny returns to the starter section.

'*Oui, chef!*'

'Which of your oils are you going to use on your salad?'

Naioki hesitates.

'Which of your oils are you going to use on your salad?'

Naioki knows that this could be the last of his nine lives about to be lost. He hesitates a second longer, then stakes his professional future on a particular *extra vierge.*

'*C'est bon.*'

He is still a *commis de cuisine.*

In between the conflicting claims of dessert- and pepper-preparation, Sébastien has found time to cook the staff lunch. There are two long tables dressed with gaudy plastic tablecloths at the restaurant end of the kitchen, and next to these, on the pass, is an unappealing assortment of roasted chicken wings and legs, a pile of yesterday's rolls reheated and a saucepan full of unsauced pasta tubes. Lionel mentioned earlier that I could have some lunch while I watched the lunchtime service but perhaps, after all, I'll not insist on the point.

Claude sits for a helping at one of the tables. Two waiters and the *plongeur* settle at the other. No one suggests that I join them and I am happy to keep a low profile. Meanwhile, none of the kitchen staff has the time for anything so leisurely. Those who are reasonably on top of things manage a clumsily guzzled plateful whilst stirring a last-minute saucepan. Philippe looks as if he might have to wait until afternoon teatime at home. As twelve o'clock approaches, their unused water glasses and cutlery are cleared from the tables and, as if to emphasize that time is well and truly up, even the chairs are mostly stacked away. Lionel's lunch proposal seems to have been forgotten but I can always get a sandwich on the motorway.

Then a waiter starts covering one of the tables with starched white linen. Perhaps this is where they set the dishes up, ready for service? But no, surely they do that on the pass. And anyway, why the starched linen?

The arrival of silver cutlery, wine glasses and napkins answers my question. The table is being laid for four and Lionel's 'not too long now' makes it clear that I am to be one of them. But who are the other three? Lionel himself went nowhere near the chicken bones but surely he can't have time to eat with me, certainly not on the launch of the new menu.

'*Bonjour*, Lionel,' calls a plump, ruddy-faced figure descending the short flight of stairs that links the kitchen to the restaurant. 'Christian,' he introduces himself to me. 'I eat here two or three times a week,' he explains (although the figure and the complexion would be consistent with a dozen such visits).

'You must certainly get to know the menus.'

'Oh, I do,' he agrees with satisfaction, as a waiter brings us glasses of white wine. 'And, do you know, I've only once had to say that I didn't like a dish.'

'What did he do?'

'Said he couldn't give a damn!' he laughs heartily. 'Some

marvellous things on the new menu, though. I had a bit of a preview yesterday.'

'What do you do about the other meals?' I ask solicitously.

'Oh, well there I'm doubly lucky. I've a wife who's almost as good a cook as Lionel.' He beams with contentment, both at the adequacy of his lot in general and the herring dish set before us in particular.

Each plate – a strikingly wide oblong platter – contains a central stack of finely diced herring, mixed with onion, topped with salad leaves and flanked on either side by a line of cold potato slices. The miniature bottles of contrasting oils stand at either end and Lionel steps across with Claude to tell us which is which.

'You ought to have labels,' says Christian between appreciative mouthfuls.

'You're right,' says Claude, disappearing.

'There have to be some advantages in having a father with a printing business,' says Lionel, returning to his station. And within an incredibly short time, Claude returns with a first batch of name tags, giving all the relevant details and each with a loop of straw to hang it round the appropriate bottle neck.

In the meantime, Roger and Elliane, the other members of our quartet, have joined us. Christian knows both of them well, although Elliane's (to Christian inexplicable) decision to live outside the region prevents her from emulating the more assiduous attendance of the other two.

'We play a vital role,' says Roger.

'Couldn't function without us,' endorses Christian.

'They see themselves as official tasters,' explains Elliane, as two *Pissaladières de légumes de l'hiver* arrive for her and Roger.

'Ah, now that is outstanding. I tried it yesterday,' says Christian, looking as if he could cheerfully try it again today.

The traditional pissaladière from Provence is an onion-covered pastry base, topped with anchovies, olives and sometimes tomatoes, but Lionel has reinvented this with a topping of colourful miniature winter vegetables. Elliane applies herself to the task of identifying them but Roger is more intent on mischief.

'*C'est une pizza,*' he pronounces after a first thoughtful tasting. '*Oui, c'est une pizza,*' he affirms after a second, this time more loudly in the hope of Lionel hearing. 'Frozen, I shouldn't wonder, but impeccably thawed, you have to hand him that.' But Lionel is preoccupied with his yellow peppers. Even today, as he introduces the winter savoury dishes, he is experimenting with ideas for next week's new dessert menu.

'What's the other flavour?' he asks, distributing hot slices of pepper to the tasting panel.

While everyone puzzles, a fourth *habitué* drops in for coffee. 'Sorry, no time to eat today,' he apologizes, as if his abstinence might genuinely cause offence.

'Vanilla,' the newcomer guesses and Lionel smiles enigmatically.

Then suddenly: 'PHILOU! I'm going to kill you!'

'You know the funny thing is,' Roger chuckles contentedly over a dish of guinea-fowl, 'when Lionel says he's going to kill the boy, he really isn't very far from doing so. And yet, you'll see, at the end of the service they'll all be like the best and oldest of friends.'

*

Cheese-making and personal vanity are, I have decided, incompatible.

Robert Migairou, at the Carles establishment in Roquefort, looks silly enough – short and bespectacled, in his white mackintosh, white wellies and white hairnet, like a diminutive pantomime dame – but I know that I am about to look sillier. My disposable white coat is barely large enough to button up over the thick woollen pullover that I have worn for the underground caves; the disposable plastic overshoes make my feet look four sizes bigger than normal and the disposable shower cap . . . well, that would be better disposed of. However, no one is allowed to penetrate beyond the reception hallway without the full regalia.

'How long have you been making Roquefort?' I ask, as I swallow my pride inside the shower cap.

'Oh, I don't make any cheeses,' says Monsieur Migairou, taking my ridiculousness entirely for granted, as I shuffle awkwardly after him to the rear of the premises. 'There's not a single cheese made anywhere in Roquefort.'

'So where are they made?' I ask, sensing a wasted journey.

'In the dairy, over in Martrin. They're expecting you after lunch. No, what we do here is condition the cheeses. Every bit as important, as you'll soon see,' he assures me. 'But to answer your question, I've been doing this since 1969.'

'Is Martrin far?' I ask, now wondering whether I shall get home before dark.

'About fifty kilometres, but it could be worse,' he laughs. 'Some producers have dairies as far away as the Gard. It's a big catchment area, supporting seven hundred thousand sheep. Our cheeses come down from the dairy every three or four days,' he continues, as we reach a trolley-load of freshly delivered examples, and he shows me how a machine pierces each of them on arrival with thirty to forty spikes. 'The only mechanized step in the whole process,' he emphasizes. 'The holes help the mould develop inside, letting oxygen in and carbon dioxide out.'

Then he takes me to the first of several wooden staircases leading downwards. 'Two-thirds of this village is underground,' he tells me, as we descend. 'Two kilometres of caves, up to three hundred metres wide and three hundred deep. We've got four storeys of caves, each of them two hundred square metres; but some people have as many as eleven, all within the natural rock walls.'

It takes a while for my eyes to adjust to the dim light, but gradually the ivory white of the maturing, drum-like cheeses glows more brightly against the dark, damp background of the oak shelving.

'The floors and ceiling beams are oak as well,' says M. Migairou.

'It's an important reservoir of moisture. The cheeses take three to four months to ripen but, three weeks after they arrive, we wrap them in a stout, slightly porous tinfoil to slow down their evolution and prevent surface mould.' He looks along the shelves, as if searching for an example, but none of the new season's production has reached this stage.

'How do you know when the mould is properly developed?' I ask.

'Continuous testing,' is the answer and, using a probe, he bores deep into the heart of one of the drums, extracting a narrow 'pipe' of cheese, for checking by sight and smell; then he replaces it perfectly, so that no one need ever know. Only in cases of doubt is anything actually tasted.

'Do you get many visitors?' I ask, as we climb the four flights of stairs again. (There is a lift for the cheeses but people are not so pampered.)

'Not many,' he answers, almost regretfully. He seems to enjoy the role of guide. 'Our caves are too small. The warmth of all the bodies would raise the temperature too much.'

Three women on the ground floor are busy wrapping a last few cheeses before their lunch break. Removing the heavy-duty foil for recycling, they substitute a finer one for sale; but first they cut the cheeses in half. Not all producers do this, M. Migairou explains, but it helps identify which will best match, for instance, Madame Betty's requirements. Then the cheeses will be moved to a cold store in another building. 'Still within the Roquefort commune,' he emphasizes. 'It gives us an all-year-round supply.'

'I do hope Robert's looked after you,' says Jacques Carles, appearing solicitously in the doorway. 'And I'm sorry that my daughter Delphine can't accompany you to the dairy. I'd come myself but I've an afternoon meeting at home, in Saint Affrique. Young Frank will take care of you, though.'

As if to make amends, he asks what I am doing for lunch. He then explains that his wife is away and I sense that this is partly a case of not wanting to eat alone.

In one of Saint Affrique's brasseries, he explains how his father François, a local *avocat*, bought the business in 1928. He himself joined in 1958, having also trained as a lawyer but finding himself a bit 'shaken', he admits, after two years' military service in Algeria. His father handed over to him in 1975, much as he is gradually handing over to Delphine.

I ask him what distinguishes their 'artisanal' production from the mostly 'industrial' competition and his answer takes all of two courses.

The milk comes mainly from small farms with especially careful milking practices; they use small, thousand-litre curdling *cuves* (I'll see them later) for closer monitoring; they dice, stir and mould the curd by hand (more of all that later too); they use traditional tin moulds for better heat exchange, whereas most use plastic; they alone grow their own *Penicillium Roqueforti* in the caves, using special bread baked by the village baker in September, when the wild mushrooms start appearing; and they are almost the only producers to add the *Penicillium* in powder form, at the moulding stage – most introduce it (less labour-intensively) in liquid form, at the curdling stage.

'Papillon say they use powder,' says M. Carles dismissively. 'But it's only for a small part of their production, so that they can claim it in their publicity. It's like saying a pâté's half thrush and half horse, when it's made with one thrush and one horse!' he laughs but, by the end of the main course, he is more concerned about the time than pâté recipes. His meeting is due to start in five minutes and he needs the bill.

'Are you sure you won't have a dessert?' He tries to flag down a waitress. 'I wouldn't recommend the Roquefort. Always too cold. Needs to be stored in the salad box of your fridge, preferably in foil – nothing too hermetic: it has to breathe. Then you should bring it up to room temperature before the meal, like a good red wine. You know what Brillat-Savarin used to say?' He waves the bill and a banknote in the air. 'A meal without Roquefort is like a beauty with only one eye. And Casanova?' He gets up to go to the cash desk and I follow him. 'Said it was an aphrodisiac!' Then more seriously, as he waits for his change: 'We've got a big problem this year. We'd been building this chap up for ten years to head the dairy.'

'And he's left?' I ask on the pavement outside.

'He died of brain cancer.'

'Recently?' is all I can think of to say.

'We buried him the day before yesterday,' says M. Carles, adding further apologies for waving me off on my own.

In the forty kilometres between lunch and the unprepossessing concrete dairy, there is not a single sheep to be seen. 'They spend the winter months inside,' explains 'young Frank', in regulation white wellies, coat and hairnet. 'You won't see them in the fields till late March or early April.'

'Because of the cold?'

'And the risk of infection. They're quite delicate, this Lacaune breed. They never stay out at night, not even in summer. But inside or out, it's the same diet of grass.'

While I wriggle into another set of unbecoming hygienic over-garments, Frank explains that, for the first time in all his twelve years, production has been suspended over the last two days. 'For a reason having nothing to do with the quality of the milk or anything,' he emphasizes. 'A purely personal reason . . .'

'Because of the man who died?' I ask respectfully.

He nods, escorting me to the reception bay, where every morning (except the last two) the milk arrives in milk churns.

'Most producers use tankers, but they shake the milk up, damaging the fat globules. Churns also let us trace the consignments back to particular farmers,' he adds, as we enter a small laboratory. 'You see, they're all subjected to tests on arrival – stricter than the AOC rules require, in fact.'

'How much milk does it take? To make, say, a kilo of Roquefort?'

'Four and a half litres. A good ewe produces two hundred litres in a six- or seven-month season.'

'It doesn't sound very much,' I venture, remembering Rens's three litres per goat per day.

'Cows produce thirty times as much,' Frank agrees.

'And you start by cooling the milk?' I ask, recalling more from my Pélardon lesson.

'No, we heat it. To 33°. Then we add the rennet and leave it for a couple of hours to curdle.' He slides back a door, revealing four stainless steel tanks, like outsized sarcophagi, each filled with off-white curd. Standing silently beside the tanks are four burly, white-coated, white-wellied, white-hairnetted rugby-playing hulks, holding square metal 'paddles' strung with cross-wires, like wide-mesh tennis rackets. They nod politely; then, with a resounding clatter, they start thrashing away at the curd as if their lives depended on it, until – as abruptly as it began – the commotion ceases and Frank is able to explain.

Earlier, at the end of the two-hour curdling period, the rugby-players cut each tankful into cubes, using special cutters (he shows me one, shaped like a cricket bat but strung with sharp metal wires) dragged lengthways and widthways through the curd. At regular intervals since then, over another two hours, the hulks have been stirring the resulting dice, to separate the curd from the whey (a second frenzy of paddling erupts, in case I have forgotten the effect). 'Most people drain the whey off, to make it easier,' says Frank. 'But we prefer to leave it till the very last minute.'

Which is apparently now. A plug has been pulled on the nearest tank and some kind of race is on. A nimbler looking fifth rugby-player, the fly-half in this team, sprints from a back room with a trolley-load of moulds, like circular cake tins. Two of the four shovel curd cubes into moulds, as if trying to break a record. A third resumes paddling, even more vigorously than before. The fourth sprinkles powdered *Penicillium Roqueforti* into each mould from a large metal 'sugar-shaker', while the first two take a break from shovelling to mix this in by hand, before banging the moulds back on the trolley in pairs, with their open sides face to face.

The objective is to keep in step with the falling level of the whey. The curd about to be shovelled is conveniently just below the surface but the product arriving in the moulds remains thoroughly drenched. It takes only fifteen minutes to empty the first tank, during which time the fly-half shuttles several laden trolleys off to the adjoining 'draining room'. The whey is already fast escaping through finely pierced holes in the moulds, which he frantically offloads on to one of several long metal tables – refectory-like except for their raised edges, channelling the whey away from the floor.

'Normally two-thirds of these tables would be filled with the previous day's production,' says Frank, his thoughts returning to the bereavement that has broken their usually unbreakable routine. Then he collects himself, explaining how the cheeses sit there for three days being tipped from mould to mould, as they drain and compact. On the third day, they are moved to a refrigerated room. On the fourth, they are salted – on the sides by rolling them in a pile of sea salt, and on the tops by dusting them with a precisely measured scoop. Then, three days later, the bottoms receive similar treatment and they are ready for the journey down to Roquefort.

'Every three or four days,' I confirm, remembering M. Migairou's part of the cycle.

'Exactly,' says Frank, as we return to find the second tank nearly empty.

'But only for a six- or seven-month season.'

'Exactly,' says Frank, this time with a smile.

'So, what do you do during the rest of the year?' I ask, imagining some complimentary 'off season' activity, while the lambs are gestating.

'Nothing,' says Frank with a bigger smile, which – given the energy expended here in the last three-quarters of an hour – strikes me as entirely reasonable.

*

At first I thought it was snow on the trees. Then I saw that it was almond blossom, the first early herald of spring. The second was a telephone call from Rens: the new season's cheeses had hit the eleven-day mark and she had set some aside for me. Then, driving to Pégairolles, there is a real flurry of snow, reminding me that it is still winter.

Rens, however, is in high spirits. Seventy kids were born at the *bergerie* between 3 and 10 February. She needs only ten this year for renewing the herd and most have been sent away to be fattened up for Easter meat sales. The winter 'rest' is over, the ten-month treadmill of cheese production has started and Rens could not sound happier with life.

Unlike Laurent. 'We've no reservations but come over anyway,' he said this morning. I think we both felt that there was a lot of catching up to do, after the January *fermeture annuelle*.

The three of them were not long back from a few days in Brittany, where it rained all the time; and, hunched over his paperwork, he looks less than refreshed by the experience. 'Leah caught chickenpox,' he says, in further explanation of the holiday's qualified success.

'You had it as a child, I hope?' says Laurence, with a conspicuously spotty Leah at her side. 'They say it's always worse for adults.'

'I'm sure I did,' I reassure her, then almost immediately feel myself itching.

'Laurence had it but I'm not sure,' confesses Laurent 'It's not on my health records and my mother can't remember.'

'You'd better have had it,' says Laurence. 'We've enough problems, without the chef going sick.'

The departure of Georges, as anticipated, at New Year has made Laurent indispensable. Joris is working this week, because it happens to be half-term, and he can also cover the weekends; but he is still an apprentice. And except for him, Laurent is on his own.

'I've been advertising for a new *sous-chef* for three weeks without a single reply,' he tells me. 'And yet I know for a fact that there are five unemployed cooks on the dole in Lodève alone. They pay you so well for doing nothing in this country, help with the rent and everything . . . it's scarcely worth the cost of the petrol to go to work. Last year, I had a school-leaver here. This was before Joris. You never met him. He didn't stay long enough. After a week, he decided it was too much; said he now understood why his father spent most of his life on the dole. At least this one's not afraid of hard work,' he says, with an appreciative pat on Joris's shoulder.

Joris, as usual, says nothing. He is, however, looking more confident – perhaps because he has just turned seventeen (with a smart new uniform apparently one of his birthday presents) or perhaps because the chef can no longer afford not to be nice to him.

Georges is not the only missing face. Tired of the long commute from Lamalou-les-Bains, Eric the First has decided to hang up his tea towel. 'Just when he was starting to contribute to the cooking,' says Laurent sadly. Sadder still, the replacement is not even called Eric. Lodève's pool of unemployed *plongeurs* must be more restricted. Laurent has, however, found the next best thing: a Fréd-Eric.

To judge by the percentage of Frédéric's output sent back to him for supplementary scrubbing, his notions of purity must owe much to the school of Eric the Second; as does his innocent, giggly enthusiasm in the face of continuous criticism. His home in the hills at Saint Maurice de Navacelles – almost as remote as Eric the First's, but in the opposite direction – is the butt of constant teasing: 'This may pass for clean among your thirty fellow villagers . . .'

Laurent encourages me to stay for lunch, even though there are still no customers expected. He tells me he has had to cancel his evenings with the winemakers. He can no longer manage the projected numbers on his skeleton staff. He is also deferring indefinitely the improvements that he planned to make to the restaurant.

There is a large outdoor terrace at one end of the glazed veranda. In summer, I can imagine it was the most sought-after section of the campsite canteen but it has never been suitable for

Laurent's more formal style of service and hence never used. He intended, he explains, to extend the veranda on to this during the January closure. It would have enabled him to accommodate all of his thirty to forty covers in the 'room with the view', freeing the larger space behind for a shop and a *salon* for pre- and post-dinner drinks.

'It's too big an investment,' he says. 'Last year was disastrous and this one won't be much better. Not till they finish the road.'

'Isn't it due to open next year? Surely that'll make all the difference, having one of the motorway exits just a couple of kilometres away.'

'That's what I keep telling myself, but it'll take me a while to get back to where I was. I can't see myself affording the extension for a couple of years now.'

'Have you seen the new guides?' asks Laurence, changing the subject. Both the Michelin and the Gault Millau have just been published.

'Not much change in the Languedoc,' says Laurent, though he then admits modestly that the Michelin has awarded him a 'bunch of grapes' to indicate an exceptional wine list.

'And the Gault Millau?' I ask, wondering whether he has improved on his previous mark out of twenty.

'Still thirteen,' he says. 'And likely to stay that way for some time after the letter I wrote them last year. I was furious. All they could say about my wine list was how expensive the La Grange des Pères was. No understanding of how much it costs for a new restaurant to get hold of mature vintages. No recognition of the effort I'd made to create a serious Languedoc list in a short time. Well, I've taken down their plaque outside. I'm not giving them publicity.'

'But you'd still like a Michelin star?'

'It's not what motivates me, especially after Bernard Loiseau. You heard about him? The three-star chef in Burgundy, who committed suicide when he dropped to two? I think that made everybody reconsider. I know the stars bring thirty to fifty per cent of the business to the restaurants that have them, but

I'm much more motivated by the client who says he'll come again.'

'Or come at all,' says Laurence glumly, hugging her thick sweater closer.

For the first time that I can remember, the kitchen is cold. This is hardly surprising, given the early morning snow and the limited culinary activity, but it does nothing for morale. With the clock showing nearly one, there is little chance of any *clients de passage* and little incentive for Laurence to change into anything smarter but cooler. She reaches instead for a scruffy winter coat to take out the rubbish.

'Did I tell you about the Truffle Gala I did in Clermont l'Hérault in January?' asks Laurent. 'Two hundred and fifty covers. Four chefs – Jacques Pourcel from the Jardin, Eric Cellier from the Maison de la Lozère and Jean-Claude Fabre from Le Cap d'Agde – each of us serving a quarter of the tables in rotation. We did two courses each, all featuring truffles.'

'I thought there weren't any this year.'

'They came from Provence. Incredibly expensive, apparently. Even the desserts used truffles. Would you believe, Eric Cellier came up with a combination using blood-orange jelly and pineapple *confit*? Served with Virgile's Cartagène.'

'How did you manage sixty-odd covers on your own?'

'I borrowed from the others. They're all friends. I did a truffle minestrone, with brown vermicelli and crayfish . . .'

Before he can elaborate, Laurence rushes back inside from the bins. She closes the door behind her, leaning hard against it like a fugitive barring the path of a pursuer. 'Customers,' she announces breathlessly, looking anxiously towards the dining-room to see whether they have yet reached the entrance.

Laurent is halfway to the swing doors to greet them when he remembers something. He takes down a shoebox from the top of a cupboard and unpacks a new pair of brilliant white clogs that he quickly exchanges for the scuffed and spattered ones that he was wearing. And with that he is ready for business as usual.

*

For a week, it had really felt like spring. The almonds were flowering in earnest and the buds on the young mimosa had just started bursting. The low winter sun on the windows had finally shamed me into giving them a first ever clean and I had lunched in the courtyard every day, breakfasting nearly as often on the balcony terrace outside my bedroom. The potager even looked dry enough to activate the watering system but I had drained the pump in the autumn, to protect it from winter frosts, and (as Arnaud said, when resisting any premature resumption of activity on the wall) there could still be freezing nights to come.

I telephoned Claudette, hoping to accompany her on one of the early transhumances that she was planning for the second half of February, but I was already too late. The fine weather had encouraged her to start the season sooner than expected. 'I should have phoned you,' she apologized. 'But we've been so tied up, trying to make the house fit to live in.'

Then yesterday we received what felt like a whole month's rain in twenty-four hours. Hitherto unsuspected leaks appeared in the kitchen ceiling at the point where it runs beneath the breakfast balcony. By the afternoon, despite my efforts with a mop, the kitchen was flooded to a depth of more than a centimetre. Meanwhile, the wind sounded like a motor starting up outside the rattling back door. When I went outside to assess the damage to the almond blossom, I found several metres of terrace-retaining wall collapsed.

'Five hundred Euros a cubic metre to rebuild a wall like that,' said Manu, crossing the bridge to offer his condolences. 'But there's this cousin of the wife's, down in Saint Etienne. I could maybe persuade him to do it for four. A snip, compared to your electrician friend, who won't even finish in your lifetime!'

This morning I woke to find both rain and wind abated but the balcony terrace covered in a layer of curious reddish brown dust. At first, I thought it must have washed down from the field behind; then I realized it was the wrong colour. And anyway the front courtyard had turned the same reddish brown, as had the swimming pool and, most distressingly of all, the newly cleaned windows. It was as if someone had flown overhead, emptying sacks of coloured powder on to the house. But who would want to do such a thing?

Brushing the dust from the windscreen, I drove off to the market to find most of the vehicles in Lodève in the same condition. I was no less mystified, if anything more so: the quantities of unidentified powder dropped on our locality must have been prodigious. But I was relieved that I have not been singled out.

'Haven't seen this for years,' says Manu, appearing behind me with Mme Gros. 'It's sand from the Sahara. Imagine the wind it takes to manage that.'

'Imagine the damage to the almonds,' says Mme Gros severely, as if it were my fault.

'Better start saving,' laughs Manu. 'You'll be buying them in this year.'

'Talking of economies,' says Mme Gros, brisk and business-like. 'Did you decide about my cousin and the wall? The offer won't be on the table for ever.'

*

It is rare indeed for the village of Saint Guilhem-le-Désert to live up to its name. France's picturesque medieval gems seldom come 'deserted'. On a February Tuesday, however, there is even a choice of parking in front of the Viallas' cousin's workshop.

A man who looks more like their uncle calls from a third-storey window: 'You found us all right then?' Clearly anyone visiting the village this morning has to be me.

Upstairs, Léon Fonzes introduces me to the boss of the so-called Conserverie Occitane: his daughter, Geneviève Fonzes-Armand. (The husband and source of the hyphenation, Monsieur Armand, works somewhere down the corridor, in the *conserverie*'s laboratory.) Behind her big office desk, Geneviève looks as tough and business-like as her father seems gentle and dilettante. I cannot imagine a truffle-hunter getting more than the going rate out of her. When there is anything to sell, that is.

'The worst year we can remember,' father and daughter both agree.

'Normally we handle three to five tonnes a year,' explains Léon. 'But this year, we're merely using what's left of last year's stock.'

'For making the oil?'

'For preserving mainly. The oil's a bit of a sideline. In normal years, we also sell fresh truffles, from December through to March. That's wholesale,' he adds, in case I was thinking of coming shopping next year. 'But another season like this and we'll have no business of any kind.' He points to a sepia-tinted photograph of early-twentieth-century truffle-hunting on the wall. 'You just wouldn't believe how abundant the Hérault truffles used to be when my grandfather founded this company in 1912. He ran the *auberge* down the road there, which specialized in truffle dishes. I mean, can you imagine a simple village restaurant *specializing* in truffles today? And still needing a subsidiary business to preserve the surplus?'

Geneviève explains that they mostly buy directly, from sixty to eighty peasant truffle-hunters within the *département*, but sometimes they buy from markets further afield. The 'producer' prices this season range from 600 to 800 Euros per kilo, resulting in a wholesale rate between 1000 and 1100 Euros. She doesn't even know the retail price but it hardly bears thinking about.

'How much would I need per person?' I ask, knowing truffles to be light but unable to relate to these astronomical sums per kilogram.

'A minimum of ten grams per person,' says Geneviève, convincing me that I had better content myself with truffle oil, until the price comes down or my own little trio of truffle-impregnated saplings bears 'fruit', which Léon tells me will take at least ten years, with only a twenty per cent chance of success.

The adjacent two-hundred-square-metre workshop looks

forlornly inactive. Monsieur Armand has found some test or other to occupy his time in the laboratory section, but elsewhere there is a sense of equipment lying idle until next year.

Léon explains that the preserving process is largely a matter of sterilization. After brushing and washing, the truffles are packed into three-litre glass *bocaux* – outsized versions of the same wide-necked bottles, with rubber washers and metal clamps ensuring air-tight seals, which I use for preserving fruit in *eau de vie*. Then the bottles and their precious contents are 'cooked' in carefully temperature-controlled water to eliminate bacteria, after which they are simply left until the time comes for packaging the truffles individually in jars and tins, at which point they undergo a further sterilization. But this morning, very few untouched *bocaux* remain.

'Will the wet winter help for next year?' I ask.

'We can only hope so,' they answer sombrely. 'Otherwise the Hérault truffle is a thing of the past.'

*

Every two years, the Exhibition Park on the outskirts of Montpellier devotes its ten massive, aircraft-hangar-like pavilions to the wines of the south of France. For three consecutive days, one thousand, three hundred exhibitors – mainly from the Languedoc – come to Vinisud to show off their current vintages. It is a 'trade' event, targeted exclusively at wine merchants and restaurateurs, but exceptionally Virgile has secured me an invitation.

In fact, he has secured me two.

I told him how bitter Manu had been of late. When I first returned, he persuaded himself that it was only a matter of time, just a phase that I was going through. I naturally needed a moment to settle back into old routines and, wide though the Languedoc wine map was, our two-man campaign to colour it in could wait for a week or two. But then, as the months went by, each day not dedicated to wine-sampling bred increasing rancour. 'Plenty of time for cookery classes,' he muttered resentfully. 'Never too tired to go cheese-tasting.'

I was hoping the Wine Fair would help to make up for three lost seasons. However, I hadn't allowed for the possibility that Manu might, quite literally, try to squeeze all of those months of missed entertainment into seventy-two hours.

Of course, I should never have let him go alone on the first day. The trouble was that my water pump – the one that circulates the house water – had chosen the weekend to give up, after twenty years of struggle; and, Vinisud or no Vinisud, I simply couldn't face another chilly morning's ablutions in the fountain. I had to go and see a man about a new one. Thus, on Monday morning, we set off together (crucial to Manu's leave of absence) but in separate cars.

I never in fact saw his return, although I suspected that his coverage of the Parc des Expositions might have been over-zealous when I discovered that his exeat for Tuesday had been summarily withdrawn. It is only today, however, when we present ourselves at the ticket barrier for day three, that I learn that he was actually asked to leave on Monday.

'I'll use the spittoons,' Manu promises unconvincingly, when I have at last talked our way in, but the crowd in the foyer is so dense that he quickly gives me the slip, and I decide to seek out Virgile while I can do so alone.

Despite the vastness of the exhibition spaces, finding Virgile is remarkably easy. He and four other growers with whom he has banded together have secured what is arguably the best stand in the complex: immediately facing the entrance to the first hall.

'How ever did you get this?' I ask.

'Ask my mother,' he answers with a grin, as Mme Joly emerges from the back of the striking 'set' that, it seems, she designed for them.

'You must know someone very important,' I tell her.

'I'm just a good negotiator,' she laughs, with a shake of her youthful long red hair. 'I kept saying no, until they gave me what I wanted.'

I am reminded of the family motto, informing so much of Virgile's own achievements: *Si tu veux, tu peux*. If you want, you can.

Each of the five *vignerons* has a small café-style table with a couple of chairs, at which prospective customers can sit and taste, but for the moment Virgile's is unoccupied. We taste the finished Grenache Blanc, while he tells me about his latest problem: a Parisian lawyer's letter, written on behalf of the Virgin group of companies, demanding that he take his distinctive signature off his labels, corks and wine cases, insisting indeed that he cease to market his wines under the 'Virgile' name at all.

'They're saying it looks too much like "Virgin",' he explains.

'But it's your own name, your own signature . . .'

'It is quite similar to their logo,' he concedes.

'But surely no one could confuse a bottle of wine with an aeroplane?' I laugh, still unable to take the case seriously.

'There's a Virgin Cola. They do sell drinks, you see.'

'So what did you do?'

'Wrote back demanding that they withdraw their Cola from the market at once,' he chuckles. 'No, seriously. My *avocat*'s very good. The Parisians kept sending through compromise agreements and we kept crossing everything out. It really looked as if we were going to end up in court. Last Monday, it would have been. Then finally, at about six o'clock on the Friday before, they did a deal. They're letting me keep the signature on the Appellation Controllée, and I've agreed to take it off the Vins de Pays. Look, here's the new logo that we've designed.' He produces a bottle of red sporting the new image and pours me some.

'I'm worried that I haven't started my pruning,' I tell him.

'You've only got forty vines.'

'I know but I'm not as quick as you. I remember you said I could start at any time after the leaves had fallen in the first frosts.'

'Yes, and finish by the end of March, when the buds have formed. There's plenty of time still.'

'It takes me a long time to decide where to cut.'

'Would you like me to come up and give you a refresher course?'

I should like nothing more but, before we can fix a date, a familiar Montpellier wine-bar owner pauses tentatively beside Virgile's table and I get up to leave. With legal fees to pay, he needs the sales more than ever.

I catch a brief glimpse of Manu, homing in on some defence-less winemaker near the far side of the pavilion, and hope I was mistaken in what I saw. Could his gait really be so unsteady already? I have hardly ever seen him the worse for wear, but he is swallowed up in the crowd before I can be certain.

I feel a tap on my shoulder. It is Laurent, keen to introduce me to some of his favourite growers. He tells me how he has just met a chef who used to have a Michelin-starred hotel-restaurant up in Burgundy. 'Gave it all up,' says Laurent. 'Sick of the problems of finding and keeping staff. Fed up with fixing bedroom radiators in the middle of the evening service! Now it's just him and his wife and four tables in a village near Nice,' he adds enviously.

One or two of Laurent's contacts have tales to tell of a taster, fitting Manu's description, passing their way. There cannot, after all, be many invitees wearing blue dungarees. I really must find him; but how, amidst so many thousands?

It is nearly midday and I know that he favours regular mealtimes. Surely it cannot be long before he reappears to inform me which of the restaurants will be accepting my credit card – unless he is simply snacking at one of the stands serving light refreshments with their wines, which would be an equally economical solution to his hunger pangs. I say goodbye to Laurent, plunging deeper into the fray to pursue this line of enquiry. I find several Picpoul de Pinet producers drawing the crowds with Manu's much-loved oysters but no sign of the man himself. I find others offering cheeses and *saucissons*, some even producing hot dishes; but the object of my search appears to be resisting them all.

The most elaborate catering is undoubtedly that being served by Le Jardin des Sens. Together with the prestigious

Puech Haut wine estate in the Saint Drézéry subdivision of the Coteaux du Languedoc, the Pourcel twins have taken a stand that must be only fractionally smaller than a tennis court. On it, they are regaling favoured contacts with what looks like pasta with truffles, except that it clearly cannot be pasta with truffles, because the quantity served would have to be described as truffles with pasta, which is surely unthinkable. Yet a discreet enquiry reveals that, yes, it *is* pasta with truffles. No wonder there is a shortage throughout the *département*: they have all been requisitioned by the Jardin.

Just as I am wondering whether Laurent's goodwill might extend to an introduction, I hear a commotion from the adjoining pavilion. A minor scuffle, it sounds like, with a voice or two raised in protest; but then something worse, something that I really do not want to acknowledge. I have, however, heard it before, on the rare occasions when Mme Gros has allowed her usually tight rein to loosen and it tells me that I shall be leaving early, without my pasta.

It is the sound of Manu singing the Marseillaise.

*

It is bitterly cold again but the landscape sends a more encouraging message.

The apricots and plums have already flowered; the cherry blossom is at its most blowzy and the terraces near the house are bright with yellow forsythia and white deutzia. Even the oaks have at last shed their crackly brown leaves from last year and are putting out their infant silver-grey greenery to match the all-season colours of the olive trees.

This time, surely, the landscape tells me, spring cannot be far away; and as if to confirm it, the telephone rings.

'*C'est Arnaud*,' an almost forgotten voice informs me. '*Je recommence demain.*'

*

There is no sign of anyone in the kitchen but Laurence is in the middle room, mopping the floor.

'Medium,' she answers to my '*Comment ça va?*' and points to the mop. 'The sink's blocked. Without it, we can't run the washing-machine for the glasses or even the ice-maker. The plumber said he was coming an hour ago. We've only one couple reserved, but they could be here in an hour and a half.'

The telephone interrupts her. She now has two couples booked for twelve and no plumber. It rings again: a third couple hoping for clean glasses and ice at one o'clock. In each case, Laurence carefully talks them through the tortuous motorway access route, all the time praying not to hear the words, 'Oh well, if it's that complicated, we'll eat in Montpellier.'

'And Laurent?' I ask, feeling awkwardly superfluous without him to put me to work.

'Putting up signs with Frédéric, to help people find their way. Nearly 500 Euros they cost us.'

A third telephone call: this time three at twelve-thirty, and again the directions. Laurence immediately dials her husband's mobile, telling him the signs will have to wait. He needs to do some food preparation.

'There's water everywhere in this place,' sighs Laurence, returning to the mopping. 'With all this rain, we've had leaks in the basement as well.'

'In the flat?' I ask, with a sense of fellow feeling after the drips in my kitchen.

'In the bedroom. In the bed, in fact. *C'est pas idéal* . . . Were we expecting you?' she adds, disconcertingly.

'Sorry, I spoke to Laurent at the weekend . . .'

'Don't worry, there's a lot of things the chef forgets to tell me,' she says good-humouredly, but without making me feel any less surplus to requirements. So, when Laurent returns with Frédéric, I am doing my best to look interested in the local newspaper.

'Two out of four done,' he tells Laurence. 'Practically risked our lives, fitting the one on the roundabout! Absolutely no help we've had from the Mayor in all of this,' he adds, turning to me.

'I mean, the Mairie's got all the facilities to produce this kind of sign in its workshop . . .'

'Is this the Pégairolles Mayor?' I ask, remembering the support and encouragement given to Rens.

'No, Pégairolles have been great. They've put up a sign, directing people from their end, without us even asking. But for some reason, we fall under your Mayor and – did I say that my stepfather's the Mayor of Lodève? – well, the two of them belong to opposing parties. Need I say more? I told you: you have to be *malade* to want to run a business in France!'

Laurence silently points to the clock. *Malade* or otherwise, there is less than an hour and a half, including lunchtime, before the first of the eleven covers are due. Laurent starts reviewing the contents of the fridge. It is Thursday morning, the start of the winter working week.

'I thought, having only the booking for two, I'd do the signs, instead of going to Métro,' he explains, sniffing a partly used pineapple. He is likely to need more than this for the duck 'kebabs' on the winter *menu-carte*. 'Hey, Frédéric!' he calls, taking a note from his wallet. 'I need you to go shopping.'

Then as soon as the *plongeur* has been dispatched to Lodève, he realizes that he is also desperately short of rocket. The box in the bottom of the fridge is brimming over but most of the supply has wilted over the days when they were closed. I offer to drive into town after Frédéric, but Laurent prefers another solution: a *tri sélectif* that will take me most of the morning, salvaging less than one leaf in ten.

'You know they've closed the Larzac road?' Laurent continues to chat, as unflappable as ever, while cutting some duck breasts into cubes. 'Not the motorway, but the old road, up past Saint Etienne?'

I had seen the *Route Barrée* signs, thinking what a stupid time it was to dig up the minor road when we still had the motorway chaos, but I had yet to learn the explanation.

'A landslide,' says Laurent. 'Last Saturday. Caused by all the rain we've had. A woman was coming down for the Lodève market when a two- or three-tonne boulder landed on her bonnet. Then another on her boot, leaving her trapped in the middle.'

'Was she hurt?' I asked, startled. The news certainly puts my fallen terrace walls into perspective.

'Nothing worse than a broken leg, amazingly. They've shifted the car but the road's still closed. Poor Frédéric has to make a fifty-kilometre detour to get here and it'll stay like that for months. It's the responsibility of the village where it happened to make it safe but they haven't got the money. I told you this was a crazy country.'

The only good news this morning is the arrival of Monsieur Marnas, the plumber. He has yet to find a solution (the news is not *that* good) but at least he is on the case, covering most of the middle room floor with tools. The table that Laurence needs to lay for lunch has been pushed to one side, blocking access to the *plonge*. Nothing can now be washed until the plumber has finished but, with Frédéric still not back from the grocer's, it hardly matters.

Laurent works away methodically, refusing to be ruffled, and with half a box of rocket still to go, there is little that I can do to help.

'Still no replacement for Georges?' I ask, knowing the answer.

'Two months and not one applicant,' he confirms. 'That's when you know things can't get any worse,' he laughs. 'When it's harder to find a *sous-chef* than a plumber.'

'And Joris still at college?'

'Except for weekends and holidays. I'd offer him a permanent job like a shot. It's so rare to find anyone with his willingness to work. You know, I had another schoolboy last Saturday, only fourteen, brought along by his mother for work experience. At five to twelve, just after we'd eaten and just before the first table arrived, he threw up. All over this glass door here! We had to phone his mother to take him away.'

'Maybe not the right career choice,' I chuckle, as Frédéric

returns with some moderately bad news of his own: the small and tired-looking pineapple that he places on the worktop – the best he could find – cost all of 7 Euros 60. And Laurent only gave him five, he feels obliged to mention.

The plumber is still flat on his back beneath the sink as we squeeze our four chairs around the table. Indeed, he is still poking probes down the drainpipe when Laurence has to pick her way through the clutter to welcome the first of the twelve o'clock arrivals. M. Marnas may not have fixed the sink yet, but he must surely be the first *plombier français* to work through lunch.

'Any luck with the Jardin?' asks Laurent, still unhurriedly relaxed, as he shows me how to impale alternate chunks of duck and pineapple on wooden skewers.

'I keep getting Jacques Pourcel's answerphone,' I tell him. 'I tried several times and then finally plucked up courage to leave a message yesterday.'

'Don't worry, I'm sure he'll ring you. I told him to expect your call. He's a good friend,' Laurent chats on. 'But I hope you do get to see his kitchen. Then you'll understand what a culture shock it was, coming here,' he laughs, calmly trimming some fillets of sea perch for the fish course on the *menu-carte*.

'The first couple's in a hurry to order,' Laurence interrupts, half tripping over the recumbent M. Marnas, as she exits with glasses of Ricard for the second.

'A lobster risotto and a veal à la carte,' says Laurent, returning with the order. 'The lobster takes ages,' he tells me, still unruffled, as he rummages in the fridge. 'And yes, I thought so,' he says, closing the door. 'We've used all the potato gnocchi to go with the veal. Over to you,' he chuckles, passing some dirty-skinned potatoes and a knife.

'You're starting from scratch?' queries Laurence, dismayed, having managed a kind of long-jump over the plumber's prostrate form to deliver the second order, which she has taken herself for speed. 'And you haven't even started on the *amuses*.'

Laurent starts instead on thawing the snails that he needs for the second order, while I put the rapidly peeled potatoes on to boil.

'That reminds me,' I venture, as soon as Laurence has returned to the dining-room.

'The snails?' Laurent queries. He has been promising to introduce me to the man who supplies him with the so-called *petit gris* that have featured in several of his dishes since I started here. Laurent has yet to visit the Boisseron snail farm himself and keeps saying he would like to come with me. 'The guy says it's a complete mess,' he laughs. 'A *bordel* that he doesn't want either of us to see.'

'It's the *bordel* I was looking forward to!'

'I'll keep trying,' he promises, ladling four of his two-tier *amuses* into glasses, just before Laurence can ask for the third time. Then, with amazing speed, he purées the potatoes in a blender with some flour and seasoning, rolls the resulting product into sausage-like lengths and cuts each of these into two-centimetre pieces – all the while progressing a lobster risotto and two snail dishes.

'Now for the fiddly bit,' he says, handing me a fork. He shows me how to roll each gnocchi piece down the back of the fork, creating concertina-like ridges all around them, to make them crispen attractively under the grill, with a scattering of parmesan. 'You're squashing the side where you started,' he corrects me, as I make my first attempt.

It takes two or three rejects before I achieve a passable result.

'*Impeccable*,' says Laurence, checking anxiously on progress. 'Now can you do them ten times as fast?'

She sprints back into the dining-room to welcome the one o'clock party, leaving Laurent to receive the news that M. Marnas has been only half successful. It needs a joint that he doesn't have on the van. We can use the glass washer and the ice machine, but only if we empty the bucket under the sink every ten minutes or so. He'll sort it out properly before the evening service.

Laurence then rushes back to help Laurent serve the snails, to help me corrugate the gnocchi . . . anything to get some food into the restaurant before the customers lose patience. 'No, I'll take the order for the three,' she insists, hurrying away again.

A few minutes later, she returns with news that she hardly dares to break.

'*Et alors?*' says Laurent.

'*Trois Dégustations,*' sighs Laurence, looking almost tearfully at her watch.

Spring

'We start at the end of the frosts,' says Rock Vialla, picking up a large pair of secateurs and a pruning saw.

'When do you finish?' I ask, as we set off into his olive grove.

'We never finish,' he says with a grin. 'We stop when we run out of time, but we never finish. We try to make sure that the trees that miss out this spring are given priority next year.'

This makes me feel a little better. Except that mine have been missing out for several years.

We pass a young helper already at work on one of the trees, wearing just a T-shirt and shorts in honour of the sunshine.

'We only prune in fine weather,' says Rock, as I shed my unwanted coat.

'Is it harmful to prune in the rain?' I ask.

'No. Just unpleasant,' he laughs. 'We find something to do indoors.'

'And it's just the three of you?' I ask, meaning Rock, the youth in shorts and the absent Pierre.

'Yes, Pierre's over behind the mill, mincing up the cuttings to rot down as fertilizer. It supplements the animal dung. But you wanted to see how it's done, the pruning?'

'I've never done much more than cut off the dead wood from mine.'

'That's a start.' He makes some decisive cuts on the nearest tree. 'The most important thing is to let the light in. Olives need sunshine. You want to create a space in there, in the middle, that you could open an umbrella in. You also want to thin all these dense areas. And here, where you've got two branches doing the same thing, competing for the same space, choose the stronger. Like to have a go?'

He passes the secateurs to me. At first they seem clumsy – the handles as long as my arm, the blades as long as my fingers – but I soon get the hang of them. Or think I do.

'You could afford to be more radical,' he prompts.

I must seem pathetically tentative, thinking long and hard before even the most cautious cut, worrying that every severed twig represents a mouthful of olives. 'It's just that you can't put it back again,' I apologize, reluctant to decimate their profits.

'Never worry about cutting too much,' Rock reassures me. 'The other objective, of course, is a practical one, to stop them getting too tall. This branch, for instance, you'd never be able to pick it, even with a ladder, so off it comes.' He saws the branch back to the trunk.

'You'll stop before the flowering?' I ask as Rock snips away at smaller branches.

'Yes and no. Depending on the success of the flowering, we sometimes do a second pruning *en vert*. It helps to maximize the size of the olives.'

'I'd better get back and make a start, while I can still remember,' I tell him gratefully.

'There's rain forecast for this afternoon,' he warns.

'The story of my life,' I laugh, already resigned to the wet afternoon that the professionals will doubtless avoid.

*

'Good news!' announced Laurent. 'The snail man's said "yes". But do you mind going on your own? I'm a bit stretched. He says you can visit any time after Easter. He's tidied up,' he added disappointingly.

'I don't suppose I could come on the Wednesday before,' I appealed, when I telephoned the snail farm. 'I have to pick a friend up from Nîmes that afternoon.'

'*C'est pas évident*,' Benoît Liétar hesitated. 'There's no school on

Wednesdays. I'll have the children. But no, it's fine,' he decided. Maybe he thought the tidy-up would only last that long.

'You're sure?' I pressed, wondering whether it might, after all, be more entertaining when the *bordel* reinstated itself.

'We'll manage,' he insisted. 'Come at ten-thirty.'

I need not have worried. As soon as I see Benoît's unshaven stubble, I know that this is not a man who has had time to be house-proud: he has three-year-old twins. Vincent in yellow is curly-haired and mischievous-looking; Arthur in red is straight-haired and comparatively serious; but both constitute identical distractions from snail-breeding.

'My wife works regular hours so it's me who's in charge of the monsters,' he says, leading me over to an outdoor dining-table, half-hidden behind some overgrown greenery.

'When's he going?' asks Vincent, before I have even sat down to drink the proffered cup of coffee.

'Aren't we going to play?' asks Arthur, sounding potentially tearful.

'We're going to show the gentleman the snails and then we'll play,' says Benoît, buttering each of them a slice of bread to buy time.

'So, what attracted you to snails? I ask him.

'I have some friends who do this at Digne . . .' He is sidetracked by Vincent's arrival with three large ice-cream tubs. 'I'd finished my masters in geology in '86 . . .' Containers of pear and apricot join the apple, passion fruit and vanilla already on the table. 'At first, I worked on some ordinary farms . . .' With the arrival of melon, strawberry and chocolate, Benoît takes the hint, giving sundae-making precedence. 'I finally started the snail business in '94,' he resumes, as soon as the twins are happily smearing their selections over their faces.

'But I was wondering, what attracted you?' I try again.

'Don't you want any ice-cream?' Vincent asks me, before his father can answer. He points hospitably to the third plastic dish, which he brought from the house. Then Arthur, less hospitably: 'Are you going soon?'

'Come,' says Benoît to me. 'I'd better start showing you how it's done. We're in here,' he calls to the twins from the nearby garage, where stacks of plastic crates fill most of the space not taken by chest freezers.

The first pile of crates holds dozens of small plastic boxes, like those used for supermarket strawberry sales but, in this case, they are half-filled with a mixture of peat and soil, on top of which are six or eight balls of snails' eggs – each of the balls a little smaller than a golf ball but made up of scores of eggs. 'These are two days old but already you can see the shell forming.' He pokes one to show me how it looks different when broken. Meanwhile the twins, just a couple of minutes behind us, commence a rampage through the equipment at the back of the garage.

'They've been laying since the middle of February,' says Benoît, moving to another stack with slightly larger plastic boxes, in which ten-day-old snails have reached the size of small peas, mostly clinging upside down to the lids of their boxes. 'That's when they're ready to leave,' he says.

For ninety per cent of the population, 'leaving' means 'sold to other farmers who don't do the breeding'; for the other ten per cent, a mere thirty million snails, it means 'migrating to the park'. And 'migrating to the park', he suggests, should be the strategy for all of us, before the 'monsters' destroy the garage as well as its contents.

He gathers up a bag of toys and slings it into the back of his van.

'What toys are in the bag?' asks Arthur pickily.

'Every kind,' Benoît assures him. 'Drums, trains . . .'

But Vincent is single-handedly loading his father's small trolley into the van: clearly his chosen toy of the morning. 'Are you coming to the park?' he then asks me, sounding pleased but also surprised, as if no one outside the family circle ever goes there.

'It's only three hundred square metres,' says Benoît, as we complete the roughly half-kilometre drive to the small patch of land that he rents. 'I was hoping to enlarge it this season, but the monsters had other ideas.' He empties the toy bag outside the back of the van. 'You be good,' he says optimistically, as Vincent pushes Arthur down a grassy bank on the trolley.

Benoît takes me to see the next phase: a low-sided wooden enclosure filled with rows of close-planted radishes, the leaves of which are to be home to the next age group of snails, now grown to the size of larger peas.

'Is that what they eat?' I ask. 'The radish leaves?'

'That and a mixture of flour and soya.'

I am surprised to see a bag of slug killer leaning against the enclosure.

'It's to kill the wild snails outside the enclosure,' he explains.

'To preserve the purity of your species?'

'No,' he laughs. 'Just to stop them eating the food that's meant for my lot.'

'Papa, *c'est cassé*,' calls Vincent. The trolley, built for snails not boisterous boys, has a broken wheel. 'Papa mend,' he suggests, rattling the handlebar.

'Papa play,' adds Arthur, banging the drum.

'Soon,' promises Benoît.

'What's to stop your own snails escaping? Are they a risk to neighbouring crops?' The low-walled enclosure would surely not impede a determined absconder.

'It's the pampering.' He grins. 'Not just the food but the water.'

'Do you have a well up here?' I ask, seeing only plastic pipes.

'There's a metered supply. You couldn't raise snails without irrigation,' he says, stepping over into the next enclosure and lifting one of scores of wide wooden boards, propped on stumpy legs, just a few centimetres off the ground. The underside is tightly packed with adult snails, roughly one year old, ready to be collected. Most are snugly withdrawn inside their shells but a few have stirred themselves to investigate this unscheduled overturning of their world. 'Normally, they'd stay there all day, till the evening watering lures them out to eat,' he explains.

'But look how many wild ones have got in.' He pulls off some smaller, paler-shelled examples and throws them outside the enclosure, before pointing out the only two varieties that are meant to be here: the *gros gris* and the noticeably smaller *petit gris*. 'Not just a matter of size,' he emphasizes. 'The shell patterns are distinctly different.'

'All destined for the deep-freeze?' I ask, as we walk towards a makeshift greenhouse, a simple polythene-covered tunnel, where the twins are noisily dismantling some semi-derelict piece of machinery at the entrance.

'You're going to hurt yourselves,' says Benoît, shooing them gently back to the more conventional playthings beside the van, by which time he has forgotten what I was asking.

'The deep-freeze?' I remind him.

'Oh, yes . . . No, I keep the best back for egg-laying,' he tells me, as we enter the tunnel, which houses a couple of dozen plastic egg-laying trays. Benoît lifts the lid of one of them to see whether there are any new balls of eggs on the familiar mixture of soil and peat. He shows me a snail pressing deep into the mix in the act of laying and a pair busy coupling; but no new balls for collection just yet. 'I need to water these,' he reminds himself. 'Humidity's what attracts them into the trays.'

'Is it lunchtime?' calls Arthur from the toy pile, while his brother bangs the drum like a dinner gong.

'Coming,' says Benoît, loading everything back in the van.

'Do you only sell to restaurants?' I ask on the short journey back.

'Not exclusively, but only substantial orders that I can deliver,' he says. 'It's just not practical to sell directly from the house. I'm usually either up at the park or out on the road.'

'And you sell the snails frozen?'

'Normally, yes. I supply Le Jardin des Sens – that's how I know Laurent. They used to insist on live snails, which meant I had to drive over really early in the morning. But thank goodness they've now settled for frozen. I'm not sure I could do that any more, with the monsters.'

'Papa play now,' say the monsters, as the van turns back into the courtyard.

'Lunch first, then play,' says their father, adding, 'would you like to join us?'

'I have to get to the airport.'

'Then you must take some samples,' he insists and disappears to the garage.

'You like eating snails?' I ask Vincent and Arthur, by way of conversation.

They look at me as if I am mad, though whether this implies a diet of no snails or nothing but snails remains unclear, as Benoît returns with a small bag of frozen snail-filled vol-au-vents, another of breaded snail kebabs and a jar of slimy-looking snail mousse, for spreading on toast, he reliably informs me.

I feel grateful to my friend flying into Nîmes. I am not sure I am ready for the full Liétar snail menu.

*

'Thirty covers,' said Laurent, as we hurtled into Lodève for the Easter Sunday bread purchase. 'It's my absolute maximum these days, without proper help. I've stopped counting the number we've had to refuse.'

'But you do have some help?' I asked, having glimpsed a couple of unfamiliar faces, before he whisked me off in the car.

'Philippe, the temp, is quite experienced. Well, you've seen, he's twenty years older than me, but he's never done my kind of cooking. He's the best I could get for the weekend but not at all what I need in the long term.'

'And the boy?'

'Marc. He's on work experience,' sighed Laurent.

'Like the one who threw up and had to go home?' I asked, already thinking I'd give the new one a wide berth.

'Better than that,' Laurent chuckled. 'He IS the one who threw up and had to go home!'

'Full marks for persistence,' I conceded, now determined to keep my distance. 'He looks about ten.'

'He's fourteen,' Laurent laughed again. 'But you'd be small

for your age, if you kept throwing up at the sight of food.'

'And no Joris?'

'He's *en salle* again, helping Laurence. Today would have been much less stressful with him in the kitchen, but we couldn't get any temps at all for the dining-room. Or at least I found two waitresses, but one of them refused to work at weekends and the other broke her foot. I felt a plaster cast clumping round the veranda might detract from the Easter gaiety.'

Shortly before Sancho's, he pulled on to the kerb, outside a *tabac*. 'This is much more vital than the bread,' he explained with a grin. 'Everyone's run out of cigarettes.'

On the way back, duly stocked with Paillasses and Gauloises, he slowed near the château, first pointed out in September: the impossible dream on the other side of the water meadow (or what remains of it after the road-builders' most recent depredations to create the exit roundabout on which so many of Laurent's hopes are pinned).

'The owner came up for dinner last week,' said Laurent. 'Enjoyed his meal and asked if I'd like to take it on.'

'You mean buy it?'

'No, rent it, of course. It needs ten million francs of expenditure . . .' I quickly did the conversion into Euros, wondering what could have put him into such a bullish frame of mind. 'It would give me eight bedrooms and two suites.'

'And the dining-room?'

'Magnificent! And even nearer the new roundabout than where we are now. I'd probably still keep Le Temps de Vivre, putting an assistant in there to cook simpler country dishes, although I'd probably close them both for much of the winter. We'll see. I'm having my first serious meeting with the owner on Friday.'

'You'll be opening on the beach, beside the Pourcels, next!' I joke, as we turn down the drive and back to Easter reality.

'Have you managed to fix something with the Jardin?' he asks, unloading the car.

'The day after tomorrow.'

'I told you Jacques would ring.'

'He didn't,' I chuckle. 'It was his press attaché.'

'You see, I told you it was a different world!'

'She's offered me a room.'

'Then take it!' he laughs. 'They never offer me one!'

As before, lunch is ready on our return. Philippe, the temp, has done his best but the cauliflower cheese with our slices of lamb is not a dish to which Georges would have put his name. He will need plenty of Laurent's supervision today.

It is one of the quietest lunches that I have known at this table. Philippe is quiet from diffidence, Joris from habit, Laurence from nervous tension and Marc from fear of further gastric disturbances, leaving mainly Laurent's running gag about Frédéric's life beyond civilization, up in thirty-resident Saint Maurice de Navacelles.

The telephone rings twice between eleven-thirty and noon: two parties that have waited till now to formulate the idea of going out to Easter Sunday lunch and therefore two more refusals.

Unluckily for Laurent, twelve of his thirty covers comprise a birthday party, which would have helped to fill an ordinary, quieter Sunday, if Easter had fallen differently. And according to Laurence, they are the kind of customers who are happiest when complaining: about getting lost (despite her directions); about the fact that groups like theirs are asked to order in advance; even about the time it takes the hot water to arrive in the cloakroom.

Thirty is well below last Easter's numbers, but I have never known the restaurant so stretched. Or Laurent so stressed. Philippe tries hard but seems out of his depth. Marc looks queasier by the minute. Barely able to see over the worktop to contribute more constructively, he mainly hovers (worryingly close) beside me with a tea towel, offering it up for me to wipe my hands whenever they are less than perfectly clean and dry.

Under pressure, Laurent confuses two sauces from the fridge, letting Philippe put the herby one (intended for the *amuse-bouche* cream) into the asparagus preparation (destined for service underneath it) and has to start again from scratch. To make up for lost time, he assembles the first four himself, only to have one of the glass dishes rejected by a keen-eyed customer as microscopically chipped. He chides Frédéric for smashing all his glassware but is mainly annoyed with himself for failing to notice.

The rest of the *amuses* are down to me, but soon I run out of glasses, needing Frédéric to purify some of those from the early tables, while Laurence paces impatiently. Laurent is similarly running out of plates and starts using differently sized or coloured alternatives, while Laurence worries about the lack of consistency from table to table. I puzzle as to how they coped with over forty covers last year, unless the *plongeurs* have been exceptionally destructive in the interim.

I was hoping to be useful, lower down the *menu-carte*, having seen that the famous *tarte friande* was making an Easter come-back, but most of the preparatory work, where I know I could shine, was done earlier. And in the frantic pace of today's service, Laurent has little time to teach me the recipe's final flourishes. I content myself with planting the decorative sprig of thyme on the top of each tart.

Joris, it seems, is even more tongue-tied in the dining-room than he was in the kitchen. Not taking chances, Laurent takes time off to help him practise.

'Voici Messieurs-dames, la tarte tatin . . .'

'Voici Messieurs-dames, la tarte tatin . . .'

'. . . with its apple sorbet, accompanied by its glass of apple purée and cider jelly.'

'. . . with its sorbet . . .'

'. . . with its APPLE sorbet!'

'. . . with its apple sorbet and . . .' Joris giggles. 'Sorry, what was the rest?'

'Joris, you've made this dish yourself, a hundred times!'

'. . . accompanied by its apple purée, its GLASS of apple purée and its . . . um . . . cider jelly.'

'Bonne continuation, Messieurs-dames.'

'*Bonne continuation.*'
'*Messieurs-dames.*'
'*Messieurs . . .*'

Laurence bustles in from the dining-room, now free to take them herself, but Laurent insists that Joris goes, having learned the script. 'But hurry,' he urges, 'before the sorbet melts!'

'Could you stay till everyone's gone?' asks Laurent, when the end begins to seem in sight. 'There's something I want to show you.' But immediately, the birthday party orders another bottle of champagne.

'Don't tell me there'll be speeches,' I entreat him.

'Not in the way that you mean,' chuckles Laurent.

Instead there must be a dozen separate, loquacious, pontificating verdicts on the excellence of the lunch as each of the group takes his doorstep farewell. Then he beckons me into the dining-room.

Beside the entrance to the veranda, a table has been cleared, except for a bottle of superior champagne displayed in a dummy ice bucket and a tall, life-sized iris, cast in bronze. The table is not in fact under a spotlight, but it feels like it.

'They award one every year,' says Laurent, meaning the statuette. 'In fact they award three, one for the best tourist attraction – the Lodève museum won it once – one for the best hotel and one for the best restaurant. Le Jardin des Sens won the restaurant iris two years ago,' he adds, in case I underestimate his achievement.

'Hold on,' I interrupt. 'You mean best in the *département*?'

'In the whole of the Languedoc-Roussillon,' he tells me, still as low-key as ever. 'I wasn't even going to go to the presentation dinner. I'd been short-listed the year before and I thought it would just be the same thing, a waste of time that I haven't got. But then they rang me up to persuade me to come, so I sort of knew.'

He shows me a full-page article from the previous Sunday's edition of the *Midi Libre*, the 'local' newspaper with a circulation covering all the relevant six departments.

'But that's fantastic,' I say. 'Better publicity than a Michelin star!'

'It only appeared in the Lodève edition,' he says ruefully.

*

'You're not planting watercress?' asked Manu, spotting me kneeling beside the stream the next day. 'It's just that I thought I ought to say, your uncle tried it once. Complete waste of time. All got washed away when it rained.'

'Irises,' I told him.

Having finally cleared all the brambles and broken branches from the water's edge, I was determined now to beautify the banks of the stream, tucking close to fifty little plants into niches between the boulders. It was too late to hope for much in the way of spring colour, but the important thing was to give the plants a chance to establish themselves between the heavy rains of the last winter and those of the next.

'The wife was so disappointed,' Manu reminisced, as if my peculiar priorities had simply failed to register. 'Really loves a bit of watercress.'

'These are irises,' I repeated. 'Strictly non-edible.'

'Well, don't say I didn't warn you.' He shakes his head in disbelief.

*

'They were only twenty-four when they opened,' said Laure de Carrière, the Pourcel twins' press attaché, having steered me to one of the sleek leather sofas in Le Jardin des Sens's reception area. 'That was in 1988. Then they won their first Michelin star in 1990, the second in 1992 and the third in 1998.'

These were clearly dates that she found herself reciting several times a week. No doubt the same applied to the efficient listing of all the other ventures in Jacques and Laurent's portfolio, including two that were news to me: a restaurant called La Maison

Blanche in Paris and a third manifestation of La Compagnie des Comptoirs in Avignon.

'They don't stand still.' Laure smiled modestly. 'They're opening in Bangkok in June, Shanghai in September and London in October or November.' I sensed there might even be more; but she had long since persuaded me why the empire needed a press attaché.

'We wondered whether you might find it interesting to see both sides?' she asked. 'Spending part of the evening in the dining-room, as well as in the kitchen?'

I had been pondering the question of food on the slow drive down through heavy rain. I had made myself an unusually large lunch, just in case; but surely the fact that I was staying the night indicated some sort of sustenance. Most probably something with the kitchen staff before the service, I had told myself until a moment before.

'Part and part would be very interesting.' I tried not to sound gauchely excited. 'Is Monsieur Jacques in the kitchen now?'

'He's in England,' she said. 'Taking part in a symposium at Raymond Blanc's, comparing French cuisine with American.'

'That should be a short symposium,' I joked politely, but wondered privately where his absence now left me.

'It lasts a week,' she laughed, as baffled by the idea as I was. 'But don't worry. They're twins, remember. Monsieur Laurent's cooking tonight. He nearly always does. He prefers to leave the promotional stuff to Monsieur Jacques. I'll see if he's arrived.' And with an invitation to browse through the brothers' three cookery books, she vanished through a half-concealed door.

I flicked through *Cuisine en Duo*, their first. An introductory passage revealed a third collaborator, not yet mentioned: Olivier Château, the maître d'hôtel and sommelier since 1988. 'Just as the three musketeers were four, so the duo of the Jardin des Sens is a trio. Olivier is, as much as us, the life and soul of this house. He assures its solidity, like the olive tree planted in our garden.'

Laure, returning already through the secret door, explained

that, these days, Monsieur Château was as likely to be seen with a balance sheet as a wine list. She also explained that Laurent Pourcel was still in his office and would be taking his meal there. I might prefer to take a look at the garden – no, perhaps not, in this weather – a rest in my room maybe, until nearer the start of the service at eight o'clock?

All the hotel bedrooms face the garden, which is another way of saying that they all face the restaurant at the heart of the garden. A vast glass pavilion, closely surrounded by well-ordered plants and patios and waterfalls, it makes exciting use of limited urban space. Even well before nightfall, both dining-room and (tonight, rain-soaked) garden are fully illuminated. Even an hour and a half before the service, the waiters setting the tables are immaculate (no jeans and T-shirts at Le Jardin des Sens).

It is impossible to be in one of the bedrooms without a sense of anticipation. Would going down at seven-thirty appear over-eager? Seven-forty, perhaps? To judge by the number of diners reading menus on the leather sofas at seven-forty-five, I was not the only one reluctant to wait. But before I can drift towards them, Laure appears from nowhere to escort me behind the self-effacing panel, where I blink at the scene before me.

The dessert section, nearest to our entrance, is roughly the size of Laurent's entire kitchen; the black metal, brass-railed central cooking range in the adjoining room is surely bigger, without counting all the separate marble worktops and brushed-steel refrigerated cupboards which surround it on three sides. On the fourth side the pass must be nearly half as long as Laurent's veranda. Then a third room beyond for the *amuse-bouches* and cold dishes; another at the side for the sommeliers; and finally, somewhere far out of sight, the *plonge*.

Everything is brightly illuminated and uncluttered – the spot-lit, white-linen-covered pass especially so. Laurent Pourcel has yet to appear but everyone else wears a smart dark blue apron over pristine 'whites'; everyone but Loïc Lefebvre, the *second de cuisine*, wears a tall, almost traditional chef's hat, except that these are also blue and are topped with distinctive, trilby-like indentations. The explanation lies in a sliding glass door leading down a short dark tunnel to the glow of the restaurant. The kitchen is partially on display.

The brigade is mainly young, although I imagine that most of them must be skilled enough already to run lesser restaurants on their own – as no doubt several soon will. Someone has already explained my connection with the 'other' Laurent and many of the more senior team members send him warm good wishes. Cyril, the pastry chef, says he has even made the great journey west, to eat at Le Temps de Vivre. 'We go hunting together,' he explains. 'Laurent knows where to find *bécasse.*'

Meanwhile, Laurent's namesake has slipped in unobtrusively, waiting until I am unoccupied to welcome me. He seems unexpectedly reserved and, to break the ice, I tease him about the Jardin's truffle monopoly, uncovered at Vinisud.

'We have a few good contacts.' He smiles enigmatically. 'But you're happy to spend part of the evening in the dining-room?' he adds, and again I struggle not to appear too obviously euphoric.

The chef quietly checks that everyone is up-to-date and ready, but most of them have been up-to-date and ready since before I arrived. Only those responsible for the numerous different confections accompanying the aperitifs are currently busy.

Then the first order. The maître d'hôtel comes quietly to the pass. He has memorized the customers' selections – no scribblings at the table here. Instead, he writes out the details on a pad at the pass. It is Loïc who then studies these, makes some extra notes of his own, places the annotated sheet on a board where everyone can monitor progress and finally makes the announcement: '*Ça marche: Table Trois: Deux à Deux Cents Dix.*'

His moderate volume and tone leave me doubting whether all the relevant parties can possibly have heard, still less taken in what it signifies for them; but it will be the same throughout the evening. No one shouts, no one hectors; but if Loïc speaks, then however preoccupied you might seem to be, and no matter how many different dishes you might already have on the go, you listen.

Then you do the arithmetic. If you are in charge of meat, no one says, 'You realize this means two portions of kid, in eight courses' time.' Indeed, no one even appears to prompt you later on with a helpful, 'Table Three's reached the sole, you know. Less than half an hour to go.' As far as I can see, you check Loïc's board and work things out for yourself. But somehow, almost miraculously, whenever a waiter comes quietly to the pass, expectantly bearing an empty tray, the dish that he was hoping for seems to be ready.

In all of this, Laurent Pourcel is perhaps the least flustered and flustering presence of all, strengthening the team almost inconspicuously by discreetly doing a little of whatever takes his fancy or catches his eye but, like Loïc, ever watchful as to all that is leaving the kitchen.

Not that even the lowliest *commis de cuisine* is ever inattentive. Every station is equipped with a large supply of folded paper handkerchiefs and a bowl of pure water. No food ever touches a plate without the porcelain first being wiped. Even saucers and underplates receive the same thorough treatment. Then, once the dish is complete, a second wipe follows before it is released.

Loïc crosses to check the single chervil leaves resting on top of three cups of *bouillon mousseux* that form one of tonight's *amuse-bouches* for the less expensive menu. He quickly adjudicates one to be visually inferior and changes it; then he changes it again, condemning the first replacement as imperfectly positioned. Only then is the waiter permitted to kick the ankle-level pad that activates the electronic sliding door to the dining-room.

The pace does, of course, begin to hot up, as more orders come in and courses start overlapping. 'I'm afraid you won't see them at full throttle,' says Hicham, the assistant maître d'hôtel. He is another 'Arrazat fan' and seemingly, for that reason, keen to play the role of my protector for the evening. 'Only twenty-two covers tonight. That's out of a maximum of seventy in the main room, plus thirty in the smaller one near reception.'

'Because of the rain?'

'Partly the rain and partly the Tuesday-after-Easter effect. It's funny, but we never get less than twenty,' he says. 'Literally never. No one knows why. But when we're really full, the kitchen works like a powerful machine. It's very impressive.'

Hicham strikes me as one of the gentlest, most mild-mannered men in the catering industry and, remembering Laurence's flight from kitchen aggression, I ask him whether he has always worked *en salle*.

'I'm very shy in real life,' he confesses. 'So much so, I nearly changed to the kitchen. But Pierre Morel, Eric Cellier's partner, helped me gain confidence. Now, entering the dining-room's like walking out on to a stage. It's not me, it's some other character. Just let me know when you've seen as much as you want,' he adds, solicitously. 'Your table's ready whenever you are.'

I struggle heroically with the temptation to surge through the sliding glass door at once, flattening Hicham in my path. 'Perhaps in ten minutes,' I suggest, trying to sound genuinely torn between the first and second phases of my evening. I also need a moment to think.

Belatedly, it has occurred to me to wonder how I should handle phase two. I assume that I am the Pourcels' guest (if not, I had better feign a sudden illness and leave immediately); but once at the table, what if I am faced with the embarrassment of a menu? Would three courses show sufficient interest in their cooking, without seeming greedy? Or better to stop at two?

'Will you be giving me a "surprise"?' I ask the chef, hoping thereby to sidestep the problem.

'I'll let you taste some specialities.' He smiles, enigmatic as always.

Hicham kicks the electric door to usher me down the waiters' tunnel into the dining-room, and I see at once what he means about a sense of theatre. The room descends in tiers like a steeply raked auditorium, with five or six tables on each level. The ceiling descends in sympathy, so that the space is simultaneously intimate and epic in scale. A couple of red velvet drapes at the corners and a Venetian glass chandelier lend a Baroque, operatic note to the otherwise clean, modern lines of the floor-to-ceiling glass. At the front, where the theatre's orchestra pit should be, is a long, narrow pool of water. Beyond it, dramatically lit on the stage, is a triangular Zen-like garden, rising in steps to balance the terraced dining-room, with glittering water cascading down a formal channel from the highest and furthest point.

'Sorry about the rain,' says Hicham, as he shows me to a table by an extremely wet window, in the front row.

My delight in the room is suddenly swamped by a second anxiety. What should I do if they bring me the family-bible-like wine list that I saw in the sommeliers' room. Do restaurants like this have a 'house wine'? Or would that seem disrespectful to the food?

The youngest of the sommeliers, whom I remember as a trainee waiter at Cellier-Morel a couple of years ago, is advancing on the table. His hands, I note, are encouragingly empty of wine lists.

'What the chef proposes is that we serve you a glass of wine to accompany each course,' he says. 'Unless there's some particular bottle that you prefer . . . You're absolutely sure?'

I tell him I'm absolutely sure.

'*Et en aperitif, monsieur?* Would a glass of champagne help to revive you? . . . You're sure? *Très bien, monsieur*. I was going to propose this 1988 Moët & Chandon, but if there's something else that you'd prefer . . .'

I tell him the vintage Moët will be admirable. Laurent must be a very good friend.

I lose count of the various hot and cold accompaniments to the champagne. The most memorable is an ice-cream-style cornet, filled with chilled lobster and cream. Then come three *amuse-bouches*, including a minted pea gazpacho, served in a tall, narrow glass with a black straw, and a salad of tiny pasta shells, dressed with caviar. With these, the sommelier suggests a Picpoul de Pinet produced by the Pourcels' elder brother (they are a wine-making family by tradition). With the scallops on their chilled tomato jelly, enhanced with citrus, coriander and flowers, he brings a local Chardonnay . . .

And so on throughout three more savoury courses, then cheeses, then . . . was it three desserts? (Not counting the so-called 'pre-desserts'.) My adding-up skills grow blunter with every glass. Laurent must be an exceptionally good friend.

Each successive dish brings startling new surprises, both in flavour and technique; but almost more dazzling, in a way, is the service. Even on the simplest of menus in other restaurants, I have never known such timing, with never a hint of either haste or delay: a dish is finished; then a minimal pause and the dirty plate is whisked away; then new cutlery; then a moderate pause, just enough for pleasant reflection over the last course and spec-ulation as to the next; then a new wine, with a fractional further pause for renewed speculation; then the new dish. With food of this complexity, even after a couple of hours in the kitchen looking for the secret, I simply cannot imagine how they do it.

'I ought to thank the chef,' I tell Hicham, as I finish my coffee.

'He's back in his office,' says the assistant maître d'hôtel. 'Should I call him?'

'No, please don't disturb him,' I answer with relief. 'I'll leave him a note in the morning.'

For the moment, simply finding my way back to my room seems challenging enough; finding a suitable form of words out of the question.

*

'It's all starting,' said Manu, intercepting me enthusiastically at the top of my drive the next morning. 'The nightingales are back, a few days earlier than usual. Woke you up again, did they?' He had noticed that I was less than usually wide-awake. 'No, not in that storm, I suppose. Probably washed away, poor things.'

'I spent the night in Montpellier,' I told him without elaborat-ing.

I could see him looking troubled by this 'life of my own' but he had more important things on his mind. 'Time you were getting that plough out,' he told me, pointing to the potager. 'You need to get your seedlings in. There were tomato plants in Clermont this morning, so you ought to get yours in Lodève at the weekend.'

'I've got the party at the weekend. And anyway, I've sown my own tomato seeds in the greenhouse. I bought them from Pascal Poot, up at Olmet. And I'm going to grow them his way – flat on the ground.'

Manu looked once again rattled by this show of independence but remained, as ever, focused on the priorities. 'Have you sorted out the wine for the weekend? This cousin of mine, the one who takes his grapes to the co-op in Pégairolles . . .'

'I'm serving Virgile's wine. A bit expensive but it's a special occasion.'

More independence but Manu shrugged, as if to say he'd drink it out of politeness; then back to practicalities. 'What about furniture? There's this chap in Saint Etienne . . .'

'I'm borrowing trestle tables and benches from the Mairie. They're free,' I added, before he could promise to undercut the Mayor on price. 'I was hoping you'd help me collect them in your van. Seven o'clock on Friday morning, it needs to be.'

Further momentary loss of composure – Manu was unused to being organized; but he grunted in agreement. It *was* a special occasion – special enough, indeed, for Mme Gros to have offered to help with the catering. 'You will keep her contribution to the minimum, won't you?' he urged. 'And Garance – your English friends don't want to come all this way for a lot of her silliness. If you fancied a sucking pig, for instance . . .'

'All in hand,' I told him, adding that I was on my way down to the stream. Everything was, as he rightly said, 'starting' and I wanted to check the progress of the newly planted irises.

'What are you going to do if it rains?' he asked, as if hoping to introduce me to a marquee supplier. 'Imagine another day like yesterday.'

'I'm trying not to think about it,' I laughed, as he followed me through the orchard. 'I wasn't going to invite so many people, but somehow it grew.'

'Maybe the ones who are staying could help with the potager after the party?' suggested Manu brightly. Then suddenly he gasped, as we took in the scene at the waterside. '*Mon dieu!* That storm was worse than I thought. Your irises have started and finished.'

They had in fact vanished, swept away by what must have been an exceptional volume of water for any time of year and simply undreamt of in mid-April. Everything within a couple of metres of the stream that was smaller than a tree but well-established had been flattened; anything not well-established had been uprooted. My carefully planted irises were well on their way to the sea.

*

'You're so lucky with the weather,' says almost everyone at the lunch.

Not Garance, of course. We have erected the trestle tables in a single line beneath the principal cherry tree and, incredibly, this provides shade enough for all of us. Or rather, all except Garance, on whom a flicker of sunlight somehow shines, no matter where we try to seat her.

'Magical,' says everyone else, as they carry their food to the sun-dappled tablecloth.

Or rather, everyone but Sarah who grumbles that there are no seats *in* the sun. And Mme Gros who complains that there are no proper seats. She would never have helped with the cooking, had she known it was benches. 'If only we'd told her,' chuckles Manu, glugging Virgile's Grenache Blanc with laudable generosity of spirit.

The Vargases' only protest is that I didn't tell them it was my birthday. Most of my English friends came with presents and they feel embarrassed. 'An important number too,' they scold me in characteristic unison.

'It isn't,' I tell them hastily. 'My birthday's not for a couple of weeks. We're celebrating the fact that I've been back here for exactly a year.'

'Rubbish,' laughs Virgile, joining the group. 'What we're celebrating is the completion of the Wall.' He casts an eye down to where Sarah has gone to sunbathe – lying, somewhat less fully attired than she was at the start of the meal, between the glazed terracotta pots on the pristine, mathematically horizontal top of Arnaud's edifice.

Virgile himself is likewise pretending that it's high summer. Wearing a white panama hat and matching white suit, he looks like a gangster at a Sicilian wedding. 'I'm off to London next month,' he tells me more mundanely. 'For the Wine Fair.'

'On your own?' I ask, with a glance across to Magda, sipping water in the shade with Garance. 'Is everything okay?' Magda has always accompanied him on his previous marketing trips; and she has always drunk his wine.

'Everything's fine. In fact...' He blushes slightly. 'Magda's expecting a baby in November. That's why she's taking things easier.'

'Anything to get out of the *vendange*,' I tease him, but I'm delighted. He adores children and they adore him.

'We needed someone to inherit the overdraft,' he jokes, on his way back to Magda.

'The Vargases tell me this isn't the day,' says Mme Gros, with a wink that, if I didn't know her better, I might have construed as flirtatious. She is much too mellowed by an unaccustomed second glass of Noilly Prat to mind whether the candles on her lop-sided, pink-iced cake are apposite or not. Indeed, she is much more interested in whether I have already made a restaurant booking to mark the true date. 'We could always try your new man, if Le Mimosa's outside your budget these days,' she tells me magnanimously.

As if on cue, my new man's Subaru roars up the drive at this point.

'Sorry, I couldn't get away any earlier,' says Laurent, jumping

276

out and accepting a glass of Virgile's Coteaux du Languedoc red. 'It's the first busy Saturday lunch for as long as I can remember. I've left the desserts to Joris,' he adds, with a 'Heaven-help-me' grimace that reveals this to be a supreme act of faith for my benefit.

'Don't worry. Look, I've saved you some *caviar d'aubergines*.'

He smiles as he bites into an aubergine-covered crouton. 'So, you did learn something then! Maybe sieve it next time, to get the seeds out, do you think?' He picks a couple from between his teeth. 'But tell me, what's happened to your lane?'

'I forgot to warn you. It was never very solid, what they left us with, but that rain on Tuesday seems to have finished it off.'

'There's a gaping crevasse between the lane and somebody's olive grove.'

'I know. It belongs to that elderly couple having a snooze by the pool.'

'They're going to break something, jumping across!'

'They're being very philosophical.'

This is more than can be said for all of my guests. Garance, having exhausted the Vargases with her motorway woes, has now cornered William. He speaks minimal French – and Garance not a word of English – but none of that deters her. My friend has the look of a man who wishes he had booked an earlier return flight.

'And the château?' I ask Laurent, as he takes some more food and, restless as ever, steers me off for a walk round the back of the house. 'How did your meeting go?'

'Oh, that,' he says, as if yesterday were long ago. 'The usual Code Napoléon story. It turns out this guy doesn't own it all. He owns a share, along with about ten of his relatives. It could take months, even years for everyone to agree. I told you this was a crazy country.'

'But it's a start?'

'It's a start . . . Hey, look at your vineyard – a bit of an improvement!'

Each of the forty vines has been neatly pruned to a single stem;

each of the stems has been carefully tied to a tightly stretched wire between well-braced, well-regimented wooden posts; and the fluttering of the first intensely green leaves shows, in the words of another vine grower, that it's all starting.

'I did have a bit of help,' I confess, as we return towards the house, where Virgile is the latest to undergo the Garance treatment.

'I see his wines are getting a good press,' says Laurent, needing no further clues as to where the help came from. 'The wine we're drinking gets two stars in this year's Hachette guide.'

'Is that good?' I ask, never having consulted it.

'Only two Coteaux du Languedoc get three.'

'Well, it's a special occasion,' I tell him, refilling his glass.

'You're only young once,' wheezes Manu, rushing forward to proffer his own glass.

'You should do this more often,' declares Mme Gros, bearing down on us, just a fraction unsteadily, with what must surely be a record-breaking third glass of her private tipple. 'I hope you're going to give us a good table,' she says to Laurent, with something unnervingly close to a giggle.

Before he can ask anyone what she means, Virgile joins our group with Magda. 'We must leave you,' he apologizes. 'At least, I'm going to drop Magda back home and then I'm coming back.'

'Good stuff this,' endorses Manu, as if he imagines that Virgile is driving back up just to drink more of his own production.

'No, I'm coming back with the tractor.'

'Whatever for?' I ask incredulously.

'It's your other neighbour,' he says. 'The poetess. She wanted a bit of land ploughed up for a potager. It just seemed quicker to say yes,' he laughs. 'Otherwise, I'd still be trapped under the cherry tree, saying no.'

'I told you,' snorts Mme Gros to no one in particular. 'It's take, take, take with that one.'

Contact details

Restaurants

Le Temps de Vivre
Quartier 'Les Rials'
Route de Poujols
34700 Soubès
Tel/Fax: 0 (033) 4 67 44 20 98

Cellier-Morel (La Maison de la Lozère)
27 Rue de l'Aiguillerie
34000 Montpellier
Tel: 0 (033) 4 67 66 46 36
Fax: 0 (033) 4 67 66 23 61
Email: contact@celliermorel.com
Website: www.celliermorel.com

Le Tirou
90 Avenue Mgr Delangle
11400 Castelnaudary
Tel: 0 (033) 4 68 94 15 95
Fax: 0 (033) 4 68 94 15 96

La Table de Saint Crescent
Boulevard Général-Leclerc
Route de Perpignan
11100 Narbonne
Tel: 0 (033) 4 68 41 37 37
Fax: 0 (033) 4 68 41 01 22
Email: saint-crescent@wanadoo.fr
Website: www.la-table-saint-crescent.com

Le Jardin des Sens
11 Avenue Saint-Lazare
34000 Montpellier
Tel: 0 (033) 4 99 58 38 38
Fax: 0 (033) 4 99 58 38 39
Email: contact@jardindessens.com
Website: www.jardin-des-sens.com

La Compagnie des Comptoirs
51 Avenue de Nîmes
34000 Montpellier
Tel: 0 (033) 4 99 58 39 29
Fax: 0 (033) 4 99 58 39 28
Website: www.lacompagniedescomptoirs.com

Le Mimosa
34725 Saint Guiraud
Tel: 0 (033) 4 67 96 67 96

Le Pressoir
34725 Saint Saturnin de Lucian
Tel: 0 (033) 4 67 88 67 89

Food and drink producers

Domaine Virgile Joly
22 Rue de Portail
34725 Saint Saturnin de Lucian
Tel/Fax: 0 (033) 4 67 44 52 21
Email: virgilejoly@wanadoo.fr

La Bergerie de Pégairolles de l'Escalette
34700 Pégairolles de l'Escalette
Tel: 0 (033) 4 67 88 00 78 (House)
Or: 0 (033) 4 99 91 43 16 (Bergerie)
Email: rens.van-doorne@wanadoo.fr

Pisciculture Cirque de Labeil
34700 Lauroux
Tel: 0 (033) 4 67 44 09 55

La Mielerie de Soumont
Dominique and Claudette André
34700 Soumont
Tel: 0 (033) 4 67 44 46 30
Email: dominique.andre10@wanadoo.fr

La Conservatoire de Tomates
La Roque
34700 Olmet
Tel: 0 (033) 4 67 96 69 83

Compagnie des Salins du Midi
30220 Aigues-Mortes
Tel: 0 (033) 4 66 73 40 23
Fax: 0 (033) 4 66 73 40 21
Email: salins@salins.com
Website: www.salins.com

Ricard
Chemin Cave Coopérative
345500 Bessan
Tel: 0 (033) 4 67 01 05 00
Fax: 0 (033) 4 67 77 54 59
Website: www.ricard-sa.com

Le Moulin de l'Oulivie
Mas de Forques
34980 Combaillaux
Tel/Fax: 0 (033) 4 67 67 07 80
Email: domaineloulivie@wanadoo.fr

and

Moulin et Tradition
Route de Saint Guilhem
Zone Artisanale 'La Terrasse'
34150 Aniane
Tel/Fax: 0 (033) 4 67 57 96 38
Email: moulins-traditions@wanadoo.fr
Website: www.moulins-traditions.com

Author's note

In the hope of protecting both the innocent and the guilty, I have 'juggled' with a number of the places and personalities in this book, particularly those closest to home. (To have done otherwise might have shortened my life expectancy.) Nonetheless, improbable as it may occasionally seem, all of the incidents and characters described are inspired by real experience.

Acknowledgements

The words 'I'm writing a book' have a happy way of opening doors that might otherwise be closed and I am hugely indebted to all of those who let me 'see behind the scenes': Laurent and Laurence Arrazat and all at Le Temps de Vivre (with special thanks for letting me roll up my sleeves and get my hands dirty); Éric Cellier, Pierre Morel and all at La Maison de la Lozère; Jean-Claude Visentin and all at Le Tirou; Lionel and Claude Giraud and all at La Table de Saint Crescent; Jacques and Laurent Pourcel, Laure de Carrière and all at Le Jardin des Sens; Rens van Doorne and Bernard Chabrier at the Bergerie de Pégairolles de l'Escalette; Yves Jouvigné at the Pisciculture de Labeil; Claudette and Dominique André at the Miélerie de Soumont; Pascal Poot at the Conservatoire de Tomates; Patrice Cabanou at the Salins du Midi; Alain Pla and Francis Vilaro at Ricard; Rock and Pierre Vialla at the Moulin de l'Oulivie; Pierre-Yves Boissieu at Aroma-tiques d'Homs; Guy Balcou at Les Jardins de la Mer; Thierry Traup at Perrier; Jacques Carles and his colleagues in Roquefort (with special thanks to Betty's cheese shop in Toulouse); Léon Fonzes and Geneviève Fonzes-Armand at the Conserverie Occitane; Benoît Liétar at the Domaine de Planchenault; and especially Virgile and Magda of the Domaine Virgile Joly (not least for helping to open Laurent Arrazat's door).

Others – too numerous to catalogue here – have helped to make this book possible with many different kinds of advice and encouragement. I hope that they will forgive me if I single out only three: my agent, Mandy Little; my editor, Gail Pirkis; and my unfailing support in all things, Andrew McKenzie.

Les Aromatiques d'Homs
Les Homs du Larzac
12230 Nant
Tel: 0 (033) 5 65 62 22 56
Fax: 0 (033) 5 65 62 17 37
Email: contact@pastisdeshoms.fr
Website: www.pastisdeshoms.fr

Les Jardins de la Mer
34140 Bouzigues
Tel: 0 (033) 4 67 78 33 23

La Source du Perrier
30310 Vergèze
Tel: 0 (033) 4 66 87 61 01
Fax: 0 (033) 4 66 87 61 03
Website: www.perrier.com

La Maison Carles, Roquefort
6 Avenue de Lauras
12250 Roquefort-sur-Soulzon
Tel: 0 (033) 5 65 59 90 28
Fax: 0 (033) 5 65 59 94 44
Email: roquefort.carles@wanadoo.fr

La Conserverie Occitane
12 bis Avenue Saint Benoit d'Aniane
34150 Saint Guilhem le Désert
Tel: 0 (033) 4 67 57 46 59
Fax: 0 (033) 4 67 57 46 59
Email: conserverie-occitane@wanadoo.fr

Aux Trois Escargots
Domaine de Planchenault
1800 Route de Montpellier
34160 Boisseron
Tel: 0 (033) 4 67 86 42 30